COASTING
the MOUNTAINS

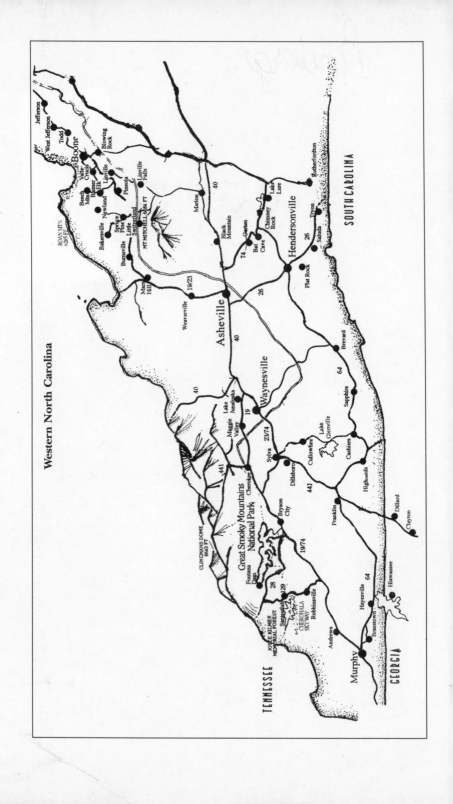

Western North Carolina

COASTING
the MOUNTAINS

A Guide to
Western North Carolina

By Judy Barnes, Jolane Edwards,
Carolyn Lee Goodloe, and Laurel Wilson

PELICAN PUBLISHING COMPANY
Gretna 2001

*The word "Pelican" and the depiction of a pelican are trademarks
of Pelican Publishing Company, Inc.,
and are registered in the U.S. Patent and Trademark Office.*

Library of Congress in Cataloging-in-Publication

Coasting the mountains : a guide to western North Carolina / Judy Barnes
... [et al.].
    p. cm.
Includes index.
ISBN 1-56554-829-9 (pbk. : alk. paper)
    1. North Carolina—Guidebooks. 2. Asheville Region (N.C.)—Guidebooks.
I. Barnes, Judy, 1938-

F252.3 .C55 2001
917.5604'44—dc21

2001034347

*Information in this guidebook is based on authoritative
data available at the time of printing. Prices and hours
of operation of businesses listed are subject to change
without notice. Readers are asked to take
this into account when consulting this guide.*

Printed in the United States of America
Published by Pelican Publishing Company, Inc.
1000 Burmaster Street, Gretna, Louisiana 70053

Contents

	Acknowledgments	7
	Introduction	9
Chapter 1	Asheville	13
	Biltmore Estate	35
	Golf Courses	52
Chapter 2	Black Mountain	53
	Marion	59
	Crossnore	62
	Linville	62
	Grandfather Mountain	64
Chapter 3	Banner Elk	67
	Sugar Mountain	70
	Beech Mountain	71
	Golf Courses	73
Chapter 4	Highway 105	75
	Valle Crucis	79
	Boone	82
	Todd	87
	West Jefferson	88
	Jefferson	89
	Shatley Springs	91
	Glendale Springs	92
	Blowing Rock	94
	Golf Courses	107
Chapter 5	Blue Ridge Parkway	109
	Little Switzerland	113
	Mount Mitchell	116
Chapter 6	Spruce Pine	117
	Penland	120
	Bakersville	125
	Roan Mountain	127
	Burnsville	128
	Weaverville	134
	Golf Courses	136

Chapter 7   Waynesville 137
             Maggie Valley 144
             Cherokee Reservation 146
             Great Smoky Mountains National Park 151
             Golf Courses 153
Chapter 8   Sylva 155
             Dillsboro 158
             Bryson City 163
             Nantahala Outdoor Center 166
Chapter 9   Robbinsville 169
             Joyce Kilmer Memorial Forest/
             Joyce Kilmer-Slickrock Wilderness 170
             Fontana Dam 171
             Cherohala Skyway 172
             Andrews 173
             Murphy...............................174
             Brasstown 174
             Hayesville 175
             Golf Courses 175
Chapter 10   Franklin 177
             Highlands 181
             Cashiers 200
             Sapphire 211
             Lake Toxaway 212
             Golf Courses 216
Chapter 11   Brevard 217
             Pisgah National Forest 225
             Cradle of Forestry 227
             Hendersonville 230
             Flat Rock 240
             Golf Courses 245
Chapter 12   Bat Cave 247
             Chimney Rock 249
             Saluda 251
             Tryon 255
             Golf Courses 258

             Index 261

Acknowledgments

We are grateful to our dear friend and constant advisor Thea Atkinson. For patience and encouragement, we especially thank Roy Barnes, Jack Edwards, and Bill Goodloe.

The North Carolina Chambers of Commerce, Ranger Stations, and Visitors Information Centers were invaluable resources as was Christine Mackey, Director of Public Relations of the North Carolina Department of Commerce. We also thank Carolyn Howser, Judy Geary, Jay Garner, Beverly Shearer, Winston and Anne-Clinton Groom, Wren Murphy, Alice Jorgensen, Tut Riddick, David Tucker, Marilyn Brannon, George Ellison, and Laura Delegal.

Artwork and covers by Erin Fitzhugh

I began again to ascend the mountains, which I at length accomplished, and rested on the most elevated peak from whence I beheld with rapture and astonishment a sublimely awful scene of power and magnificence, a world of mountains piled upon mountains.

—William Bartram, Western North Carolina, 1775

Introduction

Readers may wonder how, after writing *Coasting: An Expanded Guide to the Northern Gulf Coast,* we could shift 180 degrees to Western North Carolina. It has been said that those who love the water have the same affinity for the mountains, but it is more than that.

We were captivated by the ancient Appalachians. These gentle mountains, although challenging, are not intimidating, one of the tallest being named "Grandfather" for heaven's sake. We have climbed, hiked, rafted the rivers, and stayed in the inns. As it has always been our policy to visit every place we write about, we can testify that the wholesome mountain food, frequently served with a sophisticated creative touch, is to be relished. We can also vouch for the quality of the many fine fishing streams and golf courses in the area. The good roads that wrap around the mountains gave us the unusual opportunity to "hike" by car and revel in the spectacular Blue Ridge Parkway.

Many books have been written about this area, covering waterfalls, parks, biking, rafting, and camping in great detail, but *Coasting the Mountains* is more than a book. It is a lighthearted, personal guide to the whole, covering what we liked best about everything. This includes the renowned crafts of the region, which we delved into with great delight.

Western North Carolina is at its height and we helped ourselves to the bounty. We invite you to join us to do the same and "coast" this fabulous corner of the state.

North Carolina, which achieved statehood in 1789, stretches west from the Atlantic Ocean across swamps and fertile farms. The land rises through sand hills all the way to Mount Mitchell, which, at 6,684 feet above sea level, is the highest peak in the eastern United States. North Carolina is the leading tobacco-growing state in the United States. It also manufactures more cloth and makes more wooden furniture than any other state.

In 1861, North Carolina left the Union and did its best to help the Confederate cause. During one fierce battle, some Confederate troops retreated, and the North Carolinians threatened to put tar on the heels of the other troops to keep them sticking in the next fight. From this came the name, the "Tar Heel State."

Western North Carolina is an enchanting corner of the state and its northwest boundary is hugged by the 514-acre Great Smoky Mountains National Park. This corner, renowned for a variety of crafts and a mild climate, lures thousands to the mountains; many Northerners come for relief from the cold winters, while Deep Southerners come to escape the summer heat and humidity. In addition, blossoming mountain laurels and rhododendrons in the spring and the beautiful autumn colors are making Western North Carolina a well-known year-round resort.

COASTING
the MOUNTAINS

CHAPTER 1

Asheville

William Davidson, a lone pioneer who settled in Western North Carolina with his wife and children in 1784, unknowingly established what would one day become Asheville. A permanent settlement followed the next year, the county was established in 1791, and what is now Pack Square was home to a small log courthouse. The area was incorporated in 1797 and named for Gov. Samuel Ashe.

Asheville is the economic and cultural center of eighteen counties in Western North Carolina. Bordered by the Pisgah National Forest, the city lies in the midst of recreational areas covering over a million acres and it also serves as the agricultural wholesale center for the surrounding area.

Visitors are drawn to the city's Art Deco abundance, the Grove Park Inn Resort, indigenous arts and crafts, and the splendor of the Biltmore Estate.

Asheville is an ideal walking city and if you want to explore on foot you should begin at the beginning . . . **Pack Square.** In the center of the square is an obelisk and fountain; these two monuments commemorate Zebulon B. Vance, Asheville's first native son, and George Willis Pack, a multimillionaire who contributed much toward the progress of the city. The square is a meeting place for all types of people. Every kind of lifestyle is represented, from old age to middle age to young age to New Age. In the summer, the square looks like a patchwork quilt with all shapes, sizes, and colors of human beings sitting in the warm sun.

Across the street to the south of the square is **Pack Place.** Upon entering Pack Place, Asheville's arts and science complex, you will encounter an enormous, vivid butterfly mobile hanging from the ceiling. It was created by schoolchildren with the help of local artists for the opening in 1992. Originally, the building housed the Pack Memorial Library and is now headquarters for the Colburn Mineral Museum, Health Adventure, the Diana Wortham Theatre, and the Asheville Art Museum. Hours are from 10:00 A.M. to 5:00 P.M., Tuesday through Saturday, and from 1:00 to 5:00 P.M., Sunday, June through October.

The **Asheville Art Museum,** where a minimal entrance fee is charged, has an interesting frieze—it is a copy of the *Entry of Alexander into Babylon* from an old palace in Rome, painted in 1811. The first two floors are changeable exhibits such as "Off the Wall Sculpture." The second floor has examples of the Ashcan school. On the third floor is a small permanent collection with contemporary and traditional works of such artists as Gorky, Grant Wood, Innis, and the Asheville favorite, Will Henry Stevens.

The **Health Adventure** branch of Pack Place is a world of hands-on exhibits that is both fun and educational for children. At the entrance you will see Mr. Bones, a skeleton riding a bicycle, showing how our bodies work in motion. One mind-boggling little niche has Shaquille O'Neal's uniform and shoes displayed. (The "Shaq" weighs 300 pounds with less than 7 percent body fat, is 7 feet 1 inch tall, and his shoe size is 23EEE with shoestrings $5^{1}/_{2}$ feet long.) This informative display shows children the role that genes play in our body makeup. At the Health Adventure, you will usually find a traveling exhibit that stays several months.

Also in Pack Place is the **Colburn Gem and Mineral Museum,** which the *Washington Post* called "a mini Smithsonian of gems." The gems, minerals, and stones are displayed very effectively with information available alongside. In addition to glass cases, there are many "hands-on" displays; adults as well as children can touch as much as they like. There are fabulous exhibits of old jewelry—stickpins, watch fobs, brooches, and shirt studs. The museum also sponsors programs all through the year for children and families. Recent offerings included "How to Be a Rockhound," "Dinosaur Days," and "A Geologic Walking Tour of Downtown Asheville."

North Carolina has the largest variety of mineral species in the United States. More than 300 minerals are known to exist in the state and many are here for you to see. While you are at the museum, you can pick up brochures giving locations and directions to gem mines and shops in Western North Carolina. The museum is handicapped accessible. Call for group rates and programs. (828) 254-7162. www.main.n.c.us/colburn.

Gold

America's first authenticated gold discovery occurred in 1799 when a 17 pound nugget was found in a creek bed in Cabarrus County, North Carolina by the 12 year old son of John Reed. Unable to identify the "bright yellow stone," his family used it for a door stop until 1802 when Mr. Reed took the nugget to a jeweler who paid him $3.50. At the time it was worth $3600.00. Spurred on, the Reed family began a mining operation and the following year they unearthed a 28 pound nugget, said to be the largest ever found in the United States.

North Carolina was the nation's only gold producing state from 1803 until 1828 and continued as a leading producer until 1849 when gold was discovered in California. At today's market, Mr. Reed's 28-pound nugget would fetch a handsome price—$120,000.00!

—a plaque in the Colburn Mineral Museum

In 1900, Reverend T. M. Myers from Louisville, Kentucky, bought what would later become the **Thomas Wolfe Home.** The 18-room wooden house had been built in 1883 and became a boardinghouse in 1889. The Reverend Mr. Myers named his house "My Old Kentucky Home" and today the original sign still hangs on the porch. Later Wolfe fictionalized the house as "Dixieland" in his classic first novel,

Look Homeward, Angel. Sadly, the house became a victim of arson in 1998 and suffered extensive damage; however, many of the original furnishings were saved or are salvageable. In spite of the damage, the house is still structurally sound and restoration of this historic site is planned.

Behind the home is the **Thomas Wolfe Memorial Visitor Center,** a small but excellent museum dedicated to Wolfe's life. Exhibits and photographs of Thomas and his family, from his earliest days to just before he passed away in 1938, are effectively displayed. A 20-minute video in a small theater completes the fascinating story of the life of this literal giant in literature. A gift shop offers a wide variety of books by and about Wolfe, sketches, note cards, and prints of the home and the famous Look Homeward angel statue. Everything here is good quality and the staff is very informative. The memorial is located at 52 North Market Street and is open at 10:00 A.M., Tuesday through Saturday, and at 1:00 P.M., Sunday, March through October. (828) 253-8304.

Around Pack Square are three distinctive restaurants, which you would do well to try. First is **Café on the Square,** a fine small restaurant with a big menu. A shiny bar runs almost the full length of the café, with intimate high tables for two across the aisle. The decor is sparse with thick, white tablecloths and white walls with black accents. There is usually a good exhibit of photographs for sale by Pete Smith.

Bubble Bread is one of the special appetizers at the café, consisting of a French baguette topped with bleu cheese, oregano, tomatoes, and mozzarella cheese. Another specialty is the fried calamari with hot-n-spicy cocktail sauce. Stick with the favorite dishes and you will not be disappointed.

At Christmas, an upside-down tree is hung from the ceiling with upside-down ornaments and an electric train around the base.

Hours at the café are from 11:30 A.M. to 4:00 P.M. for lunch and from 5:00 to 10:00 P.M. for dinner, seven days a week. (828) 251-5565. Moderate to expensive.

Next door to Café on the Square is **Bistro 1896** and the owners have a menu of "creative American cuisine" with a bite. To start, the soup of the day is always homemade, with New England Clam Chowder as a mainstay. Bistro does not have a set menu but always has a fine beef, game, and poultry selection, as well as fresh seafood, pasta,

and vegetarian fare. Locals contend you cannot make a mistake ordering anything from the menu at Bistro, so don't be afraid to go after
the dish you like best. Call for seasonal hours as well as reservations.
(828) 251-1300. Moderate to expensive.

If blindfolded, you would know you were in **La Caterina Trattoria**
by the delicious aromas wafting from the kitchen. The owners and
hosts are Robbin and Victor Giancola, doing what they do best—offering an authentic Italian menu in
Asheville. Victor trained at the
famous Maria's restaurant in New
York; however, he draws from a
family background of Italian
recipes handed down by his immi-
grant parents and grandparents.

All pastas at La Caterina are made in-house, as is the fresh mozzarella. The menu changes daily to ensure the season's best ingredients. From the rich-colored mural to the daily menu, La Caterina is
totally Italian with a family atmosphere, both comfortable and fun.
Lunch begins at 11:30 A.M., Tuesday through Saturday, and dinner
starts at 5:00 P.M., Monday through Saturday. A noon brunch on
Sunday is served until 3:00 P.M. (828) 254-1148. Moderate to expensive.

Salsas is a hideaway just around the corner from Pack Square at 6
Patton Avenue. Chef Hector Diaz is hot on the Asheville scene, with
his tasty Mexican-Caribbean menu.

Everything at Salsas starts with salsas, five to be exact, and all are
served with corn chips. The menu has
tapas, tacos, enchiladas, quesadillas, and
burritos, but the likes of which you have
never tasted before. Diaz is without peer
when it comes to blending foods to give
new tastes to old dishes. He likes rice,
beans, and ripe plantains as a base for
many of his creations and he piles on
grilled veggies, roasted pumpkin, dried
tomatoes, goat cheese, or anything else in

season. On top of it all he puts a local trout, chicken, flank steak, or
Russian boar. It will not matter to you that only organic products are
used in all Hector's dishes—like free-range chickens, organic cheeses,
sour cream, and hormone-steroid-free beef. You will be delighted with
this new adventure in eating.

Salsas is open for lunch from 11:30 A.M. to 2:30 P.M., Monday through Friday, and from 12:00 noon to 3:00 P.M., Saturday. Dinner hours are from 5:30 to 9:30 P.M., Monday through Saturday. (828) 252-9805.

Hector also has an even bigger and better creation, **Zambra,** his Spanish tapas restaurant and wine bar located at 85A Walnut Street. The menu has plenty of new tastes, a lot of them perfected during a vacation in Seville. The Sevillena Fire Roasted Tomatoes, an appetizer served with bread for sopping up the last bite, is just a hint of what's to come.

The menu, which changes each night, features a number of small dishes—paella, scallops with salami dressing, mushroom ravioli, small pizzas that Diaz calls Gallettas, or Gypsy bread, to name a few. Homemade sangria is served and there is a superb wine list. The imaginative dining rooms feature the paintings of Asheville artist Sally Bryenton. Zambra is open all year, six days a week at 6 P.M. Call for reservations. (828) 232-1060.

If this isn't enough to keep Hector busy, he is now marketing his fabulous hot sauces that he has been making and bottling in small quantities for several years. Watch your local stores for Hector's Smokin' Habanero Sauce and Hector's Smokin' Jalapeno Sauce or buy them on the Internet at www.HectorSauce.com.

Quilts

While you are in the Western North Carolina area you will see lots of quilts; they will be in museums, antique shops, hanging as decorations in homes and inns, and occasionally used as bed coverings, which was the original intent. Quilting has been practiced for thousands of years. Soldiers of the Middle Ages wore quilted coats and hoods under their armor. The Dutch and English colonists brought quilts to America to protect themselves from the cold winters. Quilting was a favorite art in frontier homes and beautiful designs were developed and passed on from generation to generation. Some quilt patterns portrayed historical events while others had sentimental significance. Other beautiful and long-lasting designs include Wedding Ring, Dresden Plate, and Log Cabin.

Just down the street and around the corner from Pack Place is Spruce Street. There are several shops of interest as well as the **Appalachian Craft Center.** The center has changing exhibits by national and international artists. Regional artist Laura Teague, a fifth-generation potter, uses five different glazes and samples of each are on display. Her pieces are ovenproof and dishwasher safe. Handmade looper rugs made by Ida Freeman, now in her eighties, as well as quilts made by Western North Carolina artisans add to the exceptional collection of the best mountain crafts in the area. The center is located at 10 North Spruce Street. For information about exhibits, please call (828) 253-8499. The center is open from 10:00 A.M. to 5:00 P.M., Monday through Saturday.

A few doors down at 28 Spruce Street is **Lucy Anne,** a lovely ladies' dress shop. Lucy Stella and Anne Hunter have put together a shop where "fashion is a matter of choice," and choices are what you will find in this well-stocked shop. Whether you need elegant evening wear or sophisticated casual wear, you will find a pleasing selection. Shop hours are from 9:30 A.M. to 5:30 P.M., Monday through Friday, and from 10:00 A.M. to 5:30 P.M., Saturday. (828) 251-5164.

Just a few more steps will take you into **Hunter & Coggins Clothing Co.,** which houses a full line of coats, suits, and hats for men (sorry, no shoes). Shop hours are from 9:00 A.M. to 6:00 P.M., Monday through Saturday.

Inside the same building and sandwiched in between the ladies' shop and the men's shop is **The Finishing Touch,** a fine diamond jewelry shop open from 9:00 A.M. to 4:00 P.M., Monday through Friday, and from 9:00 A.M. to 12:00 noon, Saturday.

Turn west at the corner of Spruce and Walnut to find **Magnolia's Oyster Bar & Grille.** This jivin' place has a live band, from 10:00 P.M. to 2:00 A.M., Thursday through Saturday. If you are looking for action, this would be a great place to start and end.

The menu offers light fare to full dinners. You could order the Steam Pot, which includes crab legs, oysters, clams, shrimp, mussels, crawfish, and whole lobster steamed with corn on the cob and red potatoes. You will definitely need two people to eat all of this! The grill is located at 26 Walnut Street. Lunch is served Monday through Friday and dinner is served daily. (828) 251-5211.

The words "antiques" and "Asheville" are synonymous, so if you are an antique buff, you will be happy, as antique shops and malls abound.

At 52 Broadway, in a handsome 1914 brick building that once served as a car dealer's showroom, you will find three antique shops.

On the ground floor is **Stuf Gallery,** where the owners make and repair lamps as well as sell their "stuff"—old silver, crystal, lamps, lampshades, and some furniture. Upstairs is **Magnolia Beauregard's,** with vintage clothing, antique jewelry, furniture, Civil War memorabilia, and old photos. In one area there is a "plunder section" where you can dig and paw to hopefully find a treasure. Also upstairs is **Antique Market Gallery,** an upscale antique mall with an assortment of china, crystal, and furniture.

Just across the street in another old building is **Archives Antiques,** 57 Broadway, with an eclectic selection of furniture and decorative accessories.

Walk west on Walnut Street and you will find another cluster of antique and collectible malls. **Lexington Park Antiques** at 65 Walnut is probably the largest with about 90 dealers displaying antique Christmas lights, vintage clothing, Fiesta ware, and old toys.

Upstairs in the same large building, which was once a shirt factory owned by the Vanderbilts, is **Reunions** at 51 North Lexington Avenue. This mall of 20,000 square feet is filled mainly with primitives, old cupboards, dry sinks, painted furniture, brass, and copper. Just on the corner, at 43 Rankin Avenue, is **Asheville Antiques**, with much of the same and then some.

The hours for antique shops are generally 10:00 A.M. to 5:00 P.M., six days a week, and Sunday afternoon in the summer months. Stuf Gallery, (828) 254-4054; Magnolia Beauregard's, (828) 251-5253; Antique Market Gallery, (828) 259-9977; Archives Antiques, (828) 253-5252; Lexington Park Antiques, (828) 253-3070; Reunions, (828) 236-0013; Asheville Antiques, (828) 253-3034.

When you were a child, you probably had a shoe box or cigar box full of your favorite things—a rock, a smooth piece of glass, a favorite-color crayon. **The Loft** is like a grown-up shoe box full of favorite things haphazardly collected and randomly placed around the store. If you hit it just right, you can find a most endearing gift for yourself or a friend. The Loft is open from 10:00 A.M. to 5:00 P.M., Monday through Thursday, and from 10:00 A.M. to 7:00 P.M., Friday and Saturday. In December, the shop is open on Sunday from 1:00 to 4:00 P.M. The address is 53 Broadway. (828) 259-9303.

A lively eatery in the historic downtown district is the **Mello Mushroom,** 50 Broadway. Kids love it and the vivid interior decor will entertain them while you are waiting for the good pizzas, calzones, or hoagies.

A smiling Mello Mushroom figure and a life-sized fiberglass bear greet customers in a color scheme of fluorescent purple, green, red,

 turquoise, and yellow. Giant "cookies" hang on the walls and carved wooden gas pumps are reminiscent of the site's gas station days.

One side order with a different "twist" is pretzels basted with butter and Parmesan cheese or honey and cinnamon. Diet-conscious adults need not feel guilty, as low-fat mayo is available for the hoagies. Prices are very moderate. The Mello Mushroom is open for lunch and dinner daily. (828) 236-9800.

For a change of pace, stop in at **Beanstreets** coffeehouse, known as the "home of the Java Heads." Whatever your mood, you can find a comfy spot on one of three levels. One level is up front near the door, with tables and chairs for on-the-go eating or leisurely sipping; another has video games and checkerboard tables; and the third level is filled with books and overstuffed chairs and sofas. One of the house specialty drinks is Primoccino (three shots espresso, hot chocolate, steamed milk, and lots of whipped cream). This drink is served in-house only—too large to go! A nice breakfast and lunch menu complements the easy feeling of this coffeehouse, located at 3 Broadway in the heart of town. For takeout orders, call (828) 255-8180.

Coffee

According to legend, Arabian herdsmen noticed that their flocks became frisky after feeding on coffee leaves and berries. Coffee moved from Arabia to Turkey to Italy and then to Western Europe in the 1600s, probably coming to the Americas in 1660. South America produces over half of the world's coffee supply and most coffee is named for the region where it grows or the port from which it is shipped.

If you like to meander in and out of interesting shops in hopes of finding a hidden treasure, North Lexington Avenue is a good place. Both sides of the street offer everything from a wonderful old hardware store turned gift shop to a shoestore to a shop with wooden postcards. Most shops open at around 10:00 A.M. and close between 5:00 and 6:00 P.M.

Since the 1960s, Bob and Ellen Carr have been putting together the best selection of shoes under one roof in the Southeast. **Tops For Shoes,** at 27 North Lexington Avenue, has sizes from babies' 0 to men's 16 and widths from AAAAA to EEE! Hard to fit? Not at Tops. One salesperson said they have "hard to 'fine' brands," including Mephisto, Ecco, and Arche. Six departments offer shoes, socks, purses, belts, and wallets for men, women, and children. Store hours are from 10:00 A.M. to 6:00 P.M., Monday through Saturday, and on Sunday in October. There is free parking on Rankin Avenue. (828) 254-6721.

Laura Pet-Ritz has owned the **Mystic Eye** since 1987. She specializes in American artist-made clothing. Laura designs her own fabric and offers custom designing and fitting. Original hats and scarves are of particular interest. All of the items in the shop are made by artists the owner knows personally. The **Natural Home** has unbleached, chemical-free bed linens and decorative hardware. In the back of the shop are Oriental teapots, sake sets, and lots of sushi accoutrements. **Chevron Trading Post & Bead Company** has unique beads from around the world. Classes for children and adults are offered to help you learn how to make jewelry and other beaded items.

Bet you can't come out of **T. S. Morrison** without buying something. Starting out as a livery stable in 1891, it is the oldest retail store in Asheville, where nostalgia reigns on every shelf. If you are old enough, you will recognize the small things so familiar to your everyday life when you were a child. The penny candy is in three huge containers and glass cases hold soft confections such as lemon bonbons, Neapolitan coconut slices, and all kinds of licorice, including the yard-long strawberry kind. Keith Cox, manager, says T. S. Morrison carries over 30 kinds of old-fashioned candies. Try a sarsaparilla or a ginger beer from the soft-drink cooler in the corner.

Years ago, many things came in tins that, when empty, had a million other uses. T. S. Morrison has copies of these old tins and they still have a million uses. Wonderful, exact reproductions of the old, yellow-checkered taxis, Radio Flyer wagons, and fire engines are in the children's section as well as small toys you never see anymore, such as bicycle bells for handlebars. Many people are familiar with Old

World Christmas ornaments . . . well, Morrison has shelves of these ornaments taken from molds hundreds of years old. Young and old alike love this place because the styles have become new again. It is located at 39 North Lexington. (828) 258-1891.

Two blocks to the west is Haywood Street. If you are looking for a fine piece of jewelry, **Jewels That Dance** is an established store with an excellent reputation. Paula Dawkins and her designers have a full collection of jewelry that is both timeless and contemporary. Jewels That Dance keeps regular store hours and is open all year. The address is 63 Haywood Street. (828) 254-5088.

> "**mal·a·prop** (MAL uh prop): n. a malapropism (after Mrs. Malaprop, a character in Richard Sheridan's play, *The Rivals*). A malapropism is the ludicrous misuse of a word, especially by confusion with one of a similar sound."

There's no confusion here at **Malaprop's Bookstore/Café.** This great bookstore has been a mainstay in Asheville since 1981 and shows no sign of slowing down. There is plenty of room for serious browsing—displays are eye catching and are changed frequently. Recently they were named the Publishers Weekly Bookseller of the Year. It is the first Southern bookstore ever awarded this prestigious recognition.

In the mission statement in the store's quarterly newsletter, owner Emoke B'Racz describes Malaprop's in part as: "A place where good reads, good company, good music and the best coffee complete the picture. A place where the reader and the book meet and a journey begins." In addition to fine selections and a more than comfortable atmosphere, there is a café with a roomy seating area and a counter. Soups, sandwiches, and beverages are served daily. Nearby, the wall-sized bulletin board lists café events, classes, book signings, and gatherings. This is a pleasant, helpful, and educational place to go. It is located at 55 Haywood Street. It is open from 9:00 A.M. to 9:00 P.M., Monday through Thursday; from 9:00 A.M. to 11:00 P.M., Friday and Saturday; and from 9:00 A.M. to 6:00 P.M., Sunday. (828) 254-6734. For books by phone call (800) 441-9829 or visit www.malaprops@mindspring.com.

Look for **The Open Door,** a boutique of mainly casual, fun ladies' clothes, at 35 Haywood Street. It is small, but since 1978 the shop has been packed with jewelry, candles, rugs, bedspreads, and even soap. Most enticing are the natural-fiber blouses, shirts, pants, dresses, and hand-knit sweaters in all colors and the selection of hats. The boutique is open from 10:00 A.M. to 5:00 P.M., six days a week, and from 12:00 noon to 5:00 P.M., Sunday. (828) 254-8056.

Fondue can be a fun way of dining and the **Flying Frog Café** has it on their menu. Poaching pots are also available using broth instead of oil as a cooking medium. Other menu items include Indian and Caribbean specialties. The café is located at 76 Haywood Street and is closed Tuesday. Dinner is from 5:30 P.M. Reservations recommended. (828) 254-9411. Moderate to expensive.

If the soft-sculptured mannequins don't lure you into the **Gentleman's Gallery** at 66 Haywood Street, owner Alan Levy will. Al's family has been in the clothing business for many years in Montgomery, Alabama, and he is continuing the tradition here is Asheville. Al says he runs a "fun Mom and Pop store" full of sophisticated selections of men's better sportswear and women's wear, too. For shop hours, call (828) 252-7517 and ask for "Big Al."

Constance Ensner, owner of **Constance Boutique,** has taken a small slip of space and filled it with contemporary clothes and accessories. Constance studied design at Colorado State University and has an eye for stylish, nontrendy women's wear. She shops both the East and West Coasts for just the right look. Elegance and simplicity seem to be her trademark. Shoes, purses, jewelry, and hair accessories round out this eclectic shop located at 62 Haywood Street. Shop hours are from 10:00 A.M. to 6:00 P.M., Monday through Friday, and from 11:00 A.M. to 6:00 P.M., Saturday.

Gold Hill Espresso is just right for a cup of coffee or tea or, if you prefer, the cooler is always full of chilled juices and soft drinks. A variety of sandwiches and soups are offered along with an assortment of bagels and scones. At 64 Haywood Street, the shop opens around 7:30 A.M. and closes at 7:00 P.M., six days a week. Sunday hours are from 9:00 A.M. to 2:00 P.M.

The **Asheville Urban Trail,** a self-guided walking tour of the historic downtown, was begun by the city as part of its ongoing program to improve the quality of the city through the display of public art. The trail was designed by volunteers and built with donations.

Thirty "stations" are or will be highlighted on the trail. Along the 1.6-mile loop, pink granite markers embedded in the sidewalks indicate the trail and artwork has been installed at many of the stations. These artworks include a bronze top hat and cane on a bench, a statue of a young girl at a water fountain, and an enormous flat iron, effectively placed next to a flatiron building that was built in 1926.

For a map of the trail, stop by the Chamber of Commerce on Haywood Street or Pack Place Education, Arts and Science Center at Pack Square, or call (828) 259-5855.

The section of town known as Battery Hill dates back to the Civil War, when it was called Battery Porter Hill. It was the site of the Confederate battery for the defense of Asheville and was the highest point in town.

A hotel built here in 1886 attracted the rich and famous, including George Vanderbilt. It was while he was visiting the hotel that Mr. Vanderbilt decided to build his Biltmore Estate. In the early 1920s, E. W. Grove bought the hotel and razed it—even removing some of the hill itself. He then created a commercial district anchored by a hotel, which today is the Battery Park Apartments. He also built the Grove Arcade as a public marketplace, which is still the architectural centerpiece of the district.

Today, Battery Hill is a thriving, charming area. Restaurants, shops, galleries, and the Haywood Park Hotel are set amidst the architectural charms of the 1920s.

The **Haywood Park Hotel,** located at 1 Battery Park Avenue, is in the heart of downtown Asheville. The hotel is privately owned and the minute you step inside the lobby you can feel it. The atmosphere is quiet and the decor is tasteful. (800) 228-2522. Moderate to expensive, depending on the suites.

The **New French Bar** is on the corner of Battery and Haywood in the Haywood Park Hotel. This sunny triangle has a great atmosphere. Seating is available at the bar or at tall tables with tall chairs, which provide a perfect perch for people watching. Outside seating along the sidewalk is also possible when the weather permits. Be careful not to overindulge on the French bread—it's wonderful. Try a baguette and a cup of soup with a glass of wine. (828) 252-3685.

Downstairs from the New French Bar in the Haywood Park Hotel is a dimly lit French restaurant, **23 Page.** Seating is cozy and lends itself to creating a romantic atmosphere. American and French cuisine is offered along with an ample wine list...an enjoyable evening can be expected. It is open for dinner only from 5:30 to 9:30 P.M.,

Monday through Thursday. Friday through Sunday closing time is 10:00 P.M. Reservations are suggested. (828) 252-3685.

West on Battery Park Avenue are more shops and restaurants. If you are interested in a "sit-down" lunch, the **Uptown Cafe** on Battery is a local favorite with excellent food and a nice children's menu. (828) 253-2158. Moderate prices.

Almost next door is **Julie Mar Needlepoint Studio.** Although the shop is small, the inventory is large. Julie has filled it with an amazing variety of needlepoint and counted cross-stitch canvasses and skeins of thread in every color. You can buy just about any design and any size canvas imaginable, from Christmas ornaments to rugs. Julie does some custom painting of canvasses. It is open from 10:00 A.M. to 4:00 P.M., Monday through Friday. (828) 254-8893.

Old Europe, at 18 Battery Park, is appropriately named. White lace curtains hang in the small bay windows up front. As you open the door, you get the feeling of the "old country"—lovely French melodies softly playing contribute to the European atmosphere. A tempting array of fine pastries is displayed in an old-fashioned case.

Since 1994, Zoltan and Melinda Vetro, both from Hungary, have been baking handmade delicacies each morning. Fresh strudel, tortes, and cakes, along with a fine egg salad croissant, will delight your taste buds. European-style coffees and liquors complete the scene. It is open seven days a week.

A Faraway Place represents many ethnic cultures from all over the world. Owner Mark Fields goes deep into the heart of Africa, the Amazon Rain Forest, and Saudi Arabia to gather exotic objects that speak of the people and customs from whence they came. Faraway has wonderful CDs and the beautiful music you hear in the shop will stay with you a long time after you leave. (828) 252-1891.

When you are strolling down Wall Street, you may see a figure scaling the "Wall"; this is not Spider Man, but someone honing his rock climbing skills at **CliMax,** the indoor climbing center. Whether you are a beginner or advanced rock climber, this facility offers a simulated mountain, with all degrees of difficulty, and a foam rubber floor to catch you when mistakes are made. Groups often come for fun, celebrating birthdays and other occasions, and qualified instructors stand by to ensure safety for everyone.

After you take your first steps at CliMax, the staff hopes you will pursue this exciting sport further in the vertical world of the Western North Carolina Mountains. Call Stuart M. Cowles, president of

CliMax, for information about programs and certified Boy Scout merit badge training. The telephone number is (828) 252-9996. Hours are from 3:30 to 10:00 P.M., Tuesday and Thursday; from 12:00 noon to 10:00 P.M., Wednesday and Friday; from 10:00 A.M. to 10:00 P.M., Saturday; and from 1:00 to 6:00 P.M., Sunday.

Some say vegetarians have more fun. If so, the **Laughing Seed Café** is the place to have it. This is strictly vegetarian and you will find no pink or blue "sugar" here. The delicious herbal tea is made with honey and, for $.50 extra, soy protein powder can be added to any of the extensive juice and smoothie selections.

Some of the international favorites include a vegetarian Reuben sandwich, Tofuna sandwich, and Asian Fusion salad—it's not exactly the average menu. The bread is homemade and heavenly and can be purchased here as well as at the Fresh Market (see index).

On one large wall there is a tropical landscape mural with exotic birds and animals but no laughing seeds. Downstairs is a spacious but cozy brewpub where huge vats bubble away creating the Laughing Seed signature beers. The most popular beer is "Porter," named for an Old World ale made with extra hops, ensuring a longer-lasting and richer beer. Other tap and imported beers are also available.

The upstairs entrance is closed at 10:00 P.M. and entry is then on Patton Avenue. Closing time downstairs is irregular and depends on how much fun everyone is having. The café entrance is located at 40 Wall Street. It is open from 11:30 A.M. to 9:00 P.M., Monday through Thursday, and weekends until 10:00 P.M. Sunday brunch is from 10:00 A.M. to 2:00 P.M., serving frittatas, tofu scrambled eggs, as well as a variety of omelets. (828) 252-3445. Moderate prices.

The Laughing Seed

On the Indonesian island of Bouton there is the Legend of the Laughing Seed. The seeds of a special plant were ground to a paste and eaten by the people, who became intoxicated with laughter. This deep laughter raised their spirits so they could communicate with the gods. Their appetites were satisfied as they left with a feeling of fullness and well-being that lasted many days.

Asheville's winters are similar to those in Scotland and **The Celtic Way,** 14 Wall Street, has the answer to what to wear. Since 1981, owner-manager Betty Daughtridge has visited Scotland several times a year to return with authentic wool capes, kilts, and sweaters (or jumpers as they are known in Scotland). Scots played a major part in settling Asheville and the surrounding area and these warm, woolly goods are much appreciated.

Also in this tiny shop you'll find waxed-cotton clothing, blackthorn canes, and perhaps your very own family plaid. The Celtic Way is open from 10:00 A.M. to 7:00 P.M., six days a week and sometimes on Sunday. (828) 254-0644.

Asheville is certainly not lacking in great restaurants, but when the best are mentioned, the **Market Place** has to be one. Since the 1980s, Mark and Kim Rosenstein have been soothing people with good food and discreet service. When asked about the restaurant business, Kim replied, "When you can turn somebody's day around, it's a good thing." The restaurant has a clean, fresh, sophisticated look with simple blush colors and the walls are accented with beautiful paintings by Scott Loury.

The food is the underscoring mark of excellence. For starters, the crispy potato cake with goat cheese topped with caramelized apples will comfort your soul, unless you select the onion tart, which will tease your taste buds. The entree selections are ample yet not overwhelming and everything is prepared to perfection. One note, however—if you order the rack of lamb, the four-chop portion is recommended as the two-chop portion is definitely small. The wine menu, with over 150 wines, is sure to have something to suit your taste as well as your purse.

The Rosensteins moved the Market Place to this location in 1990, which was formerly a print shop. Architect John Reid transformed this building into a lovely, open, and spacious dining area. The upstairs can be reserved for private parties and, if you really want a cozy spot, ask for the table under the stairs, near the wine bar. The restaurant, located at 20 Wall Street, is open for dinner only from 6:00 to 9:30 P.M. The wine bar opens at 5:00 P.M. (828) 252-4162.

The **Captain's Bookshelf** is a serious bookstore. All books are second hand, many are first editions, and most of the volumes are in excellent condition. There is a great section of books about North Carolina, but for the most part there is something here for everyone. Sturdy stools for reaching high . . . yes, books are floor to ceiling . . . and chairs for reading or studying are strategically placed. For the most part, there are no distractions.

Before you enter, be sure and notice the large bronze book with an eavesdropping bronze sparrow outside—it is one of the "stations" on the Urban Trail. The store, at 31 Page Avenue, is open from 10:00 A.M. to 6:00 P.M., Wednesday through Saturday, in the winter. Call for summer hours. (828) 253-6631.

Art Deco

Art Deco is a decorative and architectural style of the period 1925 to 1940, characterized by geometric designs, bold colors, and the use of plastic and glass. More Art Deco architecture built in the late 1920s and early 1930s can be found in downtown Asheville than in any other Southeastern city, except in Miami Beach.

An important landmark in Asheville is the **Kress Emporium** building, constructed of ceramic tile in a neo-classic motif in 1928. No more a five-and-dime, the Kress building has emerged as a showcase for over 85 local artists. Everything from tatted gloves to Russian amber jewelry is represented. Grab a cup of coffee at the small coffee bar and ramble through the stalls where the artists display their stock in trade. The Kress Emporium is located at 19 Patton Avenue and is open all year round. From January through March hours are from 12:00 noon to 5:00 P.M., closed on Sunday; April through December, hours are from 10:00 A.M. to 6:00 P.M. (828) 281-2252.

Located in downtown Asheville is **Weinhaus,** a wine shop with a great variety of labels and prices. Owner David Mallett and his staff are eager to assist you. Weinhaus is located at 86 Patton Avenue and is open from 10:00 A.M. until 6:00 P.M., six days a week. (828) 254-6453 or (800) 283-1544.

While you are in downtown Asheville you'll want to look at some of the beautiful, old churches in the area. The church community, at the heart of Asheville history and architecture, reveals powerful stories of sanctuaries and the architects who constructed them. Spanish designer Rafael Guastavino incorporated distinctive stylistic techniques to construct the **St. Lawrence Catholic Church** (97 Haywood Street) in 1909, which was recently awarded the distinction of minor basilica. Sheathed in pink, green, brown, and white tiles, two Spanish baroque towers distinguish the church as a true architectural masterpiece. Using a method called "cohesive construction," Guastavino built a dome measuring 52 feet by 82 feet—the largest unsupported tile dome in the United States.

A few blocks away on Church Street (appropriately) are three lovely old churches, all within one block of each other: the old **First Presbyterian Church,** founded in 1794; the **Methodist Central Church,** founded in 1827; and **Trinity Episcopal,** founded in 1911, where bells chime the hours.

A few more blocks away, at 5 Oak Street, is the **First Baptist Church.** It was completed in 1927 and is listed on the National Register of Historic Places. Architect Douglas Ellington based the design of the sanctuary space on the famous cathedral and dome of Santa Maria del Fiore in Florence, Italy. Santa Maria del Fiore was the first domed space built during the Renaissance and was considered an engineering feat in its day.

Basilica

A basilica was a public building in ancient Rome. The Romans used basilicas as courtrooms and for other civic activities. Early Christians held services in basilicas. Some Roman Catholic churches are given the honorary title of basilica because of their religious or historical importance. There are two kinds of basilicas, major and minor. A major basilica has a special altar that can only be used by the pope or those he delegates. St. Peter's in Rome is a major basilica.

"Hurricane" John Cram blew into Asheville in 1972 and the art world in this mountain city has never been the same. With an artist's heart and a head for business, he has developed several successful galleries filled with first-rate contemporary American crafts that cannot be equaled. Single-handedly, he has put Asheville on the map as the source for arts and crafts, with serious collectors from all over the country knocking at his door. Not only has John been a successful entrepreneur, but many civic undertakings have his fingerprints on them. He has been "Daddy Warbucks" with Asheville being his "Annie."

Cram's latest acquisition is the **Fine Arts Theater,** showing independent and foreign films that cannot be seen in many theaters. You cannot nosh on popcorn and Milk Duds, but fresh juices, espresso, tea, wine, and beer are offered. Often, John himself takes up tickets or greets people. (828) 232-1536.

Just past the Fine Arts Theater is **Blue Spiral Gallery,** where accomplished artists exhibit their work. John Cram has no boundaries on the art presented at the gallery, so you will always find eclectic work in all media. Upstairs are works by in-house artists with a good selection by Will Henry Stevens, Asheville's most famous.

Blue Spiral Gallery makes it possible for you to own an exceptional piece of art without selling the farm. Hours are from 10:00 A.M. to 5:00 P.M., Monday through Saturday, year round. The address is 38 Biltmore Avenue; the phone number is (828) 251-0202. Someday Asheville will build a monument to John Cram, but it will not be ordinary; his epitaph will probably be taken from Ernest Becker's book, *The Denial of Death:*

> Who knows what form the forward momentum of life will take in the time ahead or what use it will make of our anguished searching. The most that any one of us can see to do is to fashion something—an object or ourselves—and drop it into the confusion, make an offering of it, so to speak, to the life force.

Zone One, located at 37 Biltmore Avenue, is a good contemporary art gallery. Started in 1992, the gallery houses some permanent art but also has quality traveling exhibits. (828) 258-3088.

Ad-Lib, at 40 Biltmore Avenue, is an upscale ladies' clothing store specializing in natural fabrics. Owner Anna Sagel has geared her shop to women from 20 to 70. She can literally dress you from head to toe and accessorize with hats, scarves, belts, purses, and Nootes shoes. Hours are from 10:00 A.M. to 6:00 P.M., Monday through Saturday, and from 12:00 noon to 5:00 P.M. Sunday. (828) 285-8838.

Next door, **Barley's Taproom & Pizzeria** opens at 11:30 A.M. and closes when the crowd goes home. You can "build" your own pizza if you have a hearty appetite or you can order by the slice and wash it down with one of many varieties of domestic beer or a microbrew. Upstairs are a pool table and a bar where the younger crowd tends to gather. Moderate prices.

What smells better than bread baking? Not much. Open the door to the **Blue Moon Bakery** and you know immediately that these folks know what they're doing. The bakery has been baking artisan bread in Asheville since 1992. The dough is slowly proofed, the loaves shaped by hand and baked in the huge stone deck oven, which you can see from the eating area. From this great oven come approximately 15 varieties of bread daily—apple-currant rye, red-pepper cheddar, raisin pecan, and challah (traditionally baked on Fridays).

If you don't gobble up your purchase before you get home, all of the breads freeze well. Served daily starting at 7:30 A.M. are breakfast, brunch, lunch, and tea. Sandwiches, salads, and pastries are the fare. (828) 252-6063.

If you enjoy feathering your nest, you should not miss **Vertu,** an elegant little shop at 69 Biltmore Avenue. It is appropriately named, as vertu means "a knowledge or love for artistic objects or curios, beautiful and rare as to interest a collector." Owner Gail Armstrong certainly has knowledge of beautiful objects. She travels to France three times a year to discover objets d'art as well as French antiques. The old is mixed artfully with the new; an example is a contemporary glass-topped iron table with French antique chairs.

There is an abundance of soft French and Italian bed linens at Vertu, as well as table linens. You will also find vintage patchwork pillows, lamps, chandeliers, works of local artists, antique French drawings, and other irresistible accessories. Hours are from 10:00 A.M. to 5:00 P.M., Monday through Saturday. (828) 253-0099.

American Folk Art and Antiques at 64 Biltmore Avenue is a unique gallery. From functional wood-fired pottery to folk art carvings and important examples of American antique furniture, this gallery celebrates the handmade and centuries of creativity. The variety here is wonderful and unusual. Be sure and look for the mud paintings by renowned artist Jimmy Lee Suddeth. It is open from 10:00 A.M. to 5:00 P.M., Monday through Saturday, and from 12:00 noon to 5:00 P.M., Sunday, May through October. (828) 251-1904.

A few feet off of the beaten track is **Biltmore Gallery Downtown,** just three blocks south of Pack Square at 144 Biltmore Avenue. Owners Suzanne and Steven Bellich have created a light-filled, wide-open gallery that is "uniquely North Carolina." They specialize in displaying North Carolina artists, many of them from Asheville.

Although Suzanne is not an artist she has been a serious collector for years; husband Steven makes beautiful furniture as a hobby. The artists they feature fill this gallery with jewelry, paintings, turned and carved vessels, pottery, sculpture, and a large collection of blown glass.

Here is an array of fine art to fit any decor. The richness of the work will make you appreciate these "hometown" artists. Displays are always changing, so come by six days a week beginning at 11:00 A.M. and on Sunday at 1:00 P.M.

The **Screen Porch,** 115 Fairview Road, is located just up the hill from Biltmore Village and only minutes from downtown Asheville. This is an unusual but charming garden-to-porch-to-cottage warehouse. It is much too large to be called a shop.

Inside are individual booths containing reinterpretations of architectural salvage such as old weathered windows, shutters, doors, and furniture. One booth has mirror frames from molded tin ceiling pieces. Another has antique wrought iron made into handsome plate hangers and picture frames. Among the most striking items are the rusty automobile "insides" transformed into delightful planters and fountains.

This is the ultimate in recycling. Several landscape artists at the Biltmore Estate are among the very creative contributors. The spacious entrance area is occupied by the **Common Ground Distributors,** a book outlet of discounted garden and nature books. Save time for a good browse here. It is open from 10:00 A.M., six days a week, and from 1:00 P.M., Sunday. (828) 274-0370.

A true Victorian bed and breakfast, **Cedar Crest Bed and Breakfast,** located at 674 Biltmore Avenue, is listed on the National Register of Historic Places. If you are looking for a place to stay that is authentic in style and furnishings, Cedar Crest is the one for you. This historic mansion was built by architect Richard Morris Hunt and is one of the largest and most opulent residences surviving from the 1890s.

Ten guest rooms in the main house are all furnished with antiques. The house is air-conditioned and a full breakfast is served. There is also a circa-1915 bungalow containing two suites, a one bedroom and a two bedroom.

Rates are expensive, but if you want to be near the Biltmore Estate and downtown Asheville, the location is ideal. (828) 252-1389. www.cedarcrestvictorianinn.com.

Heading south on Biltmore Avenue toward the Biltmore Estate, you will see Biltmore Station in a cul-de-sac one block north of Bilt-more Village. Here you will find the **Interiors Marketplace,** Asheville's answer to an Eastern bazaar. It opened in 1994 and is in a former building-supply house.

Over 200 spectacular exhibits display furniture and accessories for the home in styles contemporary or traditional, casual or formal, whimsical or utilitarian. There is everything here—china, glassware, furniture, rugs, linens, garden accents, paintings, and prints. With over 100 artists represented, the walls are well covered.

The Interiors Marketplace is fertile ground for interior decorating ideas and inspiration. After you tour all the vignettes, a neat little café will provide a light lunch or coffee and rest for foot fatigue. The Interiors Marketplace is open from 10:00 A.M. to 6:00 P.M., Monday through Saturday, and from 1:00 to 5:00 P.M., Sunday. (828) 253-2300.

*Voted Best Italian Restaurant
in Western North Carolina*

Trevi, named after the famous fountain in Rome, is a lively, good place to dine. Owners Barbara and Richard Laibson have furnished the dining room "bistro" style, with an open high ceiling, a few twin-kling lights, chest-high dividers that furnish dining privacy, and red-checked tablecloths. Through a long, slim opening at one end of the room, you can glimpse the kitchen just enough to know that the chef is serious about cooking.

The style of cooking here is from the Apulia region of southern Italy, which features light sauces, fresh herbs and produce, lots of seafood, and great olive oils. You might want to begin your meal with the steamed mussels or a sample of the great assorted olives to go with the house bread and oil. There is a fine marinated salad, but the "Insalate Trevi" is hard to beat.

Pasta is featured and the selections are impressive, as are the house specialties that are labeled "Trevi." If you prefer a somewhat light meal, try the fabulous spinach/artichoke pizza. There is full bar service and a good wine list.

Before you leave be sure to walk in the **Baba Riche** gourmet market. Part of the market is actually in the restaurant, anchored by a chunk of a column. Specialty items used in the kitchen are available and you may also buy bread, oils, soups, sauces, and pestos. Trevi, located at 2 Hendersonville Road at the Biltmore Station, is open for lunch weekdays and for dinner Thursday through Sunday. (828) 281-1400.

If "a thing of beauty is a joy forever," you will be eternally happy at **Village Antiques,** located at 755 Biltmore Avenue. This is where you can find exquisite, serious investment furniture and accessories. Owners Zenda Addis and Terry Powell comb Europe several times each year for their treasures, but they focus mainly on France. A favorite of Ms. Addis's are French commodes, hand carved, hand rubbed, and often inlaid with satinwood.

Two old warehouses are filled with 17th-, 18th-, and 19th-century furniture, paintings, sculpture, porcelains, books, lamps, and reliquaries—an art form in itself. Since 1990, these partners have searched out the dramatic, the unusual, and the highest quality of every item and their clientele now reach from California to New York. They work with homeowners as well as dealers and designers. Hours are from 10:00 A.M. to 5:00 P.M., six days a week, or by appointment. (828) 252-5090.

Biltmore Estate

Any season is the right time to visit the incredible Biltmore Estate. Volumes have been written about the mansion but you must make the journey yourself. Seldom, if ever, has an estate in Europe or the United States been so lavishly kept true to the times, with thousands of priceless antiques that have stayed with the mansion all these years.

After purchasing 125,000 acres of land around Asheville, George Washington Vanderbilt engaged two of the most distinguished architects of the day, Richard Morris Hunt and Frederick Law Olmsted, to build the legendary Biltmore. On Christmas Day 1895, the house opened with family and guests celebrating one of the marvels of the century. They lived and played in a home with "4 acres of floor space with 250 rooms, 34 family and guest bedrooms, 43 bathrooms, 65 fireplaces, three kitchens, and an indoor swimming pool," states *A Guide to Biltmore Estate,* by The Biltmore Company. "The grounds covered a 100,000-acre forest, a 250-acre wooded park, 6 pleasure gardens, and 30 miles of paved roadways."

Take the better part of the day and scour the mansion, grounds, and winery, and then purchase the guide and read about it. Hours at the Biltmore Estate are from 8:30 A.M. to 5:00 P.M. Biltmore House opens at 9:00 A.M. Please call about seasonal events at (800) 543-2961 or visit www.biltmore.com.

Visitors can now know what it might have been like to spend the night on the estate. In March 2001 the luxury **Inn on Biltmore Estate** opened to raves. The 213-room French country-style inn is located on a hill above the winery. It is not a replica of the house; instead the design was inspired by other estate structures. The focus of the inn is to offer the same kind of hospitality that George Vanderbilt offered his guests a century ago. Packages combine a stay at the inn with admission tickets to the Biltmore House, gardens, and winery. (800) 858-4130.

Constructed in the late 1890s as a picturesque village at the entrance to the Biltmore Estate, **Biltmore Village** is a classic planned community. The designer of the Biltmore House produced the fan-shaped landscape plan for the village and Richard Smith designed the cottages, school, infirmary, and post office.

Biltmore Village is truly one of North Carolina's most enjoyable shopping environments. Village shops are in the original homes, many built for the artisans who worked at the Biltmore House. Nearly 40 buildings house over 100 merchants. Renovation of the village began in 1960 and it was declared a local Historic District in 1989.

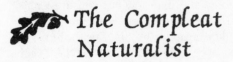
The Compleat Naturalist

The **Compleat Naturalist** is *complete* also! This fun/serious shop can equip you to monitor the weather, gaze at the stars, study plants and insects, feed and observe the birds, and feed or repel the squirrels. Here you will find a really good selection of telescopes and microscopes, a small but nice selection of outdoor clothing, and books on every nature subject. You'll also find tapes and CDs, wind chimes and tumbled stones, pocket knives, compasses, and walking sticks. A smallish, young naturalist room has puzzles, coloring books, and plenty of "critters." Owners Hal and Laura Mahan have thought of everything. Located at 2 Biltmore Plaza, the shop is open daily. (828) 274-5408 or (800) 678-5430.

www.CompleatNaturalist.com.

The **Biltmore Depot,** like the Biltmore House and All Souls Church, was designed by Richard Morris Hunt. It was completed in 1894 and, at Christmas of 1895, it welcomed the friends and relatives of George Vanderbilt who came for the grand opening of the Biltmore Estate. It continued as a station until 1972.

The depot was declared a National Historic Landmark in 1976. While the interior has been renovated and modernized repeatedly over the years, the exterior looks the same as it did when the Vanderbilts debarked here in 1895 to celebrate the holidays. Inside the depot now is a restaurant that serves lunch and dinner seven days a week. (828) 277-7651.

The **Biltmore Village Historic Museum** is located at 7 Biltmore Plaza and is open from 12:00 noon to 4:00 P.M., Monday through Saturday. Here you will find information about the Village from the 1800s to the present. Admission is free.

New Morning Gallery has been a talisman for John Cram—it was his first business and has always been successful. Downstairs are garden accessories with fountains bursting with every kind of water pattern, heavy iron chimes that make rich Tibetan sounds, and cheerful items to tuck into the garden. Upstairs is overwhelming but so efficiently presented you can browse with ease in the different sections of glass, wood, iron, jewelry, clay, and steel crafts. New Morning Gallery is located at 7 Boston Way, in Biltmore Village. Hours are from 10:00 A.M. to 6:00 P.M., daily, and from 12:00 noon to 5:00 P.M., Sunday. (828) 274-2831.

Next door is **Bellagio,** featuring wearable art where the discerning buyer can feast. Exquisite handmade clothes—silk kimonos with pants and blouses, suits with inlaid designs, swing jackets in bright reds and yellows, woven sweaters, and catchy accessories of purses and scarves—are all here. John

Cram has melded these things with a gallery of art objects to purchase. Bellagio (meaning "beautiful leisure") is costly, but the quality of merchandise and the timeless designs in clothes are worth every penny. Hours are from 10:00 A.M. to 6:00 P.M., daily, and from 12:00 noon to 5:00 P.M., Sunday. (828) 277-8100.

For you early risers, **Hathaway's Village Café and Market** is a comfy spot. At 8:00 A.M., daily pastries, bagels, muffins, and gourmet breakfasts are offered along with a huge coffee and tea menu (coffee is roasted daily in the store). Soups, quiches, sandwiches, and desserts are also served for lunch in a big glassed-in room reminiscent of your grandmother's porch.

Hathaway's has an extensive mail-order menu. Coffees (Continental, South American, Far Eastern, or African), flavored coffees, organically grown coffees, and bulk tea can all be ordered. Call (888) JAVA-BILL for more information. Hathaway's is located at 3 Boston Way and is open from 8:00 A.M. to 5:00 P.M., Tuesday through Saturday, and for brunch, Sunday.

With all the shops and galleries in Biltmore Village to keep you busy, be sure to save time for lunch at **Chelseas.** A quaint cottage, at 6 Boston Way, is decorated in typical English style with English rose printed damask table skirts covered with white, cut linen cloths. Lots of English china is displayed around the rooms. Choices for lunch include soups, salads, sandwiches, and quiche. Luncheon hours are from 11:30 A.M. to 3:00 P.M., and a Sunday brunch is served from 10:30 A.M. to 3:00 P.M. An even better idea would be to take time for afternoon tea, served in proper English form. You can relax and enjoy a pot of tea with authentic scones served with Devonshire cream and jam along with finger sandwiches and a variety of sweets, including English trifle. If you prefer, a cheese and fruit board is also available. Tea is served from 3:30 to 5:00 P.M. After lunch or tea, browse through the gift shop and food hall. (828) 274-4400. Moderate prices.

The **Baggie Goose,** at 3 Swan Street, has a good selection of stationery, invitations, and wonderful wrapping paper. (828) 274-3333. A small goldsmith shop, called **Blue,** sits at 1 Swan Street. Lynn Danies and Susan West have tempting collections of handmade platinum, plus gold and silver jewelry. Several artworks by locals are very affordable. (828) 827-277.

Good, easy clothes are what you get at the **2 On Crescent** shop (easy to remember because the shop name is the address as well). Flax, Joan Vass, and Bluefish are some of the lines carried here as well as Birkenstock shoes. These established lines of clothes have four or five pieces to each ensemble, giving you several different looks.

2 On Crescent also carries jewelry, some of which is made by local artists. Hours are from 10:00 A.M. to 5:30 P.M., Monday through Saturday, and from 10 A.M. to 5:00 P.M., Wednesday. (828) 274-6890.

If you have an interest in children's books, **Once Upon a Time,** at 7 All Souls Crescent, has over 6,000 titles along with fun toys and games and a full range of children's clothing. For mail orders call (800) 561-KIDS.

In the midst of scurrying from shop to shop, do take time to visit the beautiful old Episcopal church, the **Cathedral of All Souls.** It was established in 1896 and became the Cathedral of the Western North Carolina Diocese in 1995. A cathedral is a parish church in which the bishop, the chief pastor-leader of the diocese, has his seat or chair (*cathdra* in Latin). All Souls was conceived as a congregation and a building by George Vanderbilt to be the central focus of the village.

The design of the church is said to have been inspired by abbey churches in northern England. The windows were designed and made by David Armstrong and his daughter Helen, contemporaries of Tiffany, and the kneeling cushions are original. New needlework on them has been designed and stitched by parishioners and friends as memorials. Located at 3 Angle Street, All Souls welcomes visitors. Coffee is served on the porch or in the parish hall after the 11:15 A.M. Sunday service. Call for other worship times. (828) 274-2681.

"The best things come in small packages" is an apt quotation for **The Gardener's Cottage,** a nook located at 34 All Souls Crescent. Of course, the shop bursts with beautiful flowers, plants, and all that goes with them, but the small, quiet artifacts will catch your fancy. Owner Bee Sieburg takes one flower, an orchid or a sweet pea, and puts it into every kind of vessel imaginable. You will see a pansy peeking out of an antique salt shaker or violets in a silver jigger. What could be a more thoughtful gift than a beautiful flower in an antique keepsake? The Gardener's Cottage is open from 10:00 A.M. to 5:00 P.M., Monday through Saturday. (828) 277-2020.

Fireside Antiques and Interiors is an attractive shop of 18th- and 19th-century furniture and accessories, as well as tasteful reproductions. Although European antiques are featured, old porcelain is the specialty of vice-president Ronald Clemmer, who often lectures on Imari and Rose Medallion china.

Fireside Antiques has been providing their customers with that special accent piece since 1981 and is located at 30 All Souls Crescent, just across from Biltmore Village. Hours are from 10:00 A.M. to 5:00 P.M., six days a week. (828) 274-5977.

If you continue south on Biltmore Avenue and take Interstate 40 West to Brevard Road, you will find the **Western North Carolina Farmer's Market,** a 36-acre "roadside stand" featuring year-round selections of produce, cheese, honey, flowers, country cured hams, butter, cider, and handcrafted items. In season, the booths are a riot of fruits, vegetables, and plants. Five truck sheds provide space for farmers and dealers to sell their crops. One truck shed is for farmers to sell directly to the consumer.

Aside from fresh produce, you can purchase jellies and jams, hard-to-find mountain black walnuts, dried plants, wreaths, Christmas trees, gourds, birdhouses, baskets, squirrel corn, and herbs. The Spring Herb Festival, held here in late April, is the largest of its kind in the Southeast. Take the time to browse among the beautiful displays of canned goods—green tomato pickles, pickled eggs, chow chow, and jalapeno relish abound. Among them hang blue ribbons won at fairs and the effect is a colorful patchwork quilt of edibles.

Whether you want a pound, a peck, or a truckload, you'll find it here. The address is 570 Brevard Road. It is open seven days a week, from 8:00 A.M. to 6:00 P.M., April to October; and from 8:00 A.M. to 5:00 P.M., November to March. (828) 253-1691.

Blue Ribbon Grated Apple Pie

1 cup butter or margarine	1 tsp. cinnamon
1 large egg (beaten)	2^1/$_2$ cups shredded apples
Dash of nutmeg	(drained)
1 cup sugar	

Mix together and fill 9-inch uncooked pie crust. Bake at 350 degrees for 1 hour. Serves 6-8.

—North Carolina Apple Growers Association, Inc.

The front of the menu reads in part: "The **Moose Café** features fresh food served with a smile at a reasonable rate." What an understatement! This uncomplicated building, sitting on the grounds of the Farmer's Market complex, is owned by the state and opened as a restaurant in 1993 when the market wanted to highlight the produce sold there.

Upon sitting down, whether for breakfast, lunch, or dinner, you'll be immediately served a basket of fluffy biscuits and homemade (on the premises) apple butter. In two comfy rooms overlooking the Farmer's Market and the grounds of Biltmore, you can order from an extensive menu. Eggs can be cooked any way and are served with grits, sawmill gravy, and country ham. For lunch, the market will provide collards, cabbage, and beans in case you want a vegetable plate. If you decide on steak, chicken, barbecue, or catfish, be sure to order the *real* mashed potatoes. This is award-winning food and they have the awards to prove it! The address is 570 Brevard Road. It is open from 7:00 A.M. to 8:30 P.M., daily. (828) 255-0920.

Four miles south on Brevard Road is the **North Carolina Arboretum,** a dream of Frederick Law Olmsted, who designed the gardens of the Biltmore Estate. The arboretum spreads over 426 acres within the Pisgah National Forest. It serves as a regional and international resource for education, conservation, and enjoyment, hosting a wide variety of classes, workshops, and tours.

You don't have to be a scholar or even a gardener to enjoy it here; visitors come simply to appreciate a day of natural beauty. The stunning visitor's center will furnish you with information and maps . . . look around the center at the beautiful meeting rooms and lounges with mountain views. A state-of-the-art greenhouse is also open to visitors and here is one of only two public bonsai displays in the Southeast.

Outside the visitor's center are several pools and small waterfalls, surrounded by lush native plants and flowers—though not your "garden variety." Literally spilling out of containers are blackberry lilies, cat's whiskers, bugleweed, lablab, strawflower, and flowering tobacco to name a tiny sampling. Butterflies, dragonflies, and honeybees dart everywhere in ecstasy! Paths wind over the grounds. There is a 1-mile, "meandering" natural garden trail, a 3½-mile walking and mountain bike trail, and the Shut In Trail. This 18-mile trek, which is part of the Mountain to Sea Trail, will take you up to Mount Pisgah.

From Brevard Road, turn at the second brown arboretum sign. It is open six days a week, except Christmas, from 8:00 A.M. to 9:00 P.M., and Sunday, from 12:00 noon to 5:00 P.M. The visitor center is open from 9:00 A.M. to 5:00 P.M., Monday through Saturday. Admission is free. (828) 665-2492. www.ncarboretum.org.

Since 1979
Complements to the Chef

A cooking shop is a cooking shop is a cooking shop? Absolutely not. Ultracomplete does not begin to describe **Complements to the Chef.** From floor to ceiling, in at least eight rooms, is everything you could possibly need, want, or covet for your culinary creations. Owner Tex Van Hoefen Harrison, in business since 1979, has created a stunning shop. From walls of cookie cutters to silver-tipped chopsticks, she has it all.

When you have to leave you'll want to take home some Sharffen Berger chocolate or the house-brand spicy cheese bits in a tin; or you could order a custom gourmet basket. Compliments to Complements to the Chef! At 375 Merrimon Avenue, it is open Monday through Saturday. (828) 258-0558 or (800) 895-CHEF.

www.complementstothechef.com.

If you like to go where the locals go, the **Boston Pizza** Italian-American café is for you. You'll be lucky to get a table at lunch; but don't worry, the wait is worth it as everything is homemade and delicious. Be sure to try the Greek salad with dressing made with feta cheese (you can get extra cheese if you like). The pizza, with Asheville's largest selection of toppings, is mouthwatering and sure to please. Most anything you order will be good. Wine and beer are available. Allow 30 minutes for takeout orders. Boston Pizza is located at 501 Merrimon Avenue and is open from 11:00 A.M. to 11:30 P.M. (828) 252-9474.

Fresh Market, at 944 Merrimon Avenue, is a must stop for cooks and noncooks alike. Cooks will enjoy browsing the bins of fresh produce and the cases of fresh meats. There is a wonderful selection of grains, nuts, coffees, and teas. The noncooks will enjoy surveying the choices of already prepared items: the roasted chickens are moist and savory, the salads are fresh, and the breads and desserts are irresistible. Don't forget the freshly squeezed orange juice—it's delicious. It is open from 9:00 A.M. to 9:00 P.M., Monday through Saturday, and from 11:00 A.M. to 8:00 P.M., Sunday. (828) 252-9098. There is also a Fresh Market in Hendersonville.

Fine Friends is a *fine* place for lunch or dinner. It sits rather unobtrusively alongside the Fresh Market in the busy Northland Shopping Center. Once inside the cozy dim rooms, you will feel miles away. There are comfy booths lining the walls, and tables on different levels provide an intimate feeling.

For lunch try the Veggie Pita Pesto Pizza or the Reuben and the house soup. At night, the locally raised, whole grilled rainbow trout or a steak with caramelized onion marmalade is hard to beat. Start with the baby shrimp fritters for an appetizer. Takeouts and catering are available. Fine Friends is open from 11:30 A.M. to 9:00 P.M., Monday through Saturday; for Sunday brunch from 11:00 A.M. to 3 P.M.; and for Sunday dinner 5:00 to 9:00 P.M. (828) 253-6649.

Cumberland Falls Bed and Breakfast is located in the Historic Montford District and is just minutes from downtown. When you walk up the path to the inn, a waterfall's gentle sound will greet you. The pond under the tiny bridge is filled with koi and surrounded by lush lilies.

The five guest rooms have beautiful beds and luxurious marble bathrooms, two of which have Jacuzzis. At Cumberland Falls, breakfast (as in "bed and breakfast") has been elevated to new heights. Breakfast can be served bedside, inside, or outside in the lovely secluded backyard. This is a very pleasant place, located at 254 Cumberland Avenue. (888) 743-2557. www.cumberlandfalls.com.

The Black Walnut Bed and Breakfast Inn is also located in the Historic Montford District at 288 Montford Avenue. Architect Richard Sharp Smith built the distinctive shingle home in 1899. You can park under the porte-cochere while you register and nearby is an inviting front porch, furnished with rocking chairs, where you can sit and relax and enjoy the beautiful grounds. The property is surrounded with flower gardens and black walnut trees.

The Black Walnut
BED and BREAKFAST INN

The home was restored as a bed and breakfast in 1992. Innkeepers Sandra and Robert Glasgow are waiting to make you comfortable in one of four rooms in the main house or in the new addition, the

Ivy Garden Room, which is in a separate building. Rooms are decorated with antiques and traditional furnishings. Each room has a private bath, wood-burning fireplace, and Jacuzzi. A video library and
VCRs are available, as are complimentary bicycles.

A three-course breakfast is served by candlelight in the main dining
room and the Belgian waffles are a specialty. Refreshments are available throughout the day. Rates are based on double occupancy and
are moderately expensive. (828) 254-3878 or (800) 381-3878.

www.blackwalnut.com.

Albemarle Inn, located in a quiet and beautiful old residential area,
is a 1909 Greek revival mansion with high ceilings, oak paneling, and
an exquisitely carved oak stairway.

Totally renovated in 1998, this bed and breakfast has 11 comfortable guest rooms on three floors, all with private baths; one room has
a private balcony. Several of the rooms have king-sized beds, while
two have an additional dormer alcove containing a single bed.

Breakfast is served in the dining room or out on the spacious sun
porch looking out over the wide front yard. The inn is located at 86
Edgemont Road. (800) 621-7435 or (828) 255-0027.

www.albemarleinn.com.

The **Chestnut Street Inn,** 176 East Chestnut Street, is one of the
premier bed and breakfasts in Asheville. This large Colonial revival
home is in the Chestnut Hill Historic District. The spacious front
porch with rocking chairs, swings, and graceful ferns is occasionally
the setting for three-course breakfasts and late-afternoon teas.

The two-story house with six rooms and suites was built in 1905
and has a lovely fanlight above the entrance. Inside is some of the
area's finest woodwork, along with ornately carved mantels and a
handsome, unusual bowed staircase landing. All guest rooms are air-
conditioned. Another plus is the short walk to downtown galleries
and restaurants.

The friendly canine butler, Mr. Bentley, may greet you at the door
and see you to your room. Gracious proprietors Gene and Paulette
Dugger live on the premises. (828) 285-0705 or (800) 984-2955.
www.chestnutstreetinn.com.

Edwin Wiley Grove had a dream: he wanted to build a unique
resort overlooking the Blue Ridge Mountains. Influenced by the Old
Faithful Inn in Yellowstone National Park, he purchased a large
acreage on Sunset Mountain and began his search for an architect,
but to no avail. His son-in-law, Fred L. Seely, shared his vision and
was called in to oversee the project. Mr. Seely designed (without an

architect) and built (without a contractor) the beautiful **Grove Park Inn.** The boulders were taken from nearby Sunset Mountain and were fitted into place by the hands of Italian stone masons and hundreds of local laborers. The entire project was completed in an unbelievable 11 months and 27 days. This historic building has many notable features, the most famous of which is the Great Hall. The two massive fireplaces facing each other from each end of the hall burn 12-foot logs and each andiron weighs 500 pounds. The Mission oak furniture and period pieces from the Arts and Crafts Era make up the most extensive collection in the world.

The original purpose was to provide a serene, quiet atmosphere for busy people to get away and rest. Today you can still enjoy the restfulness of the mountains and the peacefulness of rocking chairs, but there is much, much more—golf, tennis, an indoor sports center, children's programs, and nearby shopping, hiking, and fishing. The inn has grown from its original 150 rooms to 510 guest rooms. Open year round, rates are seasonal. Children under 16 stay free in rooms with adults. (800) 438-5800. www.groveparkinn.com.

Three dining areas in the inn can accommodate your taste and mood. The most recognized, **Horizons,** rated a four diamond by AAA, serves innovative yet classic cuisine and is expensive and popular. If you want to dine at Horizons during your stay, it is advised to make your dining reservations at the time you make your room reservations. The **Sunset Terrace** is a perfect place to watch the sun set or have a relaxing lunch.

Skylights and waterfalls highlight the new underground spa at the inn. The 40,000-square-foot spa opened in the spring of 2001 and is considered to be the finest in North America. The design blends natural elements of sky, water, and rock to create an out-of-this-world facility. A large staff is available to pamper and guide you through the experience. The fee to access the pool, lounges, and terraces is $35 for resort guests and $50 for nonguests. Individual services are priced separately. (800) 438-5800.

After the Grove Park Inn was finished, many of the workmen stayed on and built homes in the nearby neighborhoods of Grove Park and Proximity Park. Take time to notice these lovely old neighborhoods; keep an eye out, too, for the beautiful St. Mary's Episcopal Church, built in 1914.

For a dining change of pace, walk over to the **Grovewood Café,** located near the Grovewood Gallery. Two small rooms with about six tables in each make for an intimate experience. On the walls are some fascinating old black and white photos of the Grove Park Inn under construction in 1914. Begin your meal with the Stilton cheese and pear salad or the Mushroom Ragout. The café serves chicken, beef, and seafood entrees, as well as two excellent vegetarian entrees. The crab cakes with roasted corn remoulade and sauteed spinach are hard to beat. Outside is a beautiful rock patio and an upper deck where larger groups are welcome. The café is open for lunch and dinner, seven days a week. (828) 258-8956. Moderate to expensive.

Seventy percent of the artists in the **Grovewood Gallery** are from northwestern Carolina, Virginia, and Tennessee. The first floor deals with crafts made from glass, wood, fabrics, and pottery, both contemporary and traditional. The hallmark of the Grovewood Gallery is its quality craftsmanship by well-known artists of the day. Several resident artists whose works are featured here are available to discuss their work and create custom pieces. Some of these include sculptors, woodworkers, glass artists, and a flute maker. If you are a collector or just shopping for a handmade souvenir, you will find something to your liking at the gallery.

Don't miss the upstairs furniture gallery. Among a rich variety, there is a carved-wood, painted set of chairs in the likeness of a butler and maid, random-weave wall hangings made from local vines, and intricate fireplace screens of brass, iron, and stained glass.

The small museum next door was once an industry started by George and Edith Vanderbilt in 1901 to revive the weaving of homespun cloth and was quite successful until the Great Depression. Some of the looms are still standing and the big weaving shed is used to harbor 20 restored cars, including a 1922 La France fire engine, 1926 Cadillac, and 1927 La Salle convertible. High above them, the massive beams are inscribed with quotations that urged quality and diligence in the weavers' efforts.

Grovewood Gallery, Homespun Museum, and the Estes-Winn

Automobile Museum are free to the public and open from 10:00 A.M. to 5:00 P.M., Monday through Saturday, and from 1:00 to 5:00 P.M., Sunday. The address is 111 Grovewood Road. (828) 253-7651.

The Botanical Gardens at Asheville

An easy way to get to the **Botanical Gardens** is to take Interstate 240 to Merrimon Avenue. The Botanical Gardens are located on a 10-acre site next to the campus of the University of North Carolina at Asheville. Construction of the gardens, organized by the Asheville Garden Club, began in 1961, with a goal of preserving and displaying the native plants and flowers of the Appalachian Mountains. The concentration of plant life found in these Southern Highlands is unequaled on the North American Continent and in all of Europe.

The gardens are open all year round and the pleasant half-mile shaded trail leads you past the Garden for the Blind, over Reed Creek, and into the woods. Plants, trees, and even ground covers are well marked as the trail takes you along earthworks from the Battle of Asheville to the Azalea Garden and the Sycamore Area.

The Botany Center on the grounds is open from March to December and contains a library, gift shop, and flower displays. Some plants, mainly orchids and African violets, are for sale. On many Sunday afternoons, from spring through fall, unscheduled guided garden walks are held. In addition, lectures, bird walks, and mountain field trips are sponsored by the gardens. Recently, Weaverville naturalist Scott Dean began leading tours offering information on animal and plant life, local genealogy, and the folklore behind native plants.

Hours are from dawn to dusk and there is no admission fee. Visitors are always welcome and are asked only to respect the natural beauty of the gardens. They are located on Weaver Boulevard between Merrimon Avenue and Broadway. (828) 252-5190.

West of the city, overlooking the French Broad River, is **Richmond Hill Inn.** Lodging here is like an overnight in the 19th century except, happily, for modern conveniences. This beautifully restored Queen Anne house was built in 1889 and the mansion rooms are tastefully furnished with antiques. The dark, mahogany-paneled foyer, with fireplace, family portraits, and memorabilia, gives it an Old World

ambience. New cottages, each with a fireplace, front on an immacu-
late croquet court and blend harmoniously with the old. A total of 36
guest rooms extend into the garden pavilion looking out over an English garden with a small brook and waterfall.

The history of Richmond Hill is interesting. If there are ghosts
here, they would have to be happy, industrious, and civic minded as
was the first owner and builder, Richmond Pearson. He was a leader
in establishing Asheville public schools, served in Congress and the
Diplomatic Corps, and was a close, personal friend of Theodore Roosevelt.

Hospitality has always been
the hallmark of Richmond Hill
house. Possibly one of the
nation's largest private Fourth
of July parties was held at Richmond Hill in 1890. The Pearson family invited the entire
town in an open letter in the
newspaper and 5,000 citizens of
Asheville attended, about one-
third of the population. Today,
Richmond Hill is owned by Dr.
Albert J. and Marge Michael,
who fell in love with the mansion at first sight in 1985.

Richmond Pearson's wife, Gabrielle, a renowned hostess, would
surely be pleased that her dining room in the mansion, where she
entertained so often and so elegantly, is carrying on the family tradition as **Gabrielle's.** This is for serious dining with coat and tie recommended for men. There are exotic menu offerings such as
roasted quail stuffed with fig chutney. It is an adventure and a bit
pricey, but fine food and charm often are.

Dining on the glass-enclosed sun porch is more casual. Also, for
guests of Richmond Hill Inn, there is complimentary breakfast and
tea, but lunch is not served. Reservations for rooms are required.
(800) 545-9238. www.richmondhillinn.com.

Congressman Pearson of Richmond Hill is also remembered for
organizing a famous international chess match in 1897 played by
transatlantic cable with teams from the United States Congress and
the British House of Commons. Since transatlantic cable was a
novelty at this time, the match created widespread interest. It ended
in a draw.

Gabrielle's Gingerbread Cookies

6 cups all-purpose flour	1 tbsp. ground cinnamon
1 tsp. baking soda	1 tsp. ground nutmeg
½ tsp. baking powder	1 tsp. ground cloves
2 sticks unsalted butter	1½ tsp. salt
1 cup brown sugar	2 eggs
1 tbsp. ground ginger	1 cup molasses

Sift first three ingredients together. Cream butter and sugar, mix in spices and salt, then eggs and molasses. Gradually add flour mixture and mix well. Pat dough into three flat discs. Wrap in plastic wrap and refrigerate one hour. Roll dough to desired thickness and cut with cookie cutters. Place on greased baking sheet and bake at 350 degrees for 8 to 10 minutes. Makes two dozen large or five dozen small cookies. Dough can be frozen, thawed, and baked later.

Heading east on Tunnel Road are several interesting places. In the **Windmill Restaurant,** 85 Tunnel Road, owner-chef Cathi Shastri has combined her heritage of a German mother and an Indian husband to serve German, Italian, and East Indian food. Cathi's specialty is "A Taste of Bangkok," which is shrimp, scallops and/or chicken, and stir-fried vegetables finished with a peanut sauce. This is tossed with pasta and topped with Mung bean sprouts and fried Chinese noodles. For dessert she recommends an Austrian Linzer torte.

The restaurant interior is a grotto with a European atmosphere and is cozy and quiet. It is somewhat difficult to find, as it is tucked away in the Innsbruck Mall. The Windmill is open daily from 5:30 P.M., except Monday, and reservations are recommended but not necessary. (828) 253-5285. Moderate to expensive.

Since 1987, an Asheville favorite, **The Greenery restaurant,** has pleased its clientele with specialties—mountain trout, crab cakes, duck, and lamb—and a good wine list. It is named for a popular old song, "Mountain Greenery," and is open from 5:00 to 9:00 P.M., daily, and later on weekends. The address is 148 Tunnel Road. Reservations are suggested. (828) 253-2809. Moderate to expensive.

Dancing Bear Toys, Ltd., at 144 Tunnel Road, has toys for all ages. If you have children with you, enjoy a stop to let them choose a special handpicked gift for themselves or a friend. Adults will have as much fun as the children. (800) 659-8697 or (828) 255-TOYS. Another Dancing Bear is on North Main Street in Hendersonville.

The Asheville mountain air is said to be healthy but it also must stimulate creativity, as the arts and handicrafts flourish here. **Guild Crafts,** at 930 Tunnel Road, features many of these rich regional crafts—hand-carved birds, handcrafted jewelry, colorful woven scarves, blankets, and linen place mats. It is open from 9:30 A.M. to 5:30 P.M., Monday through Saturday. (828) 298-7903.

B. B. Barns is billed as "outfitters for gardeners, hikers and naturalists." Gardeners will drool over trellises, swings, fountains, kneepads, and sundials—not to mention plants, flowers, and a great selection of herbs. Hikers will find a good selection of fleece jackets, socks, and rain gear. For the shopper who just wants to gaze, there are gazing balls!

"For the birds" takes on a whole new meaning here—houses, feed, and feeders of every description vie for attention with fake owls in case you want to scare the birds away from your fig tree. Out on the back porch is superior outdoor furniture: Amish rockers, Adirondack chairs, and Kingsley-Bate teak furniture ("It'll last you 200 years," said the salesman).

It is a little tricky arriving. Take Exit 8 off of Interstate 240 east of Asheville. Turn right, get in the left lane, turn left down a hill before the traffic light, and you'll see the B. B. Barns sign. It is located at 831 Fairview Road and is open from 9:00 A.M. to 6:00 P.M. (10:00 A.M. to 5:00 P.M., January and February), Monday through Saturday. (828) 274-7301.

A jeweler might say that the **Folk Art Center,** east of Asheville, is the perfect stone for the perfect setting. This gem of the Blue Ridge Parkway, a 30,000-square-foot gallery, opened in 1980 and is located at Milepost 382. The handsome gray frame, stone, and glass building has three galleries, an extensive craft library, and serves as the U.S. Park Information Center. One of the galleries is Allanstand, perhaps the nation's most popular craft shop as well as the oldest (it was started in 1895).

Among the many, many items on display and for sale are the unique brooms from Big Sandy Mush Creek, North Carolina. Made of oak, maple, and poplar, the broom handles are spiraled with honeysuckle vine. Then there are the hand-carved wooden puzzles of a winsome bear with a fish in his stomach or a dinosaur with an egg in the center. You will not be able to resist touching the soft, colorful, woven wool shawls by the Churchill Weavers of Kentucky.

The Folk Art Center is also home to the Southern Highland Handicraft Guild and was a cooperative venture of the Appalachian Regional Commission, the National Park Service, and the Guild.

As you can imagine, this is not your ordinary souvenir shop and, although many of the items are costly, there is something for every pocketbook. The main gallery features changeable exhibits of the Guild's artists such as decorative textiles, a chair show, or Appalachian basket works.

The Folk Art Center's permanent collection is devoted exclusively to the pastels and watercolors of Will Henry Stevens, an early-20th-century artist whose works so aptly depict the local landscape and nature scenes. He was represented by major art galleries nationwide and is considered the South's most important modernist.

The Folk Art Center is open daily, from 9:00 A.M. to 5:00 P.M., January through March, and from 9:00 A.M. to 6:00 P.M., April through December. It is closed Thanksgiving, Christmas, and New Year's Day. Admission is free. Take Interstate 240 to Interstate 40 East. Exit at Number 55. (828) 298-7928.

He who does creative work, whether he dwell in a palace or a hut, has in his house a window through which he may look out on some of life's finest scenes.
—Allen H. Eaton, *Handicrafts of the Southern Highlands*

Golf Courses

Good golf courses flourish in Western North Carolina and the following is a list of area municipal and public golf courses; information courtesy of Journal Communications, Inc.:

Broodmoor Golf Links. Located next to the Asheville Airport. This very flat, public course, open year round, is a Scottish-style links course. Mandatory cart. (828) 687-1500.

Buncombe County Municipal Golf Course. Located five miles east of Asheville. The front nine features a flat, wide-open course, while the back nine is very hilly. It is open year round. Walking unrestricted. (828) 298-1867.

Northwoods Golf Club. Located three and one-half miles from Asheville. This executive course with mountain views is uniquely challenging and open year round. Collars required; soft spikes only. (828) 253-1659.

CHAPTER 2

Black Mountain

Located at the foot of the Seven Sisters part of the Black Mountain Range, Black Mountain was called "Grey Eagle" by the Indians. Today this little town is known as the "Front Porch of Western North Carolina." The first train rolled through here in 1874 and the town was incorporated in 1893. Today, the old hardware store and the restored 1890s train depot are a step back to a simpler time. While strolling the streets, you may even catch a craftsman stringing a dulcimer.

Galleries, shops, studios, and restaurants are nestled into a two-block area. Over two dozen craft shops grace the town and wherever you turn are artisans. There is gem mining here as well as horseback riding and hiking. Just a few blocks from town is beautiful Lake Tomahawk, where you can jog, swim, boat, fish, picnic, and golf. Speaking of golf, at the Black Mountain Golf Course you will find America's longest municipal par 6, at 747 yards.

The area's beauty and serenity are a natural setting for a large concentration of religious conference centers. Black Mountain is just a short drive from Asheville, Lake Lure, Chimney Rock, and the Blue Ridge Parkway. The pace is slower here and you can almost hear the mountain spirit calling you to linger. For more information, contact the Chamber of Commerce at (800) 669-2301 or on the Internet at www.blackmountain.org.

Seven Sisters also refers to one of the town's most well known galleries. The Seven Sisters Gallery, located on Cherry Street, carries regional arts and crafts.

Lake Tomahawk Park is owned by the town of Black Mountain and offers a peaceful setting for an outing. The park is open from 5:00 A.M. to 12:00 midnight.

There are strict boating and fishing regulations posted at the lake: boating during daylight hours only, no fishing from boats, no motorized boats, fishing catch limit of four daily, natural bait only, and state fishing laws apply.

Bring the family for a picnic and fishing or come alone for a walk around the pretty lake. (828) 669-2052.

Soft, haunting sounds of the dulcimer can be heard coming from the **Song Of The Wood Shop,** beckoning you inside. In your travels throughout Western North Carolina, you have surely been aware of the dulcimer shops and schools along the way, but Jerry Read Smith, owner of Song Of The Wood, has made the dulcimer his life's work. Not only does he build beautiful instruments of art, but he is a master musician of his beloved dulcimer. Jerry has many CDs to his credit, one being part of the background music in Mrs. Billy Graham's *One Wintry Night.*

Music from the dulcimer will always call up remembrance of the beautiful mountains of Western North Carolina and awaken in you a new appreciation of the sounds of life and nature. Song Of The Wood, located at 203 West State Street, is open from 10:00 A.M. to 5:00 P.M., Monday through Saturday. (828) 669-7675.

The dulcimer is an ancient stringed instrument invented in Persia over 5,000 years ago. There are two types of instruments: the hammered dulcimer and the plucked dulcimer. The hammered dulcimer is the oldest of the two and is played by striking the keys with wooden hammers. The plucked dulcimer or Appalachian dulcimer is played with the fingers and was developed in the United States in the 1800s. During the peak of the folk music era in the 1960s, the dulcimer reached its height in popularity.

There are many superior woodcarvers in North Carolina and one of them is Marshall Hollifield of the **Black Mountain Gallery.** Mr. Hollifield is in his eighties and his favorite wood has always been maple. He works with his son, Eddie, and they blast the bark off of the wood using 4,000 pounds of water pressure. They then create handsome vessels of all shapes and sizes as well as animal and bird figures and lamps. In 1999, the Black Mountain Gallery was on national television (on the Discovery, Travel Log, and PBS channels) featuring these talented woodcarvers at work. They have also been featured in *Southern Living* magazine. The gallery is located up the steps at 112 Cherry Street and is open at 10:00 A.M., six days a week, and at 1:00 P.M., Sunday. (828) 669-2450.

In case of slight fatigue while walking up and down the streets and going in and out of the shops in Black Mountain, climb up the steps to **Mountain Java** and order a special coffee. Sit on the outside patio and take in the surrounding mountains. The view is so spectacular that you may want to spend the rest of the day here. But then, one reason we come to the mountains is for a little respite from the rest of the world, so why not sit here all day? In case you get hungry, across the way is **Peppers,** with good sandwiches.

Black Mountain Iron Works

©1993 D. Hawachyn

Black Mountain Iron Works is easy to find because the whole lawn in front of the workshop is filled with iron sculptures. Dan Hawachyn and his wife, Tekla, are both gifted in this difficult medium and from iron forge beautiful garden gates, andirons, chandeliers, candlesticks—anything you may want for your house or garden. They may not do horseshoes!

The city of Asheville commissioned Tekla to do the iron sculpture of three women shopping on Patton Avenue (the historical shopping area in downtown Asheville). Dan also recently completed a work for the city of Waynesville, located in front of the bank downtown. Small finished pieces at very reasonable prices are always in the shop. Black Mountain Iron Works, located at 120 Broadway, is open from 10:00 A.M. to 6:00 P.M., summer, and from 10:00 A.M. to 5:00 P.M., winter, Monday through Saturday. (828) 669-1001 or (888) 689-9021.

Angela and Eddie Wilkos have a little nook in the back of their shop, **Cherry Street Kids**, where you can find vintage handmade baby clothes as well as a random selection of handmade doll clothes. The shop is located at 118A Cherry Street Square. (828) 669-1171.

At the end of Cherry Street is **The Old Depot.** Since 1976, the building has been home to The Old Depot Association, a thriving organization showcasing heritage crafts of the region. Profits have been turned back into the restoration of the circa-1898 building. The waiting room and ticket office are now full of pottery, woodcarvings, rugs, quilts, and watercolors. The Old Depot gallery is open from 10:00 A.M. to 5:00 P.M., Monday through Saturday, April through December. (828) 669-6583. A couple of blocks away on Richardson Boulevard is the Visitor's Center. (828) 669-2301.

If you like small, off-the-beaten-path restaurants, look for **Berliner Kindl German Restaurant** and Deli at 20 Ball Street-just ask any local for directions. Owners Friedhelm and Sharon Trube see that authentic German cuisine is served here Tuesday through Saturday. Friedhelm is from Darmstadt and has lived in the United States since 1981. Sharon is from Maiden, North Carolina.

The menu includes soups, sandwiches, and sausage dinners along with a daily special. The side dishes of potato salad and red cabbage are exceptional. The house special is a Reuben sandwich and is highly recommended. You may want to select an imported German beer to complete your meal. The strudel, made locally at the Black Mountain Bakery, is delicious. When the chef was asked about the red cabbage recipe, he replied that sliced apple and butter were added to "this," holding up a can of red cabbage. He contends that this particular variety of red cabbage is not grown in the United States.

Check out the small deli for other German specialties. The hours are from 11:00 A.M. to 8:00 P.M., Monday through Saturday. (828) 669-5255.

Red Cabbage

3¼- to 4-lb. head red cabbage	½ tsp. salt
1 large or 2 small apples	¼ tsp. pepper
2 tbsp. butter	2 whole cloves
1 medium onion, sliced	1 bay leaf
½ cup red-wine vinegar	Juice of half a lemon
½ cup sugar	1½ tbsp. flour
2 cups water	

Wash cabbage. Shred as for coleslaw. Peel and slice apples. In large saucepan melt butter and saute apples and onions gently for 3-4 minutes. Stir in cabbage, vinegar, sugar, water, salt, pepper, cloves, bay leaf, and lemon juice. Cover and simmer 45 minutes or until cabbage is tender. Sprinkle flour on top. Cover and simmer 5 minutes. Mix well and simmer 5 minutes longer. Serves 6-8.

A couple of blocks from the heart of town, at 102 Church Street, is **Black Mountain Bakery.** Besides offering a tempting selection of freshly baked desserts and breads, the bakery serves homemade soup, chicken salad, and a variety of sandwiches from 8:00 A.M. to 4:00 P.M., Tuesday through Saturday. To place a special order, call (828) 669-1626.

There are quite a few bed and breakfasts in Black Mountain, all conveniently located. The **Inn Around The Corner,** a gracious bed and breakfast, is one of the newest and the closest one to downtown shopping. The restored 1915 Victorian home has beautifully tiled fireplaces in many of the common rooms and in the dining room, which is bright and cheery. The bedrooms are named and many have canopied beds; all have private baths. The "Summertime" room is furnished with wicker and has a private entrance to the second-story porch. This mountain-view porch also has a bed, complete with mosquito netting. Unwind overlooking the mountains. Special rates and packages are available. The inn is located at 109 Church Street. (828) 669-6005 or (800) 393-6005.

The **Red Rocker Inn** is one of the oldest bed and breakfasts. It has been an inn for nearly a hundred years and has been meticulously restored. There are 18 guest rooms, most with private baths.

Even if you are not a guest, you can eat breakfast, lunch, dinner, or Sunday midday dinner with reservations. Hours change with the season so please call ahead. Also inquire about seasonal specials. You'll be glad you stopped at 136 Daughtery Street—those red rockers on the porch are waiting! (828) 669-5991 or (888) 669-5991. www.travelbase.com/destinations/black-mtn/red-rocker.

Once a spiritual center for the Cherokee Indians, Black Mountain is now the center of the largest concentration of religious retreats in the United States. There are 20 in a 35-mile radius. **Montreat Conference Center** is probably the largest and best known. In addition to being a retreat, Montreat is a resort, town, history center, and college.

Nestled into 4,000 beautiful acres, two miles north of Black Mountain, are two hotels and seven group lodges. There are also meeting rooms and auditoriums seating from 250 to 2,000 people. Located in the main inn is the Galax dining room, which serves three buffet meals daily. In addition, there are campsites for tents, tent trailers, and small campers—all tucked in along the banks of the Greybeard Stream. All sites have picnic tables and grills and there is a centrally located bathhouse.

The recreational activities are nearly unlimited! Besides the normal offerings, you will find a crafts center, canoe and paddleboats, and great hiking and walking trails for all levels. There is also a good playground for kids.

Up above Lake Susan is the **Chapel Of The Prodigal,** a 212-seat sanctuary that many have described as "an architectural treasure." The actual treasure is a fresco of the *Return of the Prodigal Son* by internationally known fresco artist Ben Long. It is painted on plaster applied over bricks on a wall that has complete air circulation. The 16-foot by 17-foot fresco portrays the entire parable story and creates an intimate and uplifting worship space.

Once you leave, you will long to return. Surrounded by hemlocks, laurels, and rhododendrons, Montreat is a relaxing place where you can enjoy all of the beauty that the Blue Ridge Mountains have to offer. (800) 572-2257. www.montreat.org.

In the mountains near Black Mountain and secluded from the noise of everyday life is the cozy campus of the **Ridgecrest Baptist Conference Center.** Ridgecrest began in 1907 as a summer retreat for Southern Baptists. Today it is a year-round conference center that welcomes a variety of groups that meet its mission statement.

Although the center is used primarily for religious programs, if space is available, Ridgecrest is open to the public for family vacations and reunions. Accommodations include hotel rooms, apartments, cottages, dormitories, and campgrounds with sites for tents and recreational vehicles. The main dining room offers three meals a day, buffet style, and three smaller spots offer ice cream, pizza, and snacks. Guests in cottages and apartments may choose to cook their own meals.

Nature and hiking trails on the grounds are in a beautiful setting with outstanding views. On the grounds also are tennis, basketball, and volleyball courts. Ridgecrest is alcohol and tobacco free. It is located one mile east of Black Mountain on Old U.S. Highway 70, off of Interstate 40 at Exit 66. (800) 588-7222.

Marion

If you are headed east from Black Mountain, you absolutely do not want to miss **Max Woody Chair Shop,** located on U.S. Highway 70 five miles west of Marion. Chair making has been a tradition in the Woody family for five generations and their fine chairs can be found in homes throughout America and Europe. Methods of chair making have changed very little over the years. Modern tools enable the chair maker to make a chair quicker and maybe a bit nicer, but no more durable. Woody chairs are superbly crafted of such native hardwoods as black walnut, wild cherry, maple, oak, and ash.

Mr. Max (nickname "Pat") will graciously talk to you about his craft. "First of all," he says with a grin, "I only work half a day . . . you know, twelve hours!" Downstairs in the workshop crammed with fragrant wood, sawdust, and wood filings, son Myron works efficiently bending ladders for the chair backs, while another worker mans the antique mortise used for forming joints. In addition to ladderback chairs, the Woodys make rocking chairs, benches, stools, tables, and buffets and all work is custom done. This is a good place to visit, open "early to late," five days a week and some Saturdays. (828) 724-4158.

When asked how long the **Harvest Drive In** had been in business, the pleasant waitress said, "Forever." Well not quite, but Burger King was not even a twinkle in someone's eye when this landmark began.

Drive up, pull in, and order breakfast, lunch, or supper (the Double Barrel Hamburger with cheese and Thousand Island dressing is hard to beat any time of day). Or you can park and go in. Booths line the walls and in each one is a phone so you can . . . yes, phone in your order! Your meal then efficiently appears and is it good. Harvest is located in Marion at 423 Main Street and is open from 10:00 A.M. to 9:00 P.M., six days a week. (828) 652-4155.

Linville Caverns are located between Marion and Linville on U.S. Highway 221 North, three and a half miles south of the Blue Ridge Parkway. You can see huge limestone caves, 2,000 feet under Humpback Mountain, at North Carolina's only caverns. There is an informative guided tour of about half an hour, leading you through the beauty inside featuring centuries-old stalactite and stalagmite formations. There is also an underground stream and several lighted chambers. Rates are reasonable and there is a good gift shop. The caverns are open daily, March through November, and on weekends only, December through February. (828) 756-4171 or (800) 419-0540. www.linvillecaverns.com.

Beautiful views of **Linville Falls** are easily found just off of U.S. Highway 221. Paths are accessible to all ages and the rock-viewing areas allow close contact with this raging waterfall that crashes down from Linville Gorge, churns and swirls, then drains into a lower falls.

Several short paths are available for different views of the falls and mountains. If you are not driving by way of U.S. Highway 221, you can reach the falls at Milepost 316.3 on the Blue Ridge Parkway.

Don't ignore the old country stores on the North Carolina highways and byways. They are a bit of the flavor of the mountain country and you can find tasty jams, jellies, preserves, all manner of crafts, and the friendliest store clerks in the state.

The old **Three Oaks Country Store** is in Newland at 7645 Linville Falls Highway (U.S. Highway 221), just outside of Linville. It is a neat rest stop. You can gas up your car, buy moonshine jelly or a birdhouse, and hear some of the local lore or gossip. This family-owned store is open most of the year, from 6:00 A.M. until 8:00 P.M., six days a week, and from 8:30 A.M. to 6:00 P.M., Sunday. (828) 733-4781.

At 4312 Linville Falls Highway in Newland is **Holden's Arts and Crafts.** This is hard to miss as there is at least an acre of bark birdhouses, baskets, twig furniture, and concrete garden statuary. Inside is more. Gail Edwards has been owner and manager since 1978, while her husband constructs the well-made twig furniture and other special orders. Hours are from 10:00 A.M. to 5:00 P.M., daily, most of the year. (828) 733-4658.

Personable Bill Brown, owner of **Anvil Arts Studio, Inc.** and sculptor extraordinaire, has been a full-time studio artist since 1978. His father, also a sculptor, was the director of Penland School for 22 years, so Bill grew up exposed to and participating in the creative process with established and emerging artists.

Bill takes his traditional blacksmith skills to different avenues, combining steel with copper and bronze to produce pieces that have a softer, almost claylike quality. Dividing his artistic energy between creating individual sculptures and commission work, he sculpts pieces on every scale—suitable for home and garden, corporate and public settings. Often his clients simply show him their "space" and he goes from there, designing chandeliers, sconces, chimes, and fire screens as well as his superb sculptures.

Bill welcomes inquiries and visits to his large, serious studio with a wonderful sculpture garden. Anvil Arts is located on U.S. Highway 221 South, three miles south from the Three Oaks Country Store. (828) 765-6226. www.billbrownsculptor.com.

The nearby hills are alive with Christmas trees. Christmas tree farming is a long-term commitment; it takes 6 to 10 years from a seedling to a fair-sized tree. Trees are also a lucrative commodity, ranking about 13th in the state, between peanuts and wheat. North Carolina is first in Fraser fir production in the U.S. and second in total number of trees produced, just behind Oregon.

Crossnore

Also on U.S. Highway 221 is the **Weaving Room Gallery** at Crossnore School, a place where you can actually watch weavers at work on their looms. The gallery is housed in the Homespun House, which was built in 1936. Most of the weavers are local volunteers and the art is literally passed on from one to another. According to one of the volunteer weavers, the amount of tension is the most difficult thing to learn. Items made here in the Weaving Room are available for purchase and the selection includes shawls, pillows, rugs, place mats, and napkins.

Proceeds go to the Crossnore School, which is dedicated to "giving mountains of hope to children living in crisis situations." The pretty, 72-acre campus provides a healing environment for these children. Notice the E. H. Sloop Chapel on the hill just above the gallery. Located on U.S. Highway 221 in Crossnore, the Weaving Room is open from 8:30 A.M. to 5:00 P.M., Monday through Friday, and from 9:00 A.M. to 4:00 P.M., Saturday. (828) 733-4660.

Linville

It is probably a good bet the **Gardens Of The Blue Ridge** will continue to stay open, as they have been in business for over a century! This wildflower nursery has supplied surrounding counties (and the rest of the United States via mail) with prolific wildflower plants and seeds for years.

In 1892, Samuel Kelsey, one of the founders of Highlands, opened a nursery on U.S. Highway 221 between Linville and Pineola. An

employee, E. C. Robbins, later bought the business. Today, Mr. Robbins' granddaughter and great-grandson run this nursery, where you can choose from hundreds of plants, quite a few native shrubs and trees, and seeds by the ounce or pound.

This is not a display garden; it is a working nursery where the specialty is native plants and flower gardens, including design, installation, and maintenance. There is a small shop with a nice selection of wildflower books—some about growing, some about identifying, and some about just enjoying.

The gardens are located off of Highway 181 in Pineola, less than a half-mile from the Blue Ridge Parkway Milepost 312. Drive south on Highway 181; at Pittman Gap Road turn left; garden signs are on the right. They are open at 7:30 A.M., six days a week. Call for a catalog (828) 733-2741. www.gardensoftheblueridge.com.

Hugh McRae developed Linville as an exclusive resort area in the late 1800s and in 1926 the McRae family built the **Eseeola Lodge.** The lodge was built with chestnut-bark siding, which was commonly used in the area as it was thought to deter termites. The architecture is typical mountain style, using natural tree trunks for columns and exposed beams for the outside entry. A large stone fireplace greets you in the foyer. Thankfully, the lodge has managed to retain its original splendor and is listed on the National Register of Historic Places.

Eseeola has rooms featuring authentic antiques and handmade quilts. Each room is equipped with modern conveniences—private baths, air-conditioning, telephones, and cable TV—and most rooms have porches overlooking the beautiful gardens that surround the lodge.

An executive chef with a large staff makes dining here a true gourmet experience. The menu is rotated daily and the chef describes the food as "an eclectic blend of international cuisine with a Southern accent." Dinner is a four-course meal with a choice of seven entrees. Your taste buds will be rewarded with such choices as pan-seared salmon or sauteed loin of rabbit.

Activities abound, with a championship golf course and club with all of the amenities, including eight Har-tru tennis courts. Hiking trails are nearby and Grandfather Mountain is practically at your doorstep. Fishing is permitted in **Grandmother Creek** and Kawana Lake. The Eseeola Lodge is open from the end of May until the middle of October and rates include breakfast and dinner. (800) 742-6717. www.eseeola.com.

While you are in Linville don't miss the opportunity to stop in at the **Linville General Store,** which is over a hundred years old and was built by Ed Loven. Paul and Fay are the current owners, but Paul claims it is Fay's store and when asked about the merchandise he says, "It's the finest bunch of 'junk' you ever saw." The "junk" includes clothing, good fishing equipment, and some not-for-sale pottery made by the oldest folk potter alive, Berlin Craig.

Old Hampton Store and Grist Mill was built in 1921 and is still a meeting spot for locals and visitors alike. The store stocks lots of "old-timey" merchandise such as speckled pottery, marbles by the pound, Grandpa's Pine Tar Soap, flour-sack dishtowels, flavored syrups, and cobbler in a jar. The café, located in the back of the store, serves delicious homemade barbecue and chili. You can choose to eat inside or out on the front porch. The store is located on Russin Street. (828) 733-5213.

Grandfather Mountain

Your first visit to Grandfather Mountain should begin at the main entrance off of U.S. Highway 221 and the Blue Ridge Parkway. This route allows you to cover all of the interesting attractions up to the swinging bridge close to the summit. After entering the gate, you will see McRae Meadows on the left; this rich green area is where the famous Highland Games and Gathering of Scottish Clans are held each July. You will also pass Half Moon Overlook and, in late spring, white blooming serviceberry trees accented by rhododendrons will give you pause. Farther along you will reach Split Rock, the Nature Museum, and Animal Habitats—a great stop for children. Allow at least 30 minutes to take in the museum and to see such animals as black bears and cubs, eagles, otters, and some endangered species in natural settings. Lunch is served in the museum's family restaurant but having a picnic is more fun.

Park your car at Black Rock Parking Area and follow the Bridge Trail to the swinging bridge, the highest swinging footbridge in America. You will feel as though you are on top of the world on a tightrope, skipping across mountain peaks—however, this indestructible steel bridge will lead you safely to the other side.

The mountain is a hiker's dream, with rugged Alpine trails as well as simple nature hikes. Go to the visitor's center and map out the best one for you. Experience is the key to some of the mountain's hardest trails; they are strenuous and sometimes require in-place ladders and cables to climb to the next level. Some hikes can take all day and can be approached from other entrances to the mountain.

Grandfather Mountain is an International Biosphere Reserve, where man is one with nature (only 24 other biospheres exist in the world). Because the mountain is privately owned, an admission fee is charged to access it by car. For other trailheads that begin at outlets around the mountain, contact Grandfather Mountain Backcountry Manager, Post Office Box 129, Linville, North Carolina 28646, or call the Ranger's office at (800) 468-7325. The Web Site, www.grandfather.com, can also give trail information. Hours are from 8:00 A.M. to 7:00 P.M., April through October, and until 5:00 P.M., November through March.

Western North Carolina celebrates everything from apples to woolly worms and every town with a population of over 25 has a festival. **Grandfather Mountain Highland Games and Gathering of Scottish Clans** has been in existence since 1956 and has flourished and become a popular event. Linville has a strong Scottish influence and the festival in July brings out families, clad in kilts and carrying beautiful tartan banners, ready to take part in games that date back centuries.

At the foot of Grandfather is a luxuriant green meadow surrounded by a 440-yard track where footraces take place. Inside the track, all manner of competitions go on all day long—sheep herding, bagpiping, fiddling, Scottish dancing, tugs-of-war, shot put, and tossing the caber (a young tree trunk). Can you imagine how many show up for the Gaelic soloist competition? Outlining the track is a row of striped tents—a finishing touch to a beautifully staged event. Two world-class races occur during the games: one is called "The Bear" and the other is "Mountain Marathon."

Being Scottish certainly helps, but people from all over the country enjoy watching the Highland Games and learning about the rich Scottish history. The festival usually takes place during the second weekend of July and tickets may be purchased for all four days or by the day. The proceeds go to a scholarship fund for local students. For information write or call Grandfather Mountain Highland Games and Gathering of Scottish Clans, Post Office Box 1095, Linville, North Carolina 28646-1095, (828) 733-1333. www.gmhg.org.

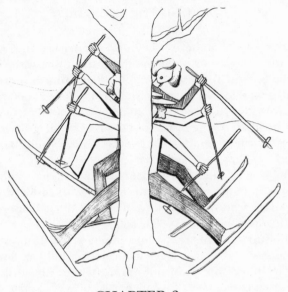

CHAPTER 3

Banner Elk

The attractive, modern shopping mall on the corner of U.S. Highways 184 and 105 is called **Shoppes Of Tynecastle** and many are noteworthy. **Tynecastle Galleria** is a spacious antique center with 18 dealers and a great variety of collectibles, china, old linens, crystal, and some furniture. (828) 898-3622. The **Centerpiece** has a large selection of serving pieces and giftware. (828) 898-6766. **Sam's Boutique,** a ladies' clothing store, features Susan Bristol sweaters, children's clothes, and a large selection of moderately priced casual wear. (828) 898-4999. Shops are open from 10:00 A.M. to 6:00 P.M., six days a week. Sam's Boutique is also open on Sunday afternoons.

Banner Elk was originally called "Banner's Elk" for Martin Luther Banner, who moved to the area in 1845. The town was so named to describe one side, or Banner's side, of the Elk River. Later, the postal service requested that the area be called Banner Elk. During the Civil War, Banner Elk was a stopping point for men who wished to reach the Union lines in Tennessee. In 1895, Edgar Tufts first came to this small village and forever altered history. He founded Lees McRae College, Grace Hospital (now Cannon Memorial), and the Grandfather Home for Children. The beauty of the stone buildings in Banner Elk stands as a tribute to this hardworking man (information from Rebecca L. Tuten's *A Guide for You*).

Although small, the town of Banner Elk has a lot to offer—great restaurants and good shopping. At the top of the list is **Morel's,** at 1 Banner Street, where chefs Dean and Donna Mitchell offer New York style dining at its best. (828) 898-6866.

For a bistro atmosphere, try **Sorrento's,** which features authentic Italian cuisine and an extensive menu with a full bar. Sorrento's is located in Village Shops in downtown Banner Elk. It is open for dinner, seven days a week; for lunch at 11:00 A.M., Friday and Saturday; and for brunch, Sunday. (828) 898-5214.

The **Corner Palate,** on the corner at 115 Shawneehaw Avenue at the stoplight, invites you to enjoy "the art of casual dining" and it is certainly art. The food is good and owner-chef Doua Usko has dozens of award-winning certificates hanging on the walls. The menu is varied and everything is tempting. The trout deserves a blue ribbon and the omelets are delicious and filling. There is a sushi bar on Thursday, Friday, and Saturday nights. This is a popular local dining spot and open most of the year, seven days a week. Lunch is served from 11:00 A.M. to 3:00 P.M. and dinner from 5:00 to 10:00 P.M. Takeout is available. (828) 898-8668.

Since the 1970s, Carolyn Ollis has owned the **Village Grocery** at the only stoplight in Banner Elk. She stocks the basics as well as wine and beer. Across the street, at **Village Shops,** are some upscale clothing and gift shops. **Eve's Leaves,** a women's shop, and **J W Tweeds,** a men's shop, share space. Both stores are open from 10:00 A.M. to 5:00 P.M., six days a week, and from 1:00 to 5:00 P.M., Sunday. (828) 898-6166. Just across from the Corner Palate is **Almost Rodeo Drive,** a ladies' casual clothing store with the handsome Coogi sweaters from Australia. It is open most of the year from 10:00 A.M. to 5:00 P.M. (828) 898-4553. There is also a twin store in Blowing Rock.

B. J.'s Resort Wear, at 145 Main Street West, is a small, elegant boutique. There is a great selection of designer outfits, including Kay Unger gowns for evening and Austin Reed's soft wool suits for day wear. You'll also find accessories and good costume jewelry. It is open from 10:00 A.M. to 5:30 P.M., daily. (828) 898-4229. Not inexpensive.

Down-home cooking packs them in at the **Banner Elk Cafe** on Highway 184. For breakfast, try the buttermilk biscuits or the fresh blueberry pancakes; for lunch, it's hard to beat the "best burger in the mountains"; and in the evening, you might want to choose country-fried steak or smoked trout. Beer and wine are served and you can dine in or take out. It is open from 7:00 A.M. to 10:00 P.M., daily. (828) 898-4040.

Village Heirlooms, Inc., 117 Shawneehaw Avenue, has packed a large, eclectic collection of furniture and accessories into small quarters. There are antiques and reproductions in a charming blend of sophistication and whimsy. Irresistible monkey lamps, bronze bears, handsome embossed silver trays, and leather chairs are just a few of the varied selections that can fit into formal or casual surroundings. It is open from 10:00 A.M. to 5:00 P.M., daily, except January and February when it is closed on Sunday. (828) 898-5632.

Creole cuisine, New Orleans style, is the house specialty at **Louisiana Purchase,** located at 397 Shawneehaw Avenue (U.S. Highway 184). It is open only for dinner and reservations are recommended. Call for hours. (828) 264-7976.

In a small stone house at 7137 Highway 194 South, you'll find **Back Roads Country Antiques.** This shop specializes in American antique furniture, pine and maple, and country accessories. Another specialty is furniture restoration and owners Frank and Sally Nooney have worked on projects with several museums. The hand-painted furniture, floor cloths, murals, and faux finishes are quite good. It is open from 10:00 A.M. to 5:00 P.M., Friday through Tuesday, April 1 to November 1. (828) 963-7347.

A fascinating shop in the Banner Elk environs is **Sheer Bliss Little Bear Rock Shop** on the old Turnpike Road. You won't have to dig, sift, or pan to see these beautiful, highly polished gems and minerals crafted into gold and silver jewelry. Since 1958, proprietor Doris Bliss, a certified goldsmith, has specialized in fine custom jewelry. Doris became a full-fledged rock hound when she and her husband lived in Cheyenne, Wyoming. Her shop is filled with a wide assortment of rocks, meteorites, crystals, and fossils, as well as pottery and baskets. Hours are irregular as the shop is in her house, but they are generally open from 10:00 A.M. to 5:00 P.M., six days a week. (828) 898-9800.

Dedicated to a lowly worm, the **Woolly Worm Festival** is surely the most uncommon celebration in the country. Since 1978, this whim-

sical festival in Banner Elk has grown in popularity and today attendance is in excess of 25,000. The founder, Jim Morton, owner of
Grandfather Mountain, apparently recognized the fascination with
the woolly worm and its weather-forecasting talent. The worm has 13
stripes corresponding to the 13 weeks of winter. If there are more
black stripes than brown, there will be a severe winter ahead. Do not
laugh! Since the 1980s, this little worm has had a 90 percent accuracy
record. The festival, with food and craft vendors, games, music, and
dancing, is held in mid-October, when the woolly worms are out along
the highways and byways. People capture the critters and, for a small
fee, enter them in races, which are held on a flatbed trailer with a
blackboard and 20 vertical strings.

Throughout the day, there are about 60 heats, with 20 worms in
each, and the winners are awarded $20. The highlight of the festival
is the final competition. There is a prize of $500 and the champion
woolly worm has the honor of having his stripes read. Thereafter the
winter forecast is official. Do be careful in Banner Elk and try not to
step on a woolly worm. It might be next year's champion.

Sugar Mountain

Sugar Mountain Resort opened in 1959 as North Carolina's largest
ski area. It boasts a 1,200-foot vertical drop and a run of one and one-
half miles. With 20 slopes and trails, it provides all levels of skiing.
Night skiing is available between 6:00 and 10:00 P.M. The Base Lodge
at Sugar conveniently houses everything under one roof. Ticket sales
and rentals, along with an adult lounge for relaxing at day's end, are
all near each other. There is a cafeteria that serves three meals a day
and, when weather permits, hamburgers are grilled on the slope-side
deck.

Professional ski instructors are available for both private and group
lessons. Sugar Bear Ski School is for children, ages 5 through 10, and

for young nonskiers there is a nursery. For information about rates and packages write to Sugar Mountain Resort, Inc., Post Office Box 369, Banner Elk, North Carolina 28604. (800) SUGAR MT (784-2768). www.skisugar.com.

There are a variety of places to stay while skiing Sugar Mountain—from chalets and condominiums located on the slopes to log cabins in the woods. For information about lodging contact Sugar Mountain Accommodations Center and Realty at (828) 898-9475 or (800) 545-9475. www.staysugar.com.

If you would rather stay in the town of Banner Elk, there are numerous motels and inns. A good choice would be **The Inn at Elk River,** located at 875 Main Street (N.C. Highway 194). The inn has eight rooms, all with private baths and four with fireplaces. There is a restaurant that is open from 5:00 to 9:00 P.M., Tuesday through Sunday (Wednesday through Saturday in winter). (828) 898-9669.

Beech Mountain

The first known inhabitants of Beech Mountain were the Cherokee Indians and this area was a favorite hunting ground. In 1774, the first white settler, Samuel Bright, led pioneer families through the Yellow Mountains on an old Indian trail that became known as "Bright's Trace." In the early 1900s, Beech Mountain was an important lumbering area and ruins of the lumber-camp cabins can still be found in some areas of Beech (information from Rebecca L. Tuten's *A Guide for You*).

The town of Beech Mountain boasts the highest elevation of any town in Eastern America.. At 5,506 feet above sea level, it is also the highest-elevation ski area. The resort has 14 slopes—3 beginner, 7 intermediate, and 4 advanced—all lit for night skiing. There are programs for children from age 3 to 12 and a nursery for infants. The Bavarian-style facility is attractively nestled at the base of the mountain and everything you need is available: ski rentals, ski school, and clothing shops. Food is served at the **Beech Tree Bar and Grill** (seated) or the **View Haus** (cafeteria style). For Ski Beech information call (800) 438-2093.

There are many inns and bed and breakfasts to accommodate you at Beech Mountain. The **Beech Alpen Inn** offers both lodging and food. The rooms are clean and uncluttered, with views of the Blue Ridge Mountains and the ski slope; some rooms have fireplaces. A complimentary breakfast is served in the lodge-style dining room. Rates are reasonable. (828) 387-2252. www.beechalpen.com.

Jordan's
Restaurant
(828) 387-9449
Closed Monday
Located in The Beech Alpen Inn

The Beech Alpen Inn is also home to **Jordan's Restaurant,** which offers a variety of gourmet ethnic cuisine and American favorites. A children's menu is available, dress is casual, and reservations are recommended, especially on weekends. (828) 387-9449.

If you prefer lodge-style accommodations, the **Top Of The Beech** is reasonable and has rooms with fireplaces. The lodge also has a great room with a large fireplace where guests can visit and relax. Children under 12 stay free in their parents' room. (828) 387-2252.

Fred's General Mercantile is located in the center of town at 501 Beech Mountain Parkway and it's the place to go to find out "what's happenin'!" The people are friendly and their motto is, "If you don't see it, ask for it; if we don't have it you don't need it." Fred's has everything you could want or need to make your stay at Beech Mountain pleasant. Ski and snowboard rentals are available along with boots and bindings, sport skis, snowblades, and bigfeet (smaller skis designed to allow turning and jumping). Also available are groceries, wine, beer, and fishing licenses. **Fred's Backside Deli** (breakfast, lunch, and dinner) features homemade breads, soups, salads, and sandwiches. It is open from 7:30 A.M. to 10:30 P.M. (828) 387-4838. www.fredsgeneral.com. Summer Sunday Sunset Concerts in the gazebo at Fred's are a treat for the entire family.

Just across the street from Fred's is **Vasarely's Restaurant,** at 502 Beech Mountain Parkway. The menu offers pasta, chicken dishes, fresh mountain trout, and steaks. A chef's specialty is the Steak Au

Poivre, which translates to Black Angus filet marinated in Jack Daniels and crusted in black peppercorns. Beer, wine, and cocktails are available and there is a children's menu for ages 10 and younger. (828) 387-4900.

An idyllic place to wine and dine is **Jackalope's View** at Archer's Inn, 2489 Beech Mountain Parkway, just outside of Banner Elk. Jackalope's View is a delightful restaurant with a panoramic view of Grandfather and Sugar mountains. The quality of the food is good and the menu includes rack of lamb, a fine filet, crab cakes, and always-fresh fish. The bar and restaurant open at 5:00 P.M. and it is advised to call for reservations. You also should check on opening dates, which vary according to the season. It is open only for dinner and prices are moderate to expensive. (828) 898-9004 or (828) 898-9007. (A jackalope is a mystical Western rabbit with horns probably created by a cowboy after too many whiskies.)

Next door, at **Archer's Inn,** the rooms are cozy and inviting with magnificent views and fireplaces of native stone. Several rooms have Jacuzzis, while the Roof Garden room boasts an outside hot tub with a mountain view. There are 15 rooms, several of which are listed as family rooms, but generally there are few facilities for children. Archer's Inn is open all year. Prices are moderate to expensive and rates are seasonal. The phone number is the same as Jackalope's View. www.archersinn.com.

Ridge Law

If you are driving around Beech Mountain (named for the beautiful and profuse beech trees) and see what looks something like a nuclear power plant on the crest of a mountain, you might be interested to know that the buildings are condominiums. The good news is that since this construction, a "Ridge Law" has been passed preventing any structure on the top ridges of any of these majestic mountains.

Golf Courses

Here are the area municipal and public golf courses; information courtesy of Journal Communications, Inc.:

Hawksnest. This mountain course with an elevation of 4,800 feet is fun to play. It is open from April through October. Mandatory cart. (888) 429-5763. www.hawksnest.com.

Sugar Mountain Golf Course. This Arnold Palmer/Francis Duane designed course is noted for the best greens on the mountain. It is open from April through October. (828) 898-6464.

CHAPTER 4

Highway 105

Take your time and enjoy driving the intriguing road between Linville and Boone (N.C. Highway 105), which abounds with tempting art galleries, antique shops, craft shops, and fly-fishing establishments. The mountain scenery comes later.

Marjon's Antiques, at 10884 N.C. Highway 105 South, is housed in a 19th-century building and served as a general store that received its supplies from Tweetsie Railroad. Marjon's is literally wall-to-wall "stuff": glass bottles, Kewpie dolls, books, magazines, old tins, tools, and car tags. The store is open from 10:00 A.M. to 5:00 P.M.(closed on Tuesday), and from 1:00 to 5:00 P.M., Sunday. (828) 063-5305 or (800) 310-6841.

Just around the corner is the **Mulberry Cat,** a shop worth seeing because of its picturesque setting on the edge of a busy, rocky stream. You enter across a bridge and the shop contains a little bit of everything—garden statuary, weather vanes, pottery, and some furniture. It is open from 10:00 A.M. to 6:00 P.M., six days a week, May through October; hours vary during the winter. (828) 963-8363.

Down the road, at 10890 Highway 105, the mountain-rustic building gives no hint as to the elegance inside the **Gilded Age Antique Shop.** Don't miss this if you're fond of Majolica china (the specialty) or very fine English and French antique furniture. A second shop is located in Hilton Head. Hours are from 10:00 A.M. to 5:00 P.M., Monday through Saturday, and from 1:00 to 5:00 P.M., Sunday. (828) 963-8633.

On Highway 105 and down the road a short distance is a series of shops framed in white with green trim. This is **Green Mansion Village.** One shop, **Finders Keepers,** has a handsome selection of antique English furniture as well as English-made reproductions and well-priced bronze figurines. It is open from 10:00 A.M. to 5:00 P.M., six days a week, and from 1:00 to 5:00 P.M., Sunday. (828) 963-7300. Another shop, **Dreamfields,** owned by Elaine and Mike Englehard, is open all year. They have put together a nice mixture of antiques and decoratives as well as some original art. Ekornes chairs are for sale here. These chairs were designed by an orthopedic surgeon and are unbelievably comfortable and *sooo* good for your back. Buy one on the spot! This is open from 10:00 A.M. to 5:00 P.M., six days a week, and from 11:00 A.M. to 5:00 P.M., Sunday. (828) 963-8333.

Follow the path around the shops to the wooden bridge and cross over the creek to **Carleton Gallery.** This modern building houses fine art, sculpture, jewelry, and pottery. Both regional and international artists are represented in an above-average collection. Don't overlook the whimsical metal sculptures of snails and dragonflies on the creek bank. Hours are from 10:00 A.M. to 5:00 P.M., Monday through Saturday, and from 11:00 A.M. to 5:00 P.M., Sunday. (828) 963-4288.

Art connoisseurs will delight in **Gallery 9,** which is right up there with the best of the galleries in the state. All of the in-house artists have already been discovered and enjoy a national reputation. Clients coming to Gallery 9 are collectors

interested in investment-type art and private or commissioned pieces. Art through every medium is represented in the best possible light—oil paintings, sculpture, ceramics, jewelry, glass, and photography.

Even if you are not in the market, you will still love visiting the gallery and seeing the fine art always exhibited here. Gallery 9 is located halfway between Boone and Banner Elk (10244 N.C. Highway 105). You cannot miss it—just look for the big red *9* and sculpture in front of the building. It is open at 11:00 A.M., Monday through Saturday, and at 12:00 noon, Sunday. (828) 963-6068.

Foscoe Fishing Company and Outfitters is located at 9378-1 N.C. Highway 105 in Foscoe. This is a full-service fly shop with endorsed Orvis guides and a licensed North Carolina wildlife agent. Owner Matt Fussell says that there are 400 miles of trout streams in the area and his goal is to help you catch more fish.

The shop has a complete selection of fly-fishing gear and accessories from Orvis, Filson, and Sportif. Fly-fishing schools for beginners to experts are offered as well as guide trips. A good selection of fly-tying tools and materials is also available and fishing licenses may be purchased here. Foscoe Fishing is open from early morning to 7:00 P.M., daily. (828) 963-7431. www.foscoefishing.com.

For gifts, accessories, and furniture, stop at the large, yellow framed house that is **Tatum Galleries,** 5320 N.C. Highway 105. Mrs. Tatum is an interior decorator and her husband makes most of the furniture. The pieces for your yard are especially distinctive. Be sure to sit down in one of the original Pennsylvanian rocking chairs; they are so comfortable you may not want to rise again! It is open from 10:00 A.M. to 5:00 P.M., six days a week, but winter hours are irregular. (828) 963-6466.

Brothers Haden, Theo, and Mark Copeland must be doing something right. Their **Appalachian Angler** guide service has spawned (no pun intended!) a full-service fly-fishing shop. This great shop carries all accessories from top manufacturers for any fishing adventure. Because of the Copelands' experience in all areas of fly fishing, they have become a worldwide destination outfitter, offering complete packages to visiting anglers.

Employing 8 to 10 experienced guides, their trips include bone fishing in the Bahamas, salmon fishing in Alaska, float trips in

Tennessee, and small-stream fishing in North Carolina. All during the year the brothers offer fly-fishing schools at their lodge in Siam, Tennessee. Go by their shop and check out all the necessities and luxuries for this exciting sport. Look over the fly-tying equipment and the fly selection—one of the largest and most comprehensive in the Southeast—then get yourself a fishing license, a rod, some waders, a "bead head pheasant tail" fly, and you're ready to . . . fly . . . fish! Their motto? "Life's Short . . . Fish Hard." They are located on N.C. Highway 105. Hours are usually from 9:00 A.M. to 6:00 P.M., seven days a week. (828) 963-5050. www.appalachianangler.com.

Before you cross the Watauga River on N.C. Highway 105, take a left onto State Road 1112 and on the right is **The Ham Shoppe.** In a rusty 1930s building, Ruth Ann Rizzo has been selling hams to both locals and tourists since the early 1990s. She says the country hams and the spiral-cut honey-glazed hams are the most popular.

The deli serves breakfast and lunch. All of the breads and pastries are freshly baked in the shop and all of the side dishes and salads are made from scratch. This is the place to stop for a picnic lunch (the sandwiches are fabulous), a ham biscuit and coffee for breakfast, or a slice of homemade cake for an afternoon snack. The shop is open from 8:00 A.M. to 6:00 P.M., daily.

Nearby is **The Arbor,** at 4416 N.C. Highway 105 South. Owners Sherri and Bill Knox have a good selection of willow and mountain twig furniture and birdhouses along with some cute wooden "critters." Be sure to go out on the back porch to see the waterfall—what a view! It is open from 10:00 A.M. to 5:00 P.M., six days a week, during the season; and Wednesday through Saturday, winter. (828) 963-7475.

Valle Crucis

Valle Crucis is a small mountain community located on the Watauga River, halfway between Boone and Banner Elk. Native Americans had lived in this region for hundreds of years when Daniel Boone traversed the area in 1760. Valle Crucis was first settled by David Hicks in 1779, but very few settlers joined him until after 1800. The early inhabitants were isolated, without even any decent roads until the 1840s. Drawn by reports of the natural beauty of the area, Levi Ives, Episcopal bishop for the Diocese of North Carolina, founded an Episcopal boys' boarding school, a theology school, and a monastic order. Valle Crucis, Latin for "valley of the cross," was named by him when he noticed two mountain streams that flowed toward each other and gave the appearance of a cross. The church's venture ended in 1862.

By the early 1900s, owners of some of the larger homes rented rooms to summer visitors who came for the scenery and cool climate. Two of these became popular inns: the lovely Mast Farm Inn and the elegant Inn at the Taylor House. In 1990 the entire community of Valle Crucis was designated a historic district. Although Valle Crucis remains somewhat isolated today, the seclusion is part of its charm (information courtesy of Chip Schwab at The Inn at the Taylor House).

Continue on State Road 1112 toward Valle Crucis until you come to the **Mast General Store Annex.** This store, built in 1909, has a great selection of casual clothes for men and women and upstairs is a complete mountain outfitter's shop with everything you need from outerwear to equipment.

The **Back Porch Deli** serves food from The Ham Shoppe, and the original **Candy Barrel** will satisfy any sweet tooth with barrels and barrels of old-fashioned candy (get some for the road!). It is open from 10:00 A.M. to 6:00 P.M., six days a week, and from 1:00 to 5:00 P.M., Sunday. Winter hours are irregular so call to verify. (828) 963-6511.

Proceeding on down State Road 1112, keep an eye out for N.C. Highway 194, where you'll find the original Mast Store. In 1882, Henry Taylor built the first rooms of the present store. In 1897, he took a partner, W. W. Mast. In 1913 Mr. Mast bought out Mr. Taylor, and the store became the **Mast General Store.** Mast attempted, successfully it seems, to stock everything his neighbors would need, "from cradles to caskets." It grew and became known as the store that has everything. In 1973, it was named to the National Register of Historic Places.

Just as you walk in the front door is the Valle Crucis Post Office, where the mail is delivered daily and the 1913 cast-iron pot-bellied stove is still warming customers. Upstairs is literally packed with housewares, earthenware, garden and bath accessories, and wonderful handmade rocking chairs for you to test—don't miss the locally crafted "gout rocker." There is much to take in, so get a nickel cup of coffee and take a break in a rocking chair on the back porch. While you're rocking, if you decide to go fishing, you can get your fishing license here. Parking in the back is recommended. It is open from 7:00 A.M. to 6:00 P.M., six days a week, and from 1:00 to 6:00 P.M., Sunday. Winter hours may vary. (828) 963-6511.

The **J & S Beaumont Pottery,** formerly the "little red schoolhouse" of Valle Crucis, was built in 1907. This pottery workshop and gallery sells bowls, vases, platters, mugs, and tiles made from local clay. If you are interested in seeing pottery artisans at work on the wheel, you'll enjoy visiting. Seasonal hours are from 10:00 A.M. to 6:00 P.M., six days, and 1:00 to 6:00 P.M., Sunday. (828) 963-6399.

Valle Fashions, a ladies' clothing outlet, is next door to the landmark Mast General. This store is a pleasant surprise as there is an amazingly large selection of clothing for the tiny town of Valle Crucis. Here you will find both casual and dressy jackets, coats, sweaters, dresses, and pants. Valle Fashions has been satisfying both locals and visitors since 1979 with wall-to-wall outfits at moderate prices. Hours are from 10:00 A.M. to 6:00 P.M., six days a week, and from 1:00 to 6:00 P.M., Sunday, during the season. It is open all year but winter hours are shorter. (828) 963-6292.

The **Mast Farm Inn** in Valle Crucis began in a simple log home in 1812 when Josie Mast moved in with her loom and began weaving. Today, this home is available as one of six private cottages. The newly restored Granary is a two-bedroom cottage and there are nine guest rooms in the three-story farmhouse. Some rooms are airy, others are cozy, and all share nearby gardens, river, and valley. Sitting on the front porch of the inn, looking over the herb and flower gardens, you'll feel at ease.

The dining rooms are intimate with fireplaces for winter and open windows for warm weather. From light summer entrees to hearty fare in cool weather, the restaurant's menu is "New Southern Cuisine." This translates to herbed trout, shrimp and white grits, or pan-seared duck breast. The food is fresh and beautifully presented. Inn guests can also enjoy a country breakfast, game tables, a gracious sunroom, and a "very civilized parlor." Innkeepers Wanda Hinshaw and Kay Phillip make you feel as if you are their personal guest. Reservations are recommended. (888) 963-5857. www.MastFarmInn.com.

Valle Landing, N.C. Highway 194, is a long gray building with white trim, which houses several interesting shops as well as one of the better restaurants in the area. The **Columbine** has been open since 1989. The chef is from Milan, Italy, so although the cuisine is generally American, the dishes have a definite Italian flair. Specialties include risotto, pasta dishes, veal, lamb, and trout. The restaurant has its own organic garden so the veggies are all fresh. Very pleasant seating is out on the porch, weather permitting. It is open for lunch at 11:30 A.M. and dinner at 6:00 P.M., May through October. It is closed on Monday. Occasionally, Columbine is open in early spring and late fall. Reservations are needed for dinner. (828) 963-6037.

A good shop here at the Landing is **Valle Crucis Rustic Furnishings,** with cabin furnishings as well as some antiques. (828) 963-4635. The **Silver Tree** is another small shop featuring gifts, home accessories, and jewelry. (828) 963-9730. Most of the shops here try to remain open all year from 10:00 A.M. until 6:00 P.M., seven days a week.

The Inn at the Taylor House, located at 4584 N.C. Highway 194, is at the top of the list when it comes to bed and breakfasts. Constructed in 1911, it was the home of Henry Taylor, his wife, and five children. In 1987, Chip Schwab transformed the farmhouse into this eight-room B & B.  When she opened the doors to the public, Chip chose the French symbol of hospitality (the rooster) for her emblem, inviting people to come as a guest and leave as a friend. The Inn at the Taylor House is beautifully decorated with a light and airy feeling and is filled with wonderful art and treasures collected over the years by Chip on her many travels. She has quite an eye for art and continues to promote regional artists.

Breakfast is the only meal served on a daily basis and it features pancakes, fruits, herbs, and vegetables from the garden and farm fresh eggs from the hen house.

The main house has seven plush bedrooms, each with private bath. A former shed barn now serves as a luxurious honeymoon or anniversary cottage and the old milk house currently displays gift items, garden accessories, and specialty foods. Rates are expensive but worth it. (828) 963-5581. www.highsouth.com/taylorhouse.

"A dreamy spell which hangs over this little valley . . . ," wrote local historian John Preston Arthur at the turn of the 20th century. Valle Crucis is North Carolina's first and only rural historic district. This small community cherishes its links to the past and preserves them for generations to come.

Boone

Traveling north on N.C. Highway 194, you will find Boone, the seat of Watauga County and known as the "Heart of the High Country." Here, in a breathtaking valley, are some of the oldest and most scenic mountains in the world. The area's earliest visitors and their descendants enjoyed the region for its mild climate and abundant wildlife. The community got its first post office in 1835 and became the county seat in 1849. It is, of course, named for Daniel Boone, who traveled through the area on frequent scouting and hunting expeditions in the 1760s and 1770s. Boone subsequently became a folk hero and a monument is erected in his honor on the campus of Appalachian State University.

A good, paved trail in town is the Greenway Trail. This "leg stretcher" is located off of State Farm Road near the Watauga County Parks and Recreation Complex. Other hiking trails meander off of its paved areas near the second of the Greenway's three bridges. Call (828) 262-4530 for more information.

The **Appalachian Cultural Museum** is a must-see. It is located at University Hall Drive off of U.S. Highway 321 in Boone. There are quite a few permanent exhibits on art and the cultural and natural history of the Blue Ridge. Displays include mountain furniture, baskets, quilts, and pottery. In addition, there are musical instruments, looms, spinning wheels, and an authentic moonshine still. A huge glass case of Native American artifacts is particularly interesting—the hundreds of rock tools include knives, axes, scrapers, and adzes.

There is a good selection of Appalachian folk toys for sale. Some of the designs have been revived and many are original. You most assuredly will want to take home a whimmey diddle! It is open from 10:00 A.M. to 5:00 P.M., Tuesday through Saturday, and from 1:00 to 5:00 P.M., Sunday. (828) 262-3117. www.museum.appstate.edu.

No one knows exactly when the first whimmey diddle was carved, but it was definitely before the age of radio and television! Probably in the 19th century, some distraught father carved it to entertain his children during the long winter months. The toy is two sticks (usually rhododendron wood), one a notched rod with a propeller at the end, and rubbing the two sticks together makes the little propeller twirl. With practice, you can make the propeller whirl left or right, or "gee" or "haw" (the commands farmers still call to their mules when plowing).

18th Century
Living History Museum

Almost next door is the **Horn In The West Grounds,** home to the **Hickory Ridge Homestead.** This was founded in 1980 to give visitors a detailed look at the life of 18th-century Appalachian pioneers. The main house, the Tatum Cabin, was built in 1785 and is one of the oldest buildings in Watauga County. Five generations of Tatums lived in the house at its original site overlooking the New River near Todd.

Included at the homestead are a smokehouse, weaving house, and museum store where you can pick up a booklet for a self-guided tour. At certain times of the year, and for a nominal fee, you can have guides for groups (50 maximum) and/or workshops.

At the **Daniel Boone Amphitheater,** historical dramas are performed from mid-June through mid-August with both general and reserved seating (there's also a good Halloween program). The homestead is open all day Tuesday through Saturday, and on Sunday afternoons, from May through October. Group visits by appointment only, (828) 825-6747. For tickets to programs, call (828) 264-2120 or write to Horn Tickets, Post Office Box 295, Boone, North Carolina 28607.

Located adjacent to the Horn In The West Grounds are the **Daniel Boone Native Gardens.** These gardens feature a collection of North Carolina native plants in an informal design for education and preservation. Daniel Boone VI, a direct descendant of the great pioneer, made the handsome wrought-iron gates, a gift from the Southern Appalachian Historical Association. The gardens are open from 9:00 A.M. to 6:00 P.M., daily, May through October (weather permitting).

Last, but not least, is the **Watauga County Farmer's Market,** held in the parking lot of the grounds from 7:00 A.M. to 12:00 noon, Wednesday and Saturday, May through October, and Wednesday, July and August. This market has been supporting local farmers since 1974. In addition to fruits and vegetables of every conceivable kind, you will find honey, wildflowers, canned goods, and homemade cakes. If you want to sit right down and have a tea party, picnic tables are nearby!

Appalachian State University is located in downtown Boone. It was founded in 1899 to train teachers for the Blue Ridge Mountain schools and the campus consists of 340 acres including a 250-acre main campus. Appalachian fosters an understanding of the Appalachian regional culture through its Appalachian Cultural Museum, Appalachian Studies Program, and the Appalachian Collection, consisting of books, letters, and historic documents. The university's summer art series is considered one of the top annual arts events in the Southeast. In addition, the Department of Theatre and Dance has offered performances since its beginnings in 1929. (828) 262-3063.

The **Broyhill Inn and Conference Center** is located on a naturally wooded hilltop on the campus and this beautiful facility overlooks the surrounding Blue Ridge Mountains. Be sure and notice the native rock work on the building's exterior.

Broyhill Inn's accommodations include 7 suites and 83 guest rooms. Breakfast, lunch buffets, and dinners are served in the dining room, which provides a spectacular mountain view. In the evening, the Duggin Lounge is open for guests who enjoy a quiet, relaxing atmosphere. All facilities are available for private parties or other occasions. The center is located on Bodenhiemer Drive. The restaurant is open beginning at 7:00 A.M., six days a week; brunch is served from 11:00 A.M. to 2:00 P.M., Sunday. Dinner is by reservation only. (828) 262-2204 or (800) 951-6048. www.broyhillinn.com.

Howard Street used to be a warehouse district and has since been transformed into shops and restaurants frequented by locals and students from the university. **Wilcox Emporium** is a 1910 warehouse that now encloses a minimall of craft shops, galleries, and clothing and sport stores. **Natural Selections** has good, casual clothes for women, moderately priced, as well as beautiful, handmade silk dresses by regional artists, not so moderately priced, but "what price art?" The **Moose Mountain Trading Company** is an attractive store with objects all pertaining to the outdoors.

After shopping, have lunch at the **Grapevine Café,** which is part of the mall. Chef Nicko has a Greek and Mediterranean menu. For lunch try the gyro sandwich (pita bread stuffed with lamb, sour cream, cucumbers, and onions). At dinner, the Greek combo is made up of spinach pie, moussaka, pasticio, grape leaves, and leg of lamb. If Greek isn't your thing, the good old American hamburger is always available. On your way out is an ice cream bar. Hours for the restaurant, located at 161 Howard Street, are from 11:00 A.M. to 9:00 P.M., Monday through Saturday, and from 11:00 A.M. to 6:00 P.M., Sunday. Reservations are required for dinner. (828) 268-0434.

The **Daniel Boone Inn** is in the middle of town at 130 Hardin Street (junction of U.S. Highway 321-421). A shady, wraparound porch, bordered by flowerbeds most of the year, welcomes you to "sit

a spell" before or after your meal.

The two-story clapboard house was built around 1920 and served as a hospital and rooming house before becoming a restaurant in 1959. Renowned for its fried chicken and country ham, the Daniel Boone Inn has served millions of happy customers. The dining room, furnished in country antiques, is pleasant and it is always an adventure to eat family style. Breakfast is served on the weekends all year round. Enjoy the ham and red-eye gravy and the biscuits with black cherry preserves.

Lunch and dinner are served daily, Memorial Day through October (besides that good fried chicken be sure and get some stewed apples!). From November through May, the Daniel Boone Inn is open but hours are irregular. Reservations are accepted for groups of over 15. Children of all ages are welcome and children's portions are very reasonably priced. (828) 264-8657.

Howard's Knob is a great take-a-break park that sits on top of the city of Boone. You can drive or walk, depending on how much time you have. At the Daniel Boone Inn, take U.S. Highway 421 North, which is also King Street; drive to Council Street; turn and follow the signs to the top. Howard's Knob is maintained by the Watauga Parks Department and has a few picnic tables scattered in the woods and a pavilion with barbecue stands for cooking. The Knob is at an elevation of 4,500 feet and the view is especially beautiful in the early evening.

The **Lovill House Inn Bed & Breakfast** is the oldest house in Boone. Built in 1875, this gracious home served as Capt. Edward Lovill's law practice and family descendants lived here until the 1970s.

It is located less than a mile from the Appalachian State University campus and King Street shopping and dining. The original property encompassed 250 acres. Today there are 11 acres of woods, exquisitely landscaped grounds, and a waterfall, affording the visitor privacy as well as beauty.

There are six guest rooms, each with private bath, telephone, cable TV, and Internet access. Be sure to notice the beautiful wormy chestnut woodwork in the living room and dining room, as well as the original maple and pine flooring. Energetic hosts Tim and Lori Shahen will leave you undisturbed or they can arrange for mountain biking, fly fishing, or rafting.

The inn, located at 404 Old Bristol Road, recently received the prestigious four diamond rating from the AAA Motor Company. "We didn't set out to win the award," said Tim. "We just wanted our guests to be truly comfortable and have their expectations met or exceeded." It is closed over Labor Day for 10 days. (828) 264-4204 or (800) 849-9466. www.lovillhouseinn.com.

Almost at the busiest intersection in Boone, at 1348 N.C. Highway 105, is **Casa Rustica.** In this rustic yet elegant log cabin setting, you can get excellent Italian-American cuisine. In addition, there's a fine wine list. Rustica's also has a takeout menu. It is open at 5:00 P.M., daily. Call for reservations. (828) 262-5128.

Todd

To explore Ashe County, take U.S. Highway 421 South to U.S. Highway 221 North. From this intersection, it is about 14 miles to West Jefferson.

One of the 10 best bike paths in all of North Carolina is nearby. The **Railroad Grade Road** is a perfectly flat road that stretches and meanders for nearly 10 miles along the New River and through some beautiful country. Actually, the road begins in Todd and finishes at U.S. Highway 221 in Fleetwood. Todd can be reached from N.C. Highway 194 north of Boone. While in Todd, you won't want to miss the **Todd General Store.** This circa-1914 general store is a step back in time, open at 8:00 A.M., six days a week, and at 1:00 P.M., Sunday. It is open on Thursday night for country music jams with local musicians. No matter when you're there, get a country ham biscuit from the deli. (336) 877-1067.

West Jefferson

Make the time to drive to West Jefferson to visit the 1940 **Ashe County Cheese Factory.** If you arrive soon after 8:30 in the morning, you can have a tour; otherwise it is still interesting to watch the "cheese brigade" stirring and cutting and wrapping. Milk from local dairies is delivered daily and poured into 20,000-pound vats. When they are full, rennet is added to help the milk solidify. The resulting curds are cooked, then pressed into hoops or blocks, sealed with wax, and stored for aging.

Across the street is the retail store—stocked with cheese, cheese, and more cheese! The cheddar comes mild, medium, sharp, and extrasharp. In addition, you can buy Colby, marble, jack, and jalapeno as well as packaged curds, cheese spreads, and the house butter. On your way back to your home or headquarters, you will have a new appreciation of those grazing cows! Located at 106 East Main Street, the store and viewing room are open from 8:30 A.M. to 5:00 P.M., Monday through Saturday. Groups, please call in advance. (336) 246-2501. For a price list write to Ashe County Cheese Company, Post Office Box 447, West Jefferson, North Carolina 28694.

Cheese Facts

Asiatic tribes discovered the art of making cheese more than 4,000 years ago and the first dairy cows arrived in America in Jamestown in 1611. It takes 11 pounds of milk to make 1 pound of cheese. Different cheeses require different times to age. Cheddar usually "cures" from 60 days to two years. Shortest aging periods produce mild cheese while longer curing periods produce sharper flavors.

Jefferson

The Episcopal Parish of the Holy Communion contains two churches, **Holy Trinity** in Glendale Springs and **Saint Mary's** in Jefferson, both built in the early 1900s. During the following 70 years, the churches were served by missionaries and traveling priests. Holy Trinity was completed in 1901 and the first service at Saint Mary's was held on Christmas Eve in 1905.

In 1971, Fr. J. Faulton Hodge was appointed priest-in-charge of Ashe County. Father Hodge's interest in art and his meeting with North Carolina artist Ben Long led to the painting of the frescoes in the two churches for which the parish is now famous. When visiting the churches, be sure and take the time to sit in a pew and listen to the interesting audiotapes about the frescoes. They describe the method of painting and also point out features you may have missed at first glance. One interesting fact is that the models for the figures of the disciples and Mary were townspeople (the pregnant figure of Mary is unusual). These are the same people who cooked meals for the artist and his students while they lived and painted in the community.

Further detailed descriptions of the frescoes might detract from your enjoyment of these primitive yet extraordinary works of art. Saint Mary's and Holy Trinity are active Episcopal churches. They are open daily and you are welcome at the services. For further information call (336) 982-3076 or write to The Parish of the Holy Communion, Post Office Box 177, Glendale Springs, North Carolina 28629.

Christmas tree farms are a beautiful and important part of the North Carolina agriculture. Western North Carolina has around 34 million trees on approximately 23,000 acres; there are about 1,500 tree farms. All over this section of the state you will see them, looking for all the world like giant green and brown quilts spread out on the hillsides. You can pick from hundreds of trees in a "choose and cut" field. For a list and map of 17 "choose and cut" farms in the high country, call the Boone Convention and Visitors Bureau at (828) 262-3516 or (800) 852-9506.

Sitting in the middle of farm country is **Greenfield Restaurant,** established in 1964 and owned by Dick and Linda Copus. The restaurant looks like a ranch house, with a long front porch full of rockers. Big, family-style meals are served at Greenfield, including a breakfast menu that will fix you for the day. The owners have a creed about the way their steaks are cooked—perfectly. Boxed lunches can also be purchased, which is a good idea if you plan to visit Mount Jefferson State Park. Greenfield also has small inn facilities as well as "on-premises" campground privileges.

Things really rock on weekends with live music and "dancin'." Greenfield is located at 1795 Mount Jefferson Road. The restaurant is open from 6:00 A.M. to 9:00 P.M., Monday through Saturday, and from 6:00 A.M. to 3:00 P.M., Sunday. (336) 246-2900.

Mount Jefferson State Park has 550 acres to roam, with Mount Jefferson rising 1,600 feet above sea level in the middle of the surrounding land. The mountain, like everything else in Western North Carolina, is beautifully managed and easily accessible by car. At the summit is a superior picnic area with a covered pavilion and a big, open fireplace with stacked firewood ready for your use. Spacious flat areas make the mountaintop convenient for people in wheelchairs, enabling them to see knockout views of the whole county. Most of the year you will have Mount Jefferson to yourself.

Jefferson State Park is located off of U.S. Highway 221, about two miles east of Jefferson. Look for a brown state sign, then turn onto Mount Jefferson Park Road; continue for three miles until you reach the top.

In spite of its name, the **New River** is believed to be one of the oldest rivers in the world. Archaeological investigations suggest the presence of humans in the New River valley at least 10,000 years ago. The river itself existed before the mountains it now passes through and the waters have flowed for millions of years.

Easy paddling and gorgeous scenery make the New River a wonderful water trail for beginning paddlers. The water is shallow and gentle and the rapids are mild. The New River is part of the National Scenic Rivers System and 26 miles of it are protected. This lovely river is also the centerpiece of the **New River State Park,** which is 8 miles from Jefferson.

There are three access areas to the park (one from U.S. Highway

221) and each area provides canoe-in primitive campgrounds with tables, grills, and hiking trails. Depending on the area, other amenities include bathroom facilities, hot-water showers, picnic areas, shelters, and a building for group gatherings. Campers must register by calling (336) 982-2587.

New River Outfitters on U.S. Highway 221, nine miles north of Jefferson, can do just what their name says—outfit you for a trip on the river. New River Outfitters will provide you with canoes or kayaks, paddles, life preservers, food, and transportation to your put-in or take-out point. Trips can be from one hour to six days. Reservations are required by calling (800) 982-9190. www.canoethenew.com.

Shatley Springs

Shatley Springs has an interesting history dating back to the 1920s. Martin Shatley's doctors told him he could live only a short time so he moved from town and settled on a farm here. By chance, he dipped into the natural springs and bathed his face in the cool water. Voila! In less than one hour he was cured of all his ailments. Three weeks later he was working like a farmhand and remained working the rest of his long life. Whether you believe in the curative powers of Shatley Springs or not, bring a jug to fill with the fresh water—you'll be instantly invigorated!

For a good family-style restaurant, have lunch at **Shatley Springs Inn.** Fried chicken and country ham are mainstays, accompanied by steamed veggies and homemade cobblers.

Shatley Springs Inn is a restaurant with a few cabins to rent. Take U.S. Highway 221 North from West Jefferson for seven miles, turn onto N.C. Highway 16 North for five miles, and look for the sign. Hours are from 7:00 A.M. to 9:00 P.M., daily, late April to late October. Reservations are recommended for lunch and dinner, especially on the weekends. Breakfast is first come, first served. (336) 982-2236 or (336) 246-5332.

Glendale Springs

For over a hundred years, visitors have come to the location of the **Glendale Springs Bed and Breakfast.** The center portion of the inn was constructed about 1892 and Daniel Weisinger Adams II added the north and south wings between 1902 and 1905. While building his "hotel" to spur development, Adams also convinced the community of "Venus" to change its name to "Glendale Springs," hoping to improve the area's business prospects. In addition, he built the widely admired Episcopal Chapel (Holy Trinity) nearby. From 1936 to 1938, construction workers on the Blue Ridge Parkway occupied the hotel. It remained in the family until 1969 and was completely refurbished in 1995.

The original structure contains the restaurant and five guest rooms, all with private baths, and the Guest House across the street contains four spacious rooms. Some rooms have fireplaces and Jacuzzis. Both buildings have wonderful porches with wicker swings and rocking chairs. In summer, guests may have lunch, afternoon tea, or evening dessert on the veranda overlooking the garden.

It is located off the Blue Ridge Parkway at Milepost 259 at 7414 N.C. Highway 16. The food is fabulous! Lunch, dinner, and Sunday brunch are served; off-season meals are served only on the weekends. Restaurant and room reservations are required. (336) 982-2103 or (800) 287-1206. www.glendalespringsinn.com.

Back near Boone, the **Mystery Hill Complex** is located near U.S. Highway 221-321 (Blowing Rock Road). In the complex is a house where nothing is as it should be. You enter a room and your whole equilibrium is lost. Objects work the opposite—water runs uphill and balls bounce in strange ways. Mountain people say that this is the mystery of the mountains, where there is a gravitational pull that is natural to the area.

Whether it be truth or illusion, Mystery Hill is a place where the mind's eye plays tricks and the fun is trying to figure out how to navigate in such weird surroundings. Mystery Hill is a great rainy-day place for children. It is located at 129 Mystery Hill Lane off of University Hall Drive. There is an admission fee. It is open at 8:00 A.M., daily (10:00 A.M., Sunday), June through August; and at 9:00 A.M., daily (1:00 P.M., Sunday), September through May. (828) 264-2792.

Next door is the **Appalachian Heritage Museum** in the Dougherty House, built in 1903. It was built as a school for mountain children and was the first house in the county to have running water and electricity. It was moved from its original location and brought to Mystery Hill Complex, where it is used today to depict how life was for the middle-class mountain people in the 1800s. Donations are appreciated.

The Carolinas' first theme park is the **Tweetsie Railroad,** which was founded in 1957. Old Steam Locomotive Number 12 is the star of the show and gives you a three-mile trip through some good-looking mountain scenery. Outlaws and Indians might try and "rob" the train so you need to be on the lookout at all times! Before 1957, Number 12 had a *real* job with the ET & WNC Railroad, toting passengers through the Blue Ridge Mountains from Johnson City, Tennessee, to Boone, North Carolina. The train was built in 1917 by Baldwin Locomotive Works of Philadelphia. In 1956, Grover C. Robbins, Jr., bought the rights to Number 12 from famous cowboy Gene Autry for one dollar and brought it back home to North Carolina.

Today the Tweetsie runs just for fun and the park around it resounds with music and dancing and all kinds of activities for children and adults. You can easily find the Tweetsie on U.S. Highway 321 between Blowing Rock and Boone. The summer season usually runs from May 15 through Labor Day, from 9:00 A.M. to 6:00 P.M. (8:00 P.M., Tuesday). From Labor Day until October 31, the train runs on a limited basis on the weekends. In October, the railroad is open on special evenings for the Halloween Festival and the Ghost Train. (800) 526-5740. www.tweetsierailroad.com.

The name "Tweetsie" was given to the train by local folks who became accustomed to the familiar "tweet tweet" shrill of the engine's whistle that echoed through the hills. The name stuck, and the train has been known as Tweetsie ever since.

On U.S. Highway 321, between Blowing Rock and Boone, is **Shoppes On The Parkway,** which has over 30 brand-name outlets. For all you serious shoppers, you could spend at least a half-day "baggin' the bargains." On the same highway is **Rogers Trading Post** and, just in case you want to buy your very own traffic light, there is one at Roger's—if he will sell it!

Best Cellar, housed in a circa-1940 log cabin, is located at 278 Little Spring Road. This restaurant is one of the most popular in the area, serving fine steaks and some of the freshest seafood around. It is open at 5:30 P.M., Monday through Saturday, May through November, and Thursday through Monday, December through April. Call for reservations. (828) 295-3466.

Blowing Rock

The mountain village of Blowing Rock was chartered and incorporated in 1889. It perches on the Eastern Continental Divide at an elevation of 4,000 feet and links the Shenandoahs to the north with the Great Smokies to the south. Even prior to 1889, the village was a popular community with visitors and seasonal residents looking for quiet, restful scenery and a respite from the heat of the lower elevations. Today, Blowing Rock has many beautiful inns, bed and breakfasts, and resorts. Restaurant choices are varied and the shops' offerings range from fine antiques to hand-woven coverlets. A variety of regular events includes summer stock theater, concerts, seminars, and arts and crafts shows (thank you to the Blowing Rock Chamber of Commerce for this information).

In a very beautiful setting around a lake is the **Chetola Resort.** The Manor House, which was the hub of the 87-acre Chetola Estate, was built in 1846 and serves as the restaurant. Delicious mountain specialties are served in three dining rooms or on the patio overlooking Chetola Lake. One hundred rooms and condominiums are available, as are meeting and banquet rooms. Chetola also specializes in hosting groups, special events, and weddings up to 150 people. This lovely setting is secluded but close to shopping and dining.

Along with tennis, swimming, and boating, Chetola offers direct access to hiking trails ranging from a casual stroll to a strenuous trek. Chetola's Adventure Camp offers great activities for young visitors, giving parents some time alone. Located directly off U.S. Highway 321 in Blowing Rock, Chetola can also be reached from the Blue Ridge Parkway at Mileposts 292 and 298. (828) 295-5500 or (800) CHETOLA. www.chetola.com.

The **Manor House Restaurant** at Chetola Resort maintains the standards of excellence of the resort. Both the lunch and dinner menus offer exceptional selections and the freshest of ingredients to make your meal memorable. For dinner, it is tempting to make a meal of appetizers—there are so many and they are all so good. However, the seafood is fresh and prepared with a light touch and the meats are carefully selected and cooked to perfection. (828) 295-5500. Expensive.

Roasted Pumpkin Confit

1 3-lb. pumpkin	$1/2$ tbsp. diced, peeled shallots
2 tbsp. grape seed oil	Fresh cracked, black pepper to taste
$1/2$ tsp. pumpkin seed oil	Kosher salt to taste

Preheat oven to 325 degrees. Roast whole pumpkin 1 to 2 hours in a shallow pan with 1 inch of water. Remove and cool. Cut in half and remove and reserve seeds. Scrape pumpkin meat from skin and mash with a fork. Fold in oils, shallots, and seasonings. Place pumpkin mixture on a nonstick baking sheet and bake at 325 degrees for 10 to 20 minutes. Garnish with arugula or chicory greens and serve warm or cool as a side dish. (Roasted pumpkin seeds are a good snack.)

—Ramsey Etchinson, chef de cuisine at the Chetola Resort

When entering the village of Blowing Rock from U.S. Highway 321 North, look for **Knight's On Main** on the right. The building has been a restaurant since the 1930s and the locals like to come here to keep up with each other and with what is going on in town. Knight's serves three meals daily. Standard breakfast fare, along with country ham, baked apples, and banana nut muffins, is served beginning at 7:00 A.M. Lunch favorites include Knight's well-known veggie plates. At dinner, the steaks and fish dishes are good and the ribs are hard to beat anytime. Located on North Main Street, Knight's is open from 7:00 A.M. to 8:00 P.M., six days a week, and from 7:00 A.M. to 2:00 P.M., Sunday.

Begin your visit to this mountain retreat at the pretty stone building on Main Street that houses the Chamber of Commerce. Here you can get a map for a historic walking tour of the town. After touring and spending some time here, you will want to return year after year to this peaceful, charming spot.

The season for the **Blowing Rock Stage Company** runs from June through September and on special holidays. This group of professional actors gives lively performances each night and if you are visiting the area this is a great way to spend the evening. The company is located at 152 Sunset Drive. Ticket information can be obtained by calling (828) 295-9627. The ticket office is in the old ice house, which was constructed of river, field, and Grandfather Mountain stone in the 1920s.

To do justice to Blowing Rock, your visit will take at least a day and a night. Many nice inns in the downtown area will put you in the middle of things and allow you to take in the town without getting in your car. **Crippens Country Inn and Restaurant** is a comfortable, affordable place to lay your head. Every room looks freshly painted and is squeaky clean. The restaurant has an excellent menu and stays booked, so reservations are a must. Tartar of yellowfin tuna with crispy fried ginger is an appetizer you may want to try. Let the house specialties be your guide for an entree.

Crippens, located at 239 Sunset Drive, has eight rooms with private baths, plus a cottage. Please, no smoking, no pets, and only children over 12 years of age. (877) 295-3487. www.crippens.com.

The **Inn at Ragged Gardens** is located at 203 Sunset Drive. The stone manor was built in the early 1900s as a private residence; the chestnut-bark siding was added in the 1920s. The inn is surrounded by English gardens, both formal and "ragged." Current owners Lee and Jama Hyett have lovingly restored the estate and they welcome guests to their bed and breakfast inn year round.

Upon entering the foyer one can't help noticing the beautiful "grandfather" rock, a type of local granite, which has been used for entry columns, flooring, staircases, and the huge wood-burning fireplace. The interior has been decorated in the Victorian style and each of the 11 rooms has been named and decorated accordingly. Each has a private bath and a fireplace. There are no telephones or TVs in the rooms, but both are available downstairs. Rates are expensive and a bountiful breakfast and refreshments are included. Children over 12 are welcome. (828) 295-9703. www.ragged-gardens.com.

DeWoolfson's Fine Linens has two locations, one on Sunset Drive in Blowing Rock and the other on N.C. Highway 105, south of Boone. For the finest of bed dressings, DeWoolfson's manufactures white goose-down comforters and pillows. There are imported linens from France, England, Germany, and Austria, along with Mulberry silk-filled comforters from China. The shops are usually open seven days a week but hours are seasonal so call ahead. (828) 295-0504 (Blowing Rock), (828) 963-4144 (N.C. Highway 105), or (800) 833-3696.

After a morning of shopping in Blowing Rock, you may want to cool your heels at a good lunch place. You will not find advertisements for the **Blowing Rock Café** because owner Larry Imeson doesn't have to advertise—which may be the best endorsement you can give a place. Since the 1980s this modest café has been a favorite of Blowing Rock's residents and summer folks and stays full almost every day. The decor is quiet and in good taste and the thick rug on the floor lowers the decibels of a full house of chatterboxes.

The café has three different homemade soups every day and if the special is a pasta dish, it can easily feed two. The entire menu is terrific—don't forget the muffins! At night, the signature dish is Vodka Rigatoni, but don't be afraid to take a chance on anything on the menu. In good weather you can eat on the small patio outside or sit with something to drink while you wait for your table. The café, located about three blocks off of Main Street at 349 Sunset, does not take reservations and prices are moderate. It is open for breakfast at 7:00 A.M., lunch at 11:30 A.M., and dinner at 5:00 P.M. It is closed the last three weeks in February and the first three in March. (828) 295-9474.

Expressions, a small art guild and gallery, is a showcase for some of the most talented of North Carolina's artists and craftsmen. There are lovely watercolors of mountain scenery, art jewelry, marvelous pottery mugs, jiggers with gnome faces, and whimsical fabric figures. Prices are very reasonable. This is truly a fun, interesting shop, located across the street from the post office. Don't miss it. It is open at 10:00 A.M., daily, April through December. (828) 295-7839.

Maggie and Bob Wilson, owners of **Morning Star Gallery,** have collected a great variety of art objects, some of which are local. Be sure and notice the flat stone birdbaths and the Earth and Sky Vases. The gallery is located at 915 Main and is open six days a week. Hours are seasonal. (828) 295-6991.

Vintners Restaurant and Wine Shoppe is located in the heart of town at 978 Main Street. You can eat inside the restaurant in a large glassed sunroom or outside on two covered decks, one shaded by a magnificent maple tree. You can also enjoy your meal in the big gazebo in the front yard.

Menu offerings are quite varied—sandwiches, salads, pastas, pizzas, vegetarian dishes, and some really nice entrees with a daily feature of mixed grill. If you would like a picnic for the parkway or even "Gossip Park" just across the street, you can get any of their menu items for takeout. Downstairs is a very complete wine shop. The restaurant is open at 11:00 A.M., daily. (828) 295-9376. The wine shop opens at 10:00 A.M., six days a week, and at 12:00 noon, Sunday. (828) 295-3719.

At 1007-1 Main is **Oz,** a toy store for the young and old alike. Everything you can think of connected with *The Wizard of Oz* is in this store. This is a great place to shop for kids or collectors of vintage toys. Iris and Jim Thirtle have "needful things for all ages, especially the young at heart," such as wonderful tin and wind-up toys, MatchBox collectibles, all sizes of Raggedy Anns, and Boyd and Steif bears. (828) 295-0770.

Starwood Gallery will pique your interest right away with the huge kinetic sculpture in the window. Every gadget freak will love all the ingenious creations that look as if they've been put together by Ph.D.s in erector sets. While the merchandise is quirky, the craftsmanship is excellent and a purchase will be a conversation piece. Starwood Gallery opens into another shop, **Man In The Moon,** which specializes in beautiful wooden accessories and other products for men. The two shops, located at 1087 Main, are usually open at 10:00 A.M. during the season and from 12:00 noon to 5:00 P.M. otherwise. (828) 295-9229.

Furnishing a mountain home, lodge, or cabin can be difficult; so many fine local craftsmen are available until your cup runneth over and your house can sometimes become a cliché. **Appalachian Rustic Furnishings** helps to individualize your dwelling while keeping the classic mountain feeling. Family-owned businesses always seem to have a leg up on quality and service and Appalachian Rustics is no exception. The shop keeps regular hours and is located at 1089 North Main. If you are interested in their catalog, you may write to Post Office Box 2389, Blowing Rock, North Carolina 28605, or call (828) 295-9554.

"Where to eat?" may be a question with too many answers in Blowing Rock, but a longtime local favorite is the **Village Café.** In the center of the village, on the east side of Main Street, look for the sign and walk down a narrow path toward a quaint building nestled among trees and gardens. In 1907, a mountain crafts co-op was housed here and later became the town's lending library. In 1991, the building was placed on the National Register of Historic Places.

The food is as noteworthy as the building. Breakfast (served most of the time) will entice you with crepes, waffles, and omelets, but the egg dishes are too special to miss: Scandinavian Eggs—scrambled with vodka-cured salmon, cream cheese, and chives—or Eggs Bernice—poached eggs served on an English muffin with grilled smoked turkey, fresh tomato, and hollandaise. Lunch will be just as tempting with a variety of salads served with homemade dressings and gourmet sandwiches made on Fugasa Bread, a traditional Argentinean sourdough recipe.

Full entrees can make your day. Try the roasted pork tenderloin with guava-tamarind glaze or grilled molasses-glazed salmon served with a black mustard seed vinaigrette. Had enough? Not yet! You must try the signature dessert, Café Vice, a frozen chocolate mousse pie with a flourless crust of pecans, brown sugar, and brandy. Beer, wine, and cocktails are available. Breakfast and lunch are normally served between 8:00 A.M. and 3:00 P.M., but hours are seasonal. The café is closed on Wednesday. (828) 295-3769.

If you see bubbles floating from a house on Main Street, it is probably the **Martin House,** which was built in 1870 as a private residence and is one of the oldest buildings in town. Upstairs is a delightful kitchen shop with a large selection of kitchen gadgets and some old-fashioned aprons. It is open from 10:00 A.M. to 5:00 P.M., weekdays, in season, and weekends only in the winter. Nearby, be sure and notice the squirrel tree house—in a tree, of course—in front of **Pandora's Mailbox.** Incidentally, Pandora's has an extensive collection of CDs and cards. **Pleasant Papers/Bookmasters** is a pleasant place with papers and books, albums, games, and gifts. Nearby **Kojays** has great takeout food.

Good casual wear for women can be found at the **Fig Leaf** on Main Street at Morris. This shop seems to have a knack for knowing what is comfortable and appropriate while visiting in the mountains.

Reasonable prices and helpful salespeople make the Fig Leaf worth a stop. Shop hours conform with other Main Street businesses. (828) 295-3535.

Antique buffs will enjoy **Family Heirlooms,** 1121 Main Street. It is brimming with vintage linens, English antique furniture, and the usual china and silver, but with a fun variety of colorful stuffed roosters. It is open from 10:00 A.M. to 5:00 P.M., six days a week, and from 1:00 to 5:00 P.M., Sunday. (828) 295-0090.

Gattle's, 1151 Main Street, is the store for pampering yourself with the finest-quality linens for bed and bath, lingerie, and elegant at-home wear. Beautifully embroidered handkerchiefs, guest towels, table linens, and baby gifts are just part of this top-of-the-line selection. A monogramming service is also provided. It is open from 10:00 A.M. to 5:00 P.M., six days a week. Winter hours are irregular. (828) 295-7556.

For a young one on your gift list, check out **G. Whillikers.** You'll thoroughly enjoy this fun store with whimsical gifts, 3-D puzzles, toys, rubber stamps, and children's books. It is open daily. (828) 295-9549. Another G. Whillikers is in Boone.

Among the numerous antique shops on Main a few stand out, such as **Windwood Antique**s, with the best selection of English pine furniture and some great related accessories. It is open from 10:00 A.M. to 5:00 P.M., six days a week and sometimes Sunday. (828) 295-9260.

Around the corner, at 131-8 Morris Street, is an intriguing shop called **de Provence et d'ailleurs,** which translated means, "from Provence and elsewhere." The proprietor, Danielle de Ville d'Avray Tester, explains that the shop contains "everything French."

The shop is the largest dealer in the Southeast of France's famous china, Quimper. Other items in the shop of great charm and whimsy are the "Santons de Provence" dolls, small clay figurines made and used in Provence for Christmas crèches. Each figure is different and holds a gift for the Christ child. Hours are from 10:00 A.M. to 5:00 P.M., six days a week, and by appointment in January and February. (828) 295-9989.

At the south end of Main Street is **SouthMarke,** a group of specialty shops around a garden setting. Minimall is not the word for this attractive corner of Blowing Rock, with brick paths and flowerbeds in front of each shop. You will have the pleasure of moseying in and out of each establishment, content to be shopping in an unhurried atmosphere. **Feather Your Nest** is the first shop and do not pass it up! Owner Pamela Ayoub knows her business and keeps it packed with the some of the best folk art and gifts you can find. Take down its number because you will invariably get home and want to call her to mail something you could kick yourself for not buying in the first place. (828) 295-1708.

Grandmothers beware! The **Lollipop Shop** has beautiful children's clothes, gifts, and furniture. Hours are seasonal. (828) 295-3003. **Hemingway's Book and Gift Shop** has bestsellers, local interest, and children's books. Owner Patty Wheeler also has a good variety of music and gifts in her shop. (828) 295-0666.

We're Good Sports is for all sports fans, whether they be college or pro, and this is the place for friendly rivals to obtain the best gag gifts. *Why I Hate (name of college or pro team)* books climb to the ceiling as well as birdhouses in school colors, hats, jackets, and license plates. Everything pertaining to your favorite team is here or Ken Cross, owner, will get it for you. (828) 295-9547 or (828) 679-9547. **Serves You Right** lives up to its name. Don't miss this shop just because it's at the end of the lane. You will discover many of the most popular lines of china: Portmerion, Royal Worcester, Herend, and Mottahedeh. A great gift would be the colorful, hand-painted, oilcloth place mats. It is open daily. (800) 825-1828.

With its scenic countryside, Blowing Rock has much more to offer than shopping and dining and it would be a shame not to take advantage of the natural beauty. There are several nonstrenuous walks nearby and one of the most popular near the village will provide a few hours of entertainment to those who do not wish to shop (like daddies and children). **Glen Burney Trail** is a two-hour round-trip walk into a virgin hardwood forest with wonderful waterfalls. Follow the signs to Cannon Memorial Gardens and park at the gardens; at the south end is the trail entrance. The trail skirts the cascading New Year's Creek and provides vistas of both **Glen Burney Falls** and **Glen Mary Falls.**

There are other walks nearby that range from nonstrenuous to moderately strenuous, as well as a number of vigorous hikes. For information and maps, stop in at the Chamber of Commerce on Park Avenue. (828) 295-7851 or (800) 295-7581.

St. Mary of the Hills Episcopal Church was built in 1918 of native stone. In 1921, the church was dedicated as the Susie Parker Stringfellow Memorial Church. Well-known New York artist Elliot Daingerfield became a summer communicant in 1883 and when he generously donated his painting of *St. Mary the Virgin*, the name was changed to St. Mary of the Hills. The painting hangs behind the altar.

The Mary Garden, to the right of the church, contains a sculpture by Elliot's daughter, Marjorie Daingerfield Howlett. *The Offering* is a statue of the Virgin offering her Son to the world. St. Mary's is located on the south end of Main Street at the corner of Chestnut. (828) 295-7323. As you leave, notice the exquisite della Robbia wreath outside of the Main Street door.

Luca della Robbia was an Italian sculptor during the Renaissance. He is known for his work in terra cotta, which he covered with glazes in brilliant colors. His nephew, Andrea, carried on the secret process. In deference to their technique, similar works by modern artists are allowed to use the name della Robbia.

Blowing Rock is named after the phenomenon of strange rock formations overlooking John's River Gorge. **"The Rock"** lies south of town on U.S. Highway 321 and is a 4,000-foot-high cliff. This rocky cliff catches a northwest wind and forms a powerful flume—you can throw light objects over the abyss and they will return to you. However, if the wind is not just right you may be guilty of littering . . . so maybe just having knowledge of this fact is enough.

The tourist area is perfectly planned and the observation deck sits out from the rocks, making it possible for you to see Hawksbill Mountain and Table Rock. Grandfather Mountain and Mount Mitchell can also be observed. Walk the nice railed path underneath Blowing Rock for another view of this natural marvel. The admission ticket is worth every cent and can be obtained at the attractive gift shop, which is also the information center. The Rock is open from March through November and on weekends in the winter, weather permitting. (828) 295-7111.

Almost across from the entrance to the Rock is the **Green Park Inn,** circa 1882. This proud Victorian beauty is painted sparkling white with many gables and a bright green roof. At the entrance you will see the signature horse and surrey—which finally had to be painted green too, as people thought a real horse was tied there eternally! Many dignitaries have signed the registry through the years: Grover Cleveland, Calvin Coolidge, Franklin and Eleanor Roosevelt, John D. Rockefeller (who always tipped a dime to everyone), and Herbert Hoover, to name a few. Green Park Inn offered a luxurious opportunity for all the potentates of the day to escape city heat and frolic in the cool fresh air of the mountains—some would even go target shooting with Annie Oakley herself.

Today, the Green Park Inn is still a luxury with modern conveniences at affordable prices, welcoming families much as it did in the 1800s. From May to October, golf and tennis can be arranged at the Blowing Rock Country Club, casual dining is available in the Laurel Room or the Divide Tavern, and most of the attractions in the region are not more than half an hour away. There are 85 rooms in the inn, from standard to suites, and prices range accordingly.

The Green Park Inn stands in defiance of the years and gives testimony to its rich and colorful past. (828) 295-3141 or (800) 852-2462. www.greenparkinn.com.

Mrs. Bertha Cone built a private home in 1939 for her nephew. It was a beautiful structure of Boston architectural design and built of stone from Grandfather Mountain. Today, the home, one of the near-perfect inns that dot Western North Carolina, is the **Gideon Ridge Inn,** owned and operated by Cobb and Cindy Miller.

When you enter the inn, located just out of the buzz of Blowing Rock, you will have the feeling of being a guest in someone's delightful home. Five acres of woods and gardens surround you with paths where you can walk and discover the 30 varieties of trees or enjoy the planted beds of fragrant flowers. Gideon Ridge's elevation is 3,900 feet. Wide-open terraces and big chairs with fluffy pillows make it pleasant for you to sit and enjoy the view of Mount Pilot to the east and Mount Mitchell to the southwest. Teatime is a high point of each day and can be served either on the terrace or in the library in front of the fire. It is a foregone conclusion that the Gideon Ridge Inn is the place where writers like to stay, especially during the Appalachian State University's visiting writers' series.

Gideon Ridge, located at 6148 Gideon Ridge Road, is popular every weekend of the year, so make reservations long in advance (a minimum of two nights is the rule). Children over 12 are allowed, but the environment is more conducive to adults. (828) 295-3644. www.ridge-inn.com. Rates are moderate to expensive and change according to the season and days of the week.

Moses and Bertha Cone came to Blowing Rock in 1897 to build their summer house in the middle of 3,516 acres of land. Mr. Cone was a textile manufacturer who produced the highest grade of denim, giving him the name "Denim King." Because of poor health, Moses came to Blowing Rock to take advantage of the fresh water and clean air in the mountainous region. He built a magnificent 20-room Queen Anne style home, which you can visit today. In 1950, the **Moses H. Cone Memorial Park** was donated to the National Park Service and the Southern Highland Craft Guild began exhibiting fine American crafts in this beautiful manor house.

The Cones were naturalists and extensively planted thousands of species of trees, including 40,000 apple trees yielding prize fruit. As a gift to his wife, Moses built 25 miles of carriage roads so that she could revel in the beautiful surroundings they had created.

To enjoy the estate to the fullest, you need to hike the Craftsman Trail, which takes you to the Cone Cemetery and to Flat Top Tower for the view. You can then amble around Bass Lake and on to the apple barn and the maze. Bass Lake can also be reached by car off of U. S. Highway 321. This is a beautiful place to walk, cross-country ski, or fish! If you choose, you may explore the estate on horseback. The stables are adjacent to the estate on Laurel Lane. (828) 295-7847.

The Moses H. Cone Memorial Park can be reached from the Blue Ridge Parkway at Milepost 294.1, from U.S. Highway 221 from Linville, or from U.S. Highway 221/321 from Boone. Manor House hours are from 9:00 A.M. to 6:00 P.M., late March through October, and from 9:00 A.M. to 4:00 P.M., November. (828) 295-7938.

Located on U.S. Highway 221 South, just minutes outside of Blowing Rock, is the **Westglow Spa,** a European-style destination spa that promises leisure, recreation, rejuvenation, and scenery.

The spa, which opened in 1991, is situated on a 20-acre estate that artist and writer Elliot Daingerfield built in 1916. He named his colonial manor "Westglow" because of the vistas, which he described as "never glaring but always glowing." Today, this beautiful manor house includes seven guest rooms upstairs, while across the road are two cottages providing comfort and privacy for additional guests.

The Life Enhancement Center is a state-of-the-art facility offering complete fitness and therapeutic programs for both men and women. Mealtimes bring "cuisine naturelle," which translates as seasonal, wholesome fresh food. A staff

member says, "We help our guests assess their wants and needs and then try to fulfill them." The center provides a really large range of services.

This is an expensive and beautiful place to stay. If you live nearby, you may apply for membership; otherwise spa services are restricted to guests. However, dinner at the manor house is open to the public. (800) 562-0807.

The majestic Grecian columns on the porch of the manor house were shipped by barge from Italy and hauled by oxen up the mountainside.

Exactly halfway between Boone and Blowing Rock is the **Yonahlossee Resort and Club.** Yonahlossee, Cherokee for "Trail of the Bear," was a girls' riding camp, which was founded in 1922 and in existence for 60 years. Today, it is a high-caliber tennis resort with six outdoor clay courts, three indoor Deco-Turf courts, and two pros on staff. In addition, Yonahlossee has one of the finest equestrian centers in the mountains. Over 130 acres are devoted to the Saddle Club and its facilities. Riding lessons are available, as well as pony rides for children, or you may bring your own horse. There is a cross-country jumping course.

The inn offers spacious rooms, cottage suites, and townhouses in wooded settings. A swimming pool and Buttermere Tarn, a beautiful small lake for swimming, fishing, and canoeing, will further enhance your visit. There is conference and banquet space and many health amenities. A continental breakfast is served daily in the inn while dinner is served across the street in the inn's **Gamekeeper's Restaurant.**

This outstanding, year-round resort is protected on three sides by the Moses H. Cone Memorial Park and it is located just off the parkway on Shull's Mill Road. (828) 963-6400 or (800) 962-1986. www.yonahlossee.com. The Gamekeeper's Restaurant is open Tuesday through Saturday evenings for the public. (828) 963-7400.

Golf Courses

Here are the area municipal and public golf courses; information courtesy of Journal Communications, Inc.:

Boone Golf Club. Located at Boone city limits. *North Carolina* magazine has listed this club as one of the top 10 best public courses in North Carolina. Listed as a three-star award winner by *Golf Digest,* it is a fun course to play. It is open from April through October. Walking restricted. (828) 264-8760. www.boonegolfclub.com.

Mountain Aire Golf Club. Located three miles south of West Jefferson. This newly remodeled course has a friendly atmosphere, spectacular views, and reasonable prices. It is open from March through November. (828) 877-4716.

Willow Creek. Three miles south of Boone. Featuring nine holes with lots of water and 27 sand traps, this is open from April through October. (828) 963-6865.

CHAPTER 5

Blue Ridge Parkway

Rivers served as the first highways in North Carolina. Roads began to appear in the 1700s but remained poor well into the 1900s. In the mid-1930s, construction began on the **Blue Ridge Parkway**, which connects the Great Smoky Mountains National Park (in North Carolina and Tennessee) with the Shenandoah National Park (in Virginia). This 469-mile parkway, often called "America's most scenic drive," is like a historical corridor lined with breathtaking vistas and recreational opportunities. Originally, the parkway was to run through Tennessee, but a mountaintop-to-mountaintop route through North Carolina was finally chosen because of the breathtaking views.

In normal times, an undertaking like the Blue Ridge Parkway might have been impractical; but with millions left unemployed by the depression, the project promised to put thousands of people back to work at government expense. Work was begun in 1935 and continued for 32 years. By the late 1970s, the only section of the parkway not completed was the rocky perimeter around Grandfather Mountain. Hugh Morton, owner of the mountain, adamantly believed that parkway construction near the top of Grandfather would ruin its rugged beauty.

Parkway officials felt that the route should maintain the scenic qualities of the rest of the parkway, while architects and engineers agreed that the road should be elevated wherever possible to eliminate massive cuts in the mountain. The eventual compromise, the **Linn Cove Viaduct,** proved to be a triumph for everyone. The 1,243-foot-long viaduct, called the most complicated bridge ever built, cantilevers away from Grandfather using 153 precast segments weighing 50 tons each. Constructed from the top down to minimize disturbance to the mountain, the viaduct itself was the only access road for construction. It was completed in 1983.

Make the time to see this engineering marvel. A visitor center located at Milepost 304.6 at the south end of the viaduct will furnish you with information and maps. (This information was courtesy of the Appalachian Cultural Museum, Boone, North Carolina. www.museum.appstate.edu.)

The ancient Romans built the first viaducts. A viaduct is like a bridge, except that it crosses over dry land instead of water. Some viaducts do cross water, but they also cross dry land instead of merely extending from bank to bank. Some viaducts carry railroad tracks over valleys and gorges and even highways.

The toll-free parkway (253 miles in North Carolina and 112 in Western North Carolina) is no high-speed highway with commercial development. Instead it offers visitor centers, a few campgrounds, picnic spots, overlooks, and trails for all hiking levels. Listed here are brief descriptions and highlights of the attractions and the nine primary sites at the mileposts in Western North Carolina only. For information on the entire Blue Ridge Parkway, you might want to pick up a copy of the Blue Ridge Parkway Directory, usually available at visitor centers or by writing the Blue Ridge Parkway Association at Post Office Box 2136, Asheville, North Carolina 28802. The National Park Service also has a beautiful brochure with an excellent map. (828) 298-0398. www.blueridgeparkway.org.

Milepost numbers are on low concrete markers on the roadside (stars indicate the nine primary sites):

Milepost 292 to 295: Moses H. Cone Memorial Park, with horseback riding trails and a craft center (see index).

Milepost 295.1 to 298: Julian Price Memorial Park has a nice picnic area and a two-and-a-half-mile trail around a lake.

Milepost 304: Linn Cove Viaduct winds around the side of Grandfather Mountain (see index); Tanawak Hiking Trail will take you under and above the viaduct. Map is available at the visitor center here.

Milepost 308.2: Flat Rock has a gorgeous view of Linville Valley and Grandfather Mountain.

Milepost 316.3: Linville Falls. Here are several trails leading to overlooks.

Milepost 317.4: A visitors center.

Milepost 320.7: Chestoa View. From a cliff on Humpback Mountain, the altitude is 4,090 feet.

Milepost 331: Museum of North Carolina displays specimens of minerals found in the state.

Milepost 340.3: Crabtree Meadows Visitor Center with a picnic area and a hiking trail to Crabtree Falls.

Milepost 355.4: Mount Mitchell State Park, highest peak in the eastern United States (see index).

Milepost 364.4: Craggy Gardens Visitor Center with a picnic area and several trails.

Milepost 382: Folk Art Center (see index).

Milepost 408.6: Mount Pisgah was part of the Biltmore Estate, where the first forestry school in America was established, and a large portion of it became the nucleus of the Pisgah National Forest. There is a visitor center, campsites, picnic facilities, and an inn. Post Office Drawer 749, Waynesville, North Carolina 28786. (828) 235-8228 (see index).

Milepost 415: Nearby is turnoff for the Cradle of Forestry (see index).

Milepost 422.4: Devil's Courthouse has a trail and an incredible view of the mountains (see index). Note: There is another overlook called Devil's Courthouse on Whiteside Mountain between Cashiers and Highlands.

Milepost 431.1: Richard Balsam has a self-guiding trail through a forest; highest point on the parkway at 6,047 feet.

Milepost 451.2: Waterrock Knob has a visitor center and a trail to the knob, where you can see four states.

Milepost 458.2: Heintooga Ridge Road leads to a mile-high overlook and the Great Smoky Mountains National Park.

Milepost 469.1: The parkway ends here and intersects U.S. Highway 441 at the Cherokee Reservation and the entrance to the Great Smoky Mountains National Park (see index).

The Blue Ridge Parkway has very few facilities so be sure you have fuel for both your car and your passengers. Many of the overlooks are built so that you can see the view from your car and some are designed so that you have views from both sides of the road. Last, but not least, although the parkway is beautiful, you will be missing many interesting side trips if you stay strictly on the parkway (e.g., Looking Glass Falls and Sliding Rock are both on U.S. Highway 276, just off the Blue Ridge Parkway).

In the fall, "leaf lookers" might enjoy knowing which trees are which breathtaking color. Of note is the fact that, of all the trees in the mountains, only about a dozen or so are the stars of the fall color show. A fairly dry September contributes to the more vivid displays.

Orange—Sassafras is the only species with true orange leaves

Yellow-gold—Sweet Birch, Tulip Popular, Hickory, Chestnut, Striped Maple, and White Ash make yellows the prominent color

Bright red—Red Maple and Black Gum; however, the most brilliant red foliage is the rare Mountain Ash, found only at the highest elevations

Maroon to scarlet red—Sourwood, Dogwood, and Scarlet Oak

Rich brown—Fraser Magnolia, sometimes called the Mountain Magnolia

(This information is courtesy of Dr. Robert Zahner of Highlands, a forester and author of *Whiteside Mountain: The Mountain End of the Trail.*)

In 1907, the Clinchfield Railroad, working its way through the mountains toward Tennessee, bought 265 acres and established what is today the **Orchard at Altapass.** When the Blue Ridge Parkway was built, the orchard was split in two. The present orchard of 85 acres is below the parkway and the land above the parkway has reverted to woodlands. Today you can visit the orchard and the packinghouse to pick or buy apples. Early apples are ready for picking after July 4, McIntosh apples come in mid- to late August, and from then until early November is the season. You can also purchase cider, locally produced jams, jellies, and apple butter, and wonderful honey from the bees that work the orchard.

Arrangements can be made for your group to enjoy a homemade

picnic lunch served on the deck overlooking the orchard and/or a hayride with storytelling. If you prefer, you can be entertained by neighbors of the orchard with their "front porch" mountain music. This is a fun place for any age. Minimum group size is 25. The orchard is located directly on the Blue Ridge Parkway at Milepost 328.3 (three miles north of the Spruce Pine Exit, Route 226). It is open from 10:00 A.M. to 6:00 P.M., six days a week, and afternoons, Sunday, Memorial Day through October. (888) 765-9531.

www.altapassorchard.com.

There is no proof that "an apple a day will keep the doctor away," but it is a fact that apples are low in calories, high in energy, and delicious. Below are just a few of the many superb varieties grown nearby:

Red Delicious is excellent for snacks or salads; is the world's most widely planted apple

Rome Beauty is the ultimate baking and cooking apple—think Mom's apple pie!

Golden Delicious is so tender that it does not require peeling for most recipes; best for juice and jellies

Stayman apples hold up well in storage and are often used for cider and apple butter

Granny Smith apples are tart and their flavor is pronounced when baked

Gala apples are small and very sweet; excellent for kids' snacks

McIntosh apples make wonderful applesauce

Little Switzerland

Within just a few feet of the Blue Ridge Parkway, at Milepost 334, is **The Switzerland Inn.** Comfortable accommodations have been welcoming guests since 1910. The big lodge has a restful lobby with "sink down" sofas, a huge fireplace, and a wall of windows for mountain gazing. There are first- and second-floor rooms but no elevator. Several other buildings, all with mountain views, and three A-frame cottages are nestled in

THE SWITZERLAND INN

the woods. Rooms are spacious with televisions and phones and each one has a small porch or balcony.

The **Chalet Restaurant,** adjacent to the lodge, has two separate eating areas and breakfast and lunch are served facing the mountains. Breakfast is a set menu and is included in the room rate. For cocktails and dinner, there is a comfy bar and lounge and inviting dining rooms with fireplaces. The food is outstanding.

Within six miles are three hiking trails; two are moderate and one is strenuous. Just past the A-frame cottages, you can also hike an easy two-mile round trip on Ridge Road. This flat gravel road takes you through a quaint neighborhood of homes. Nearby is a lovely, active Episcopal church. The Switzerland Inn is open from the end of April through the first weekend in November. (828) 765-2153 or (800) 654-4026.

Just across the street is a nice selection of shops. The first shop in the row is **The Trillium Gallery.** Step into this wonderfully lit and artfully arranged shop and you will be greeted by vivacious manager Ermina Poyce. She has been here for quite a few years and is knowl-

edgeable about the nearby local artists as well as those represented in the gallery. Incidentally, Trillium has been here since 1982 and was the first shop in the area to represent and feature local artists. There is pottery, glass, jewelry, and porcelain. Included are David Van Noppen's glass flowers, Robert Levin's paperweights, David Wilson's trillium eggs, Val and Rich Beck's Christmas ornaments, Fiona Clark's perfume bottles, and Joe Nielander's "Saturn" bowl oil lamps.

Not to be missed either are Ermina's own things—beautifully made "quilted" jackets. These are not thick like traditional quilting, but made from random pieces of exquisite fabric put together with fine darning stitches; each is a work of art and one of a kind. Trillium is open from 10:00 A.M. to 5:00 P.M., daily, during the season.

The **Gem Shoppe** is the real thing and owner Gary Ledford knows his gems. Shelves are filled with slabs of Crabtree emeralds and chunks of emerald rock and you can see what gems are like when they come out of the mine. A rare North Carolina kyanite is on display. The shop has individual polished stones beginning at $1, up to an emerald and diamond necklace for $10,000. The jewelry selection is impressive. Shop hours are from 9:00 A.M. to 5:00 P.M., seven days a week, May 1 through October 31, or by appointment. (828) 765-0134 or (828) 765-6333. **Busy B's Collectibles** is sure to have something to take home to a grandchild or anyone else on your list.

Three bright spots nearby are worth a stop. Initially, you may think this cul-de-sac is the perfect place to pick up lunch, stick your head in the shops, and be on your way, but an hour later will find you still hanging out.

At the **Switzerland Café,** healthy fresh food is prepared daily with a delicious roasted veggie sandwich on focaccia bread being a favorite. Over 50 varieties of beer are sold here. This is an excellent place to make up a picnic lunch and then go find a view. The café is open from 10:00 A.M. to 5:00 P.M., seven days a week, April to November 15. If you want to order ahead, call (828) 765-5289.

The **Grassy Mountain Shop** is full of used, out-of-print, and "scarce" books. The shop resembles a rabbit warren with a small entrance followed by tunnels of floor-to-ceiling treasures, oh so carefully chosen and cataloged. Small electric hooded sconces and a helpful window now and then light the passageways. Cozy corners with chairs make it possible for you to while away an afternoon delving into old books that grab your interest.

Wonderful children's classics can be found in the back of the store. What better gift for a child who loves to read than a copy of *Heidi* or *Ali Baba and the Forty Thieves,* with scribblings on the pages by a child from another day? Owners Curtis and Kathryn Johnson are knowledgeable book people who have managed to create the perfect atmosphere where book lovers can "mine" the gems on the shelves to their heart's content. They also have a good resource to locate a favorite out-of-print book. They are open at 10:00 A.M., daily, April to September. (828) 765-9070.

Nancy Livingston and David Bryan show their wares in the **Pottery Garden,** next door. Nancy creates most of the pottery but other regional potters are also represented. David's bright acrylic paintings have been described as "primitive impressionism." The shop is open at 10:00 A.M., daily, May to October. (828) 765-6666.

Mount Mitchell

Mount Mitchell is the tallest mountain in North Carolina and is also the friendliest mountain for driving, cycling, or hiking. It has no rough edges and the big, swooping curves lead easily to the pinnacle. The climb is so gradual you will be astounded when you reach the first clearing and see mountains below you dropping into a crystal-clear lake. Mount Mitchell is in the Black Mountain Range and does not have the length or breadth of the Blue Ridge or the Great Smokies, but these dark, fir-clad mountains are soft and beautiful. Mount Mitchell is 6,684 feet high. Add another 100 feet to climb to the top of the tower, where on a clear day, . . . etc.

Mount Mitchell has all the amenities a state park affords. A restaurant serves state park kind of food and comes with a view and a nice gift shop. Here also are five hiking trails—moderate to strenuous—family camping, and pack-in camping (when you need to leave vehicles in the park overnight). Near the peak of the mountain you will see many of the red spruce and Fraser fir dying from natural and manmade causes. The information center's displays will give you reasons for this sad situation.

Further information can be received by contacting **Mount Mitchell State Park,** Route 5, Box 700, Burnsville, North Carolina 28714, or call (828) 675-4611. The mountain is located in Yancey County, 33 miles northeast of Asheville, at Milepost 355.4 on the Blue Ridge Parkway.

CHAPTER 6

Spruce Pine

Spruce Pine is home to many different types of artists and craftsmen. One of the most unique personalities is Mr. **Bea Hensley,** master blacksmith, who was introduced to the craft by Daniel Boone VI at the ripe old age of four. Mr. Boone was a world-famous master of ornamental iron and he taught Bea to make everything from logging gear and horseshoes to fine knives and beautiful ornamental iron. Today, along with his apprentice son, Mike, Bea makes chandeliers and massive gates for the rich and famous.

In 1995 Bea received a National Heritage Fellowship as a Master Artist and has been named a North Carolina Living Treasure. He welcomes visitors to his shop, just off the Blue Ridge Parkway, in a building located on a road just beyond the Mineral Museum. Stop and ask for directions.

The first North Carolina Living Treasure Award was presented in 1987. It was designed to honor a North Carolina citizen who transforms into art traditional handcrafts using wood, glass, ceramics, metal, and textiles. These awards are sponsored by the University of North Carolina at Wilmington's Museum of World Cultures. In addition to Bea Hensley and Arval Woody, Billie Ruth Suddeth, basket maker from Bakersville, was awarded the honor in 1997.

Gem mining is a big activity in Western North Carolina and can be an enjoyable way to entertain children. Most mines are salted, which guarantees success. One of the most reputable mines is **Rio Doce Gem Mine,** located on N.C. Highway 226 one-half mile north of the parkway in Spruce Pine. Owner Jerry Call is a graduate gemologist from the Gemological Institute of America and he and his family are master gem cutters. Buckets contain gem material from area mines and famous mines of Brazil. Buckets range in price from $10 to $100. A $50 bucket guarantees one stone cut free and the $100 bucket guarantees two stones cut free. Mine hours are from 9:00 A.M. to 5:00 P.M., seven days a week, April through October. (828) 765-2099.

It is hard to believe, but nearby is another North Carolina Living Treasure, Mr. Arval Woody, a fifth-generation chair craftsman. Mr. Woody's grandfather, Arthur Woody, was one of the early pioneers with the Penland School, giving instructions in the art of seating chairs with hickory bark. His studio stood just 800 feet behind the present **Woody's Chair Shop.** Beside the original shop was a water wheel, which was the only source of power for making chairs. (Incidentally, in those early days the price of chairs was three for a dollar!)

Mr. Woody, who has been making chairs himself for over half a century, is officially retired but the successful family business continues. They dry their own lumber, have their own sawmill, and make the chairs by an Early American method using no nails or glue in the weight-bearing structure. Before the chairs are put together, each piece of wood is hand rubbed to the equivalent of several years of ordinary waxing and polishing. There are not very many styles, but they are all tried and true and beautiful—Colonial American, Chalet, and Betsy Ross. The shop also makes bar stools and child-sized rockers. Besides having a fascinating history, these lovely chairs will last for generations. One of Mr. Woody's chairs is at the Smithsonian as part of their permanent American Crafts Collection.

Woody's Chair Shop is located on N.C. Highway 226, three miles south of Spruce Pine. Here in the showroom, besides chairs, you can purchase smaller items—salad bowls, bookends, hand mirrors, and great walking canes. It is open six days a week. (828) 765-9277.

If hunger strikes while you're near Spruce Pine, you're in luck! Watch for the pretty golf course of the **Grassy Creek Golf and Country Club.** Although the golf course is semi-private, the public is welcome at the restaurant for lunch or dinner.

The large clubhouse has a full-service restaurant that offers the peace and quiet of mountain dining, a pretty view, and an excellent menu selection. Lunch offerings include salads, sandwiches, soups, burgers, and specialties. Dinners include appetizers, pasta, seafood, beef, and chicken. Both menus offer full bar service and choices for children. Grassy Creek is located on N.C. Highway 226, just north of Woody's Chair Shop. It is open from 11:00 A.M. to 2:00 P.M., six days a week, and from 5:00 to 9:00 P.M., Wednesday through Saturday. (828) 765-6589.

Joe Nielander and **Lilith Eberle** have a studio/gallery on 876 Carter's Ridge Road in Spruce Pine. Joe is well known for his "Saturn" design for bowls and vases. He has been a glass blower since the 1980s and has developed a unique style. Lilith uses sterling sliver and 14-carat gold with lovely stones to make her delicate jewelry. The gallery, not quite complete, will have a viewing window for visitors to watch Joe blowing glass. Oil lanterns and candles, vases, bowls, and tumblers are for purchase, along with some of Lilith's jewelry. Be sure to call for exact directions. (828) 765-1686. Good prices.

As you travel from gallery to gallery in and around Spruce Pine, you may want to sit and relax with a cup of coffee and a slice of homemade coconut pie or hot fudge cake. **Cedar Crest Restaurant** at 311 Locust Street can provide all of the above. It is open for breakfast, lunch, and dinner from 6:00 A.M. to 8:30 P.M., Tuesday through Saturday. (828) 765-6124.

The **Twisted Laurel Gallery** was established by third-generation clockmaker Luther Stroup and his wife, Renita. When Mr. Stroup delivered his clocks, he could not help but notice works by local artists in his customers' homes. His interest was ignited and in 1989 he and his wife opened the Twisted Laurel to showcase the artisans of the area. The gallery is located in the heart of downtown Spruce Pine on (lower) Locust Street.

In this unassuming building near the barber shop, Mr. Stroup has gathered and displayed an amazing collection. The diversity of the art and crafts is immediately obvious and after you begin browsing, you will be amazed at the diversity of prices also. There are large and small works by known and unknown artists in ceramics, wood, and other media. It is open Tuesday through Saturday or by appointment. (828) 765-1562.

Richmond Inn is located in a scenic mountain setting in Spruce Pine, within three blocks of town. The flagstone terrace overlooks the valley of the North Toe River and has a huge overhanging blue spruce. Innkeeper Carmen Mazzagatti has furnished eight spacious guest rooms with antiques and family treasures. Each room has a private bath; a TV and VCR are available in the living room for the use of guests. A full breakfast is served daily. The inn is open year round and has reasonable rates. Children are welcome but no pets. (828) 765-6993 or (877) 765-6993. www.Richmond-inn.com.

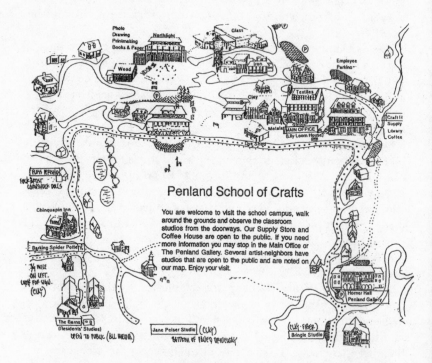

Penland School of Crafts

You are welcome to visit the school campus, walk around the grounds and observe the classroom studios from the doorways. Our Supply Store and Coffee House are open to the public. If you need more information you may stop in the Main Office or The Penland Gallery. Several artist-neighbors have studios that are open to the public and are noted on our map. Enjoy your visit.

Penland

The **Penland School of Crafts** began inauspiciously in 1920 when a young Miss Lucy Morgan arrived via train to teach at the Appalachian School in Penland, a mining region. She began making friends with the neighboring mountain women. The ancient arts of intricate hand weaving and vegetable dyeing that the women were doing in their homes soon interested Miss Lucy.

Miss Lucy became determined to preserve these traditions and to have at least the nearby Appalachian area know of the talents of these early artisans. With energy, enthusiasm, and a nonexistent budget, she procured a few looms and convinced several of the women to teach the nearly lost art. Under her direction, weaving patterns were revived and vegetable dyeing preserved. The rest is fascinating history.

From this meager beginning, a handcraft guild was formed with the John Campbell Folk School and in 1929 the Penland School was founded. Under Miss Lucy's guidance, the school grew from a simple log cabin and a few mountain women into an internationally known school. Students from every state in the union and over 60 foreign countries have come together since then to preserve and develop creative crafts, and Penland is either home or host to renowned teachers from all over the world who come to teach classes in 10 media. The school, now comprising some 400 acres and several dozen buildings, resembles not so much a campus as a big, serious camp for adults. In place of hallowed halls, students walk the wooded hills, past the old dye shed of Miss Lucy's day.

The **Penland Gallery** is housed in the original old Appalachian School building, a gracious big house that had originally been an Episcopal rectory. The gallery sells works by Penland instructors, resident artists, students, and neighbors in a light-filled four-room gallery also used for permanent exhibits and shows. Actually, all of the pieces displayed here are "shows." Blown glass, baskets, sculpture, handmade paper, jewelry, porcelain, photography, weaving, and beautiful objects of wood, iron, and copper all share space under superb lighting. Outside on the wide front porch are big rockers for you to sit and enjoy the view and contemplate which one-of-a-kind work of art you will take home with you.

The gallery is open Tuesday through Saturday, and on Sunday afternoons, mid-April to early December. Penland is located six miles from Spruce Pine and can be reached from either U.S. Highway 19 East or N.C. Highway 226. Tours of the campus are offered on Tuesdays and Thursdays. Please call ahead for reservations, (828) 765-6211. For other information about the school, call (828) 765-2359. www.penland.org.

The area around Penland has become a Mecca of sorts, where artists and fine craftsmen live, teach, and work. Their homes and studios are tucked under, over, and behind the gentle mountains, shaded by laurel and rhododendrons so thick they are next to invisible. There are many more artists in the Penland area than are profiled here and space alone dictated how many would be featured. There is no such animal as a "representative group," so please make the time to see as many of them as you can for they are all outstanding. You can get a map at the Penland Gallery.

Ceramist and painter **Tom Spleth** has a studio at Penland, but he is not always easy to find. Fortunately, Tom was working on a large abstract painting, using industrial enamel on canvas, when the *Coasting* authors visited the area. He is a very respected multimedia artist and his works are on display at the Raleigh Contemporary Gallery and the Zebulon American Crafts Gallery in Burnsville.

Jane Peiser, potter of hand-built salt-glazed porcelain, has a talent that words cannot describe. You have to see her work to really know what it is about. Her use of handmade color, her technique, and her intricate detail blend together to produce the most exquisite objects, such as medieval-looking figures used as candle holders, lamps, night-lights, vases, urns, and planters. It is worth the time to locate her studio on the Penland campus, tucked away down a narrow dirt road, with only small signs to guide you. On fence posts along the road will be some of her porcelain to let you know what's ahead. The gallery itself is enchanting. As you walk through an arched entrance into a small courtyard, the outside world disappears, and the magical world of Jane Peiser opens its door to you. When you step into her small gallery for the first time, you will gasp in awe of what you see. Jane says she "tells stories with her work." Take time to absorb it all and hopefully you will find something to take home with you to remind you of this inspiring experience.

Jane holds a B.A. in Industrial Arts Education and an M.F.A. in Art Education. Her work is in several permanent collections including the Smithsonian. She has received a fellowship from the National Endowment for the Arts. Gallery hours are from 9:00 A.M. to 4:30 P.M., daily, except Sunday morning. (828) 765-7123.

Her business card reads simply, "Clay." Her students and her contemporaries are in awe of her skill; "an amazing thrower . . . one of the best," said one. She throws with "ease and confidence," said another.

They are talking about potter **Cynthia Bringle.** The devotion to her craft is obvious when you see her work. But this is only part of the story, for it is her willingness to encourage and nourish other potters that is legendary. At a recent retrospective exhibition recognizing her 30-plus years of work, ceramist Michael Sherrill called her the "Patron Saint of Clay." A required ceramics class at the Memphis Academy of Arts redirected Cynthia's interest in painting to a love of clay. She later taught at Penland and in 1970 became a permanent part of the Penland community.

Her serene and serious studio looks past snoozing pets and a complicated bird feeder to woods and meadow. Adjoining is a cozy showroom where shelves are lined with lamps, candlesticks, bowls, vases, platters, jugs, and mugs—the diversity is amazing. Everything is wheel thrown and many pieces are wood fired and salt glazed, resulting in unusual colors and soft textures. Cynthia does a lot of custom work, sells mainly out of her own gallery, and exhibits at a few major shows.

Sharing space in the showroom are soft woven scarves, stoles, pillows, and stitched wall hangings done by Cynthia's twin sister, **Edwina Bringle,** a fiber artist. Do not miss these ladies! They are located at 160 Lucy Morgan Lane. (828) 765-0240.

Artist **Nick Joerling** says of his work in clay, "First of all, I daydream with a pencil—not drawing as rendering but simply doodling, then working hard to get that drawing to function." The resulting pieces from a complex ceramic process are functional and beautiful objects.

Like some other accomplished artists, Nick uses altering techniques. The effect of altering the pieces gives more of a soft, asymmetrical feeling. Obvious in his work is his interest in the ceremonial vessels made by the pre-Columbian potters of the Southwest

and the calligraphy of recent Japanese ware. Nick's friend, neighbor, and fellow artist, Tom Spleth, says of Nick's work, "Nick enjoys the time spent in the studio with the ware, and the reflection and care he expends on his pots are evident in the finished work." Stop by this small, unpretentious studio and you will be charmed by Nick's sensual, animated, and eye-catching work. The studio is located on Penland Road. (828) 765-5392.

He has been described as the "Picasso of Pottery," but unassuming **Norman Shulman** shrugs off the description and says simply, "Oh well, I just do pots." Norman began "just doing pots" on the advice of a friend years ago who asked what he did for fun. Norman answered by joining his friend in a ceramics class and was fascinated.

Today in his simple, narrow studio high above the Toe River near the Penland campus, soft-spoken Norman now works in midrange clay, firing at cone 3. The results are stunning, double-walled constructed pieces that look almost like ceremonial vessels. He was introduced to double-walled pots in 1950, when he saw an ancient Persian pitcher at the Metropolitan Museum. Norman imagined and later made these forms, then abandoned them for 20 years, recently returning to try them from a different perspective.

For many years he worked in porcelain, making big salt-glazed pieces—400-pound markers or "steles" that would fit suitably in an atrium or large entrance hall. These mysterious markers are displayed in Norman's gallery on his property. One piece is indeed "Picasso-esque," although Norman has named it *Great Jumping Jehosaphat!* His work can be seen in galleries in Atlanta and Chapel Hill or call for an appointment at his own gallery. (828) 765-6539.

Toe River

The Indians who occupied the area close to Penland were a branch of the Cherokee Nation who made their living by hunting and fishing along the Dashing River. The head chief was Rising Sun and his beautiful daughter was named "Estatoe," meaning *beautiful* in the language of the tribe. When she died an untimely death, her grief-stricken father renamed the river in memory of her, and until this day it is called the "Estatoe" or "Toe." You will cross over it many times as you travel and there are many places where you can stop and enjoy the beautiful water.

Bakersville

Penland School, the magnet that has attracted so many craftsmen to this area, was established to teach local women the near-lost art of weaving. Yet, today, there are not many weaving studios to visit. **Local Color Weaving Studio,** located across the street from the county courthouse in Bakersville at 1 Mitchell Avenue, is one of a few working studios.

Owners Fred Swift and Deborah Wheeler are weavers, dyers, and textile designers making handwoven and hand-dyed textiles. The mixed fiber scarves (silk and wool) are lovely as are the richly colored chenille ones. The scarves come in a multitude of designs and sizes. Studio hours are from 10:00 A.M. to 5:00 P.M., Tuesday through Saturday. (828) 688-3186.

Gay Smith Pottery Studio is located at 644 Cane Creek Road, just outside of Bakersville. Gay Smith worked part time for 20 years but has been full time since 1994. She specializes in wheel-thrown porcelain and has beautiful Caledon pieces. Her work is also at Blue Spiral, Penland, and Zebulon galleries. Her studio is open daylight hours, but call for directions as it is easy to miss. (828) 688-3686. Good prices.

Suze Lindsay has been a studio potter since 1992 but has been "playing" with clay since the early 1980s. With much hard work and commitment, she has become one of the best at once-fired and altered pottery. Much of Suze's personality is integrated into her work—it is easy to identify if you have had the pleasure of meeting this exuberant and happy person. She is probably best known for her highly decorated, warm, and earthy-colored teapots, pitchers, platters, bowls, and vases. She says of her salt-fired ceramics, "I hope my pots have a personality that will invite you to use them, whether it be for your first cup of coffee in the morning or a fancy dinner party."

Her studio/gallery, **Fork Mountain Pottery,** is located at 1782 Fork Mountain Road in Bakersville. Call for directions and an appointment. (828) 688-9297. Husband Kent McLaughlin, also a studio potter, has some of his work for sale at the gallery. Good prices.

You just go over hill and dale and a bridge or two and . . . you're there! **The Bicycle Inn,** looking like a Swiss chalet, is just there waiting for you. It's a big comfortable building with (of course) bicycle racks, small stone walls, and spearmint growing between the steppingstones. "Welcome" is what you feel. There are just five rooms (one an economy room with bunks for a family or a group of riders), a cozy downstairs dining room, and an "Oh, why didn't I come here sooner?" patio. There are no breath-stopping mountain views, just a peaceful vista of surrounding fields, hollows, and distant trees.

The original structure is a small farmhouse built in 1941 and left intact when renovations began. Salvaged materials were used and the result is a comfy mix of funk and fancy. Owners Paulette and Michael Davis have been involved in the bicycle industry since the 1960s. Amenities at the inn include a full bicycle service shop, training sessions, and excellent road-bike riding just outside. The inn also offers respite for Appalachian Trail hikers. The café is open to the public and the emphasis is on abundant, healthy local food. It is located about a half-mile off of Cane Creek Road. Watch for the sign at the Clarissa Community Center. (828) 688-9333 or (888) 4-BIK-INN. www.bicycleinn.com.

Here in Bakersville, you will also find Billie Ruth Suddeth, master basket weaver. Her extraordinary baskets are inspired by the classical forms of Shaker and Appalachian baskets. Self taught, Billie Ruth weaves many styles, using split oak and European cut-reed splints with round reed for handles. Her classical Shaker Cat's Head shapes are favorites, as are her garlic baskets and snowflakes. Billie Ruth's studio, **Jabobs,** is located at 109 Wing Road, 1.6 miles off of N.C. Highway 226. It is open year round, but please call first. (828) 688-2399.

The studio/gallery at **Cane Creek Pottery** is high on a hill behind **Diane Borde-Sutherland**'s home. From inside you can see trees and a lawn sloping toward her garden. This garden must furnish inspiration as many of Diane's pieces feature vegetables and fruits that look as if they have been sun ripened nearby.

Diane began to explore the wonders of clay in 1975 with school, apprenticeships, and many concentrated workshops and seminars. Now she produces functional pottery of red earthenware clay, which is Majolica glazed. The Majolica technique is ancient; it was developed in Mesopotamia about 900 B.C. before it spread, ending in Spain and Portugal during the 14th century.

In one corner of Diane's studio is a sophisticated electric kiln, "all computer run," she says. All of her pieces are colorful and useful for kitchen and table and her work is as uncomplicated and fresh looking as she is. Watch for her good-looking, large trivets combining glazed and unglazed work. Please call ahead to visit the gallery. (828) 688-9051.

Roan Mountain

One of the most interesting mountains in Western North Carolina is Roan Mountain, which shares its boundaries with Tennessee. The "Roan," at an elevation of 6,285 feet, is in Roan Mountain State Park and has the unusual appearance of being bald from the top down. **Carver's Gap** marks the boundary between the two states and here you may park and climb to the summit of the Roan by way of the Appalachian Trail. The steep path is bolstered with logs, making an easy trail to follow; however, the trek is strenuous and if you are not acclimated to heights, take it very slowly. From Carver's Gap you can also take in **Roan Mountain Gardens.** In mid-June, 600 acres of natural Catawba rhododendrons grow freely on the mountainside—a botanist's dream! Beyond the gardens is an area that is ideal for picnicking and nature study.

Boundaries on the Roan are so defined you can literally have one foot in Tennessee and one in North Carolina. There once stood a famous hotel, the Cloudland, at the top of the mountain. You could enter one door from Tennessee and exit another to North Carolina! Roan Mountain is on U.S. Highway 261, 13 miles northeast of Bakersville. Roan Mountain State Park is accessed from Roan Mountain, Tennessee (the town), with the steep drive to the top taking about 20 minutes. The popular state park has great facilities with 30 cabins, hiking trails, a swimming pool, and tennis courts. The park stays booked and reservations should be made well in advance. (800) 250-8620.

Burnsville

There are a few inns and bed and breakfasts near the Penland area (including NuWray Inn in Burnsville and the Chinquapin Inn at Penland), but if you'd like a change of pace you might want to try the **Alpine Village.** Located three miles from the Blue Ridge Parkway (take U.S. Highway 80), and just above the Mount Mitchell Golf Course, Alpine Village has a quiet atmosphere and panoramic views. This small restful resort has one- and two-bedroom units with dens and kitchens overlooking the mountains.

Guests receive a discount on green fees at the golf course and there is a pool and tennis court. Be aware that the area is quite isolated; the nearest supermarkets are half an hour away and the county is dry, so bring provisions. Breakfast and lunch are served at the golf club and nearby, overlooking the course, is **Albert's Inn,** a German restaurant open during the season (order the trout). Alpine Village is open from April 1 through the first weekend in December. (828) 675-4103. www.main.nc.us/alpinevillage.

"Where Springtime Spends the Summer

For space to roam and things to do and see, look into staying at the **Clear Creek Guest Ranch.** Nestled into the Pisgah National Forest at 3,000 feet, the entire ranch has a spectacular view of Mount Mitchell.

Around 1993, after visiting two of their sons on dude ranches in the West, Rex and Aileen Frederick took a chance and bought these 58 acres, once home to a campground. Then they built their ranch from scratch: guest quarters for 50, lodge, barns, stables, riding trails, pastures, swimming pool, and hot tub. The ranch has facilities for retreats, including a 1,500-square-foot conference room. It is also ideal for family reunions.

In addition to horseback riding and instruction for all riding levels, the area offers fine artists, gem mines, tubing or fishing on the South Toe River, golf, and hiking on the Pisgah Forest Trails. Children's programs are offered for all ages in the summer. Meals are served family style and adjoining the big, open dining room is a cozy sitting room with a Carolina stone fireplace and shelves of books. Entertainment includes cookouts, rodeos, line dancing, volleyball, and hayrides. Rex says, "We have activities planned for everybody if they want them. If not, they can sit on the porch and help me supervise."

Clear Creek Guest Ranch is located at 100 Clear Creek Drive (U.S. Highway 80 South), Burnsville. Be advised that the county is dry; bring your refreshments. The ranch is closed December through March. (828) 675-4510 or (800) 651-4510. www.clearcreekranch.com.

Katherine and William Bernstein's studio, an old, unfinished wooden shed, doesn't begin to allude to what is inside. The dirt floor and the handmade wooden shelves are the antithesis of the lovely pieces of hand-blown and cast glass on display. William's work can be recognized by colorful and whimsical characters molded into goblets, mugs, and tumblers. Katherine has developed a method for making cast-glass sculpture. These magnificent sculptures are one-of-a-kind works of art.

The studio, located off of U.S. Highway 80 on White Oak Creek Road, has other local artists' work on display and for sale including the Bernsteins' son, who is quite accomplished at hand-blown glass. Call (828) 675-4854 for directions and an appointment. The prices are good. The Bernsteins' work is also available at Blue Spiral Gallery in Asheville and Zebulon Gallery in Burnsville.

aft Pride Gallery is almost hidden in a bank of rhododen-
ng U.S. Highway 80. Generally there is a colorful flag flying
ad so it is easy to find. This gallery has a nice variety of local
and regional handcrafted arts with a very good range of prices. Quilts
and tin frames share shelf space with pottery, watercolors, dolls, and
kaleidoscopes. It is open at 10:00 A.M., six days a week, or by appointment. (828) 675-5470.

Woodworker **Buzz Coren** had a habit that "got out of hand." Drawing on basic woodworking skills learned from his father, school shop,
and reading, Buzz began making desk accessories and laminated jewelry before progressing to complex, multilayered bowls and vessels.
Twenty-odd years later, the still-youthful Buzz's hobby is now a passion
and these vessels attest to his dedication to and love of the craft. He
laminates domestic and imported dyed veneer and assorted hardwoods into striking patterned designs, which are further cut and
reassembled. The rough forms are then sanded, resulting in light-as-
a-feather intricate pieces.

The artist exhibits at a few galleries in Asheville but mainly aspires
to major fine craft shows. His beautiful works are one of a kind and
are priced at $75 and up. Sharing studio space is his wife, artist
Debbie Littledeer. Her note cards and limited edition silkscreen prints
focus on natural settings and whimsical animal scenes. The studio is
located on Lower Brown's Creek Road and is open by appointment
only. (828) 675-4661.

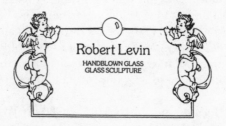

Robert Levin
HANDBLOWN GLASS
GLASS SCULPTURE

Tall glassblower **Robert Levin** has his glassblowing studio/gallery
tucked underneath an archway of evergreens on Upper Brown's
Creek Road. He has been blowing glass since 1975, mostly in this
peaceful area.

A lot of his sparkling sculptures are effectively displayed on glass shelves in the window of his small gallery, while larger, distinctive pieces sit on pedestals. Robert makes his own colors, which are vibrant and subtle at the same time. Especially beautiful are his unique frosted, sandblasted goblets; these hand-etched goblets are fused with his glass fruits and vegetables. The speckled trout goblets made in collaboration with friend and glassblower Ken Carder are absolutely stunning. Other unique pieces of Robert's are his frosted mezuzahs, made much larger than the usual ones.

The soft-spoken artist is now working on a new idea, making large, good-looking mixed-media pieces of glass and wood sculptures, and the back of his studio is half-filled with tree trunks! Please call for an appointment. (828) 675-4331. www.robertlevin.com.

Watch carefully for the discreet sign of **Ian and Jo Lydia Craven**'s gallery for hand-formed porcelain. The Cravens have worked together since 1972 and for much of that time they lived in southern Spain. Later, the couple spent three years in France, where the gentleness of the Loire Valley influenced their work.

After rolling out the clay—literally, with a rolling pin—Jo Lydia hand builds her porcelain pieces (as opposed to using a wheel). After forming the pieces, she impresses them with remnants of antique lace. Many of the pieces from her lace collection are over 300 years old. Ian then glazes and fires the forms in a gas kiln under extremely high heat, resulting in pieces with depth and complexity as well as delicacy and strength.

Upon arriving you'll be greeted by the Cravens, or the gardener, or the garden itself . . . a little bit of France and Spain with a mountain view. Although the gallery is small, it is big enough for effective displays. To elaborate further might be distracting—just go. It is located 2 miles south of U.S. Highway 19 East, 10 miles west of Spruce Pine, and 5 miles east of Burnsville at 2250 U.S. Highway 80 South, Micaville, North Carolina. It is open Friday and Saturday in season or when the gate is open, or call ahead. (828) 675-9058 or (800) 764-2402.

Burnsville has a pretty town square, centered with a statue of someone important. **The NuWray Inn,** a large, comfortable, three-story country house that has been welcoming guests since 1833, borders almost one whole side of the square. From its earliest days as a carriage stop, the inn has been a standard for Southern hospitality. Here, in the oldest inn in Western North Carolina, are 26 guest rooms with private baths. Rates include a hearty breakfast and afternoon refreshments. If you are not staying at the NuWray Inn, you can still have dinner nightly and lunch on Sunday. NuWray is open year round and is listed on the National Register of Historic Places. (828) 682-2329. For reservations only call (800) 368-9729.

The NuWray Inn
Established in 1833

"A nice place to be"

The **Hayden Gallery,** at 7 South Main Street in Burnsville, is housed in what used to be the carriage house for the NuWray Inn. The gallery has the largest selection of regional crafts in the area, representing 150 artists. Call (828) 682-7998 for seasonal hours.

A distinctive gallery is now gracing downtown Burnsville. **Zebulon American Crafts Gallery** is tucked right there across from the circa-1908 Town Hall. Owner John Stucky showcases *really* local artists—90 percent of those represented are from the two neighboring counties, Mitchell and Yancey. This translates into displays of works by many well-known Penland names as well as other nearby artisans of distinction.

The works are quite varied. Along with blown glass, pottery, and baskets are textiles, paperweights, furniture, metalwork, jewelry, and masks. Everything is effectively displayed and there is a good range of prices.

There is some eclectic stuff, too. Look for Joe's Girls Birdfeeders, Lois Simbach's "dolls," and big wooden renditions of St. Francis. A recent traveling exhibit brought some of the mud paintings of Jimmie Lee Suddeth, an invited participant in the bicentennial Festival of American Folk Life in Washington, D.C.

Zebulon is open at 11:00 A.M., six days a week, and is a "must stop by" place. Call for out-of-season hours. (828) 682-0598.

There are several good places to eat in town. The **Westside Coffee Shop** is just around the corner and nearby is the **Hilltop,** with an old-fashioned counter, where you still get a limeade. Across the square from the NuWray is the **Garden Deli,** a wide-open happy place to eat. You enter via a big deck centered by a huge weeping willow tree with branches covering the arbor above you. Sandwiches, salads, and daily specials are served in the two-level dining room or you may eat outside under the willow. It is open from 11:00 A.M. to 2:00 P.M., six days a week. (828) 682-3946.

Between Burnsville and Weaverville is the **Freedom Escape Lodge and Retreat Center.** If you want to host an intimate wedding and reception, family reunion, or company picnic, call them and you can enjoy a 650-acre mountain cove setting for your event. Just past an old grist mill and between a forest and serene pasture, the lodge offers amenities as unrivaled as the views of the Blue Ridge Mountains from the large deck (or your own private porch!).

Proprietor Ben Wax says, "Freedom Escape is an experience more than a place." Each of the 17 guest rooms has a private bath, private deck, and cable TV. Just a stroll away is a swimming pool, indoor gym, and tennis court, as well as golf privileges at nearby Reems Creek Golf Club. There is a "seats 80 theater" and the main lodge can accommodate 60 for a sit-down dinner or 150 for a reception.

Bring the children! Activities abound—from hayrides to rafting. Rates are reasonable and the food is good. When asked about the house specialty, Ben said, "Quality." The center is located at 530 Upper Flat Creek Road. Call (888) 658-0814 for directions.

www.FreedomEscapeLodge.com.

An interesting spot between Burnsville and Weaverville is the **Zebulon Vance Birthplace.** A dominant personality of the South for half a century, Zeb Vance endeared himself to the common people of the mountain coves. He also was an outstanding champion of local self-government and individual liberty.

The old homestead preserved here consists of a large circa-1795 structure containing some furnishings and household items original to the home. Clustered about are six outbuildings and a visitor center. Special events throughout the year highlight the Vance family's life. It is located at 911 Reems Creek Road. It is open year round, but hours are seasonal. It is closed on most major holidays and on Mondays in the winter. (828) 645-6706.

Weaverville

Be sure to take your camera when you visit **Gourmet Gardens Herb Farm** at 14 Bankstown Road in Weaverville. A gray, wood-frame house sits in the midst of carefully tended plants. The greenhouse has over 500 different herbs, 17 varieties of basil, and over 60 varieties of

scented geraniums. The outside gardens, lush with over 1,500 plants, meander around to the back of the house. If you happen to be here in early spring, the oriental poppy will warrant a photo. Garden statuary, markers, "bugs," and gargoyles are scattered throughout the beds. Notice the stone sculpture of a "fat lady," called *Bliss*, created by Julie Larson. You will want to take her home.

Marla and Dan Murphy, owners of the farm, have cultivated more magic in the gift shop. The small kitchen is literally running over with garden books, floral garlands and wreaths, wind-chimes, linens, framed botanical prints, herbal teas, jellies, and special seasonings. Don't miss the "Road Kill Jam"; it's delicious. The wonderful Kelvin Chen enamel miniatures (teapots, birdhouses, and watering cans) are just too enticing to leave behind. The farm is open from 9:30 A.M. to 5:30 P.M., Tuesday through Saturday. You must call for an appointment between December 1 and March 15. (828) 658-0766.

For a genuine taste of the mountains, try the **Weaverville Milling Company** restaurant on Reems Creek Road. It was actually a working mill from 1910 to 1960, producing corn, grain, and wheat products. With its weathered gray frame exterior and the original beaded wood ceiling inside, the restaurant has all the ambience of a mountain home. Fresh mint is usually growing around the front stoop and small bouquets of wild flowers grace the tables.

Two of the most popular dishes are the perfectly cooked mountain trout and the prime rib. If you're torn between the two, order the "Trail and Stream" combination. Most of the dishes offered are local products with a homemade touch.

This is a friendly family-run restaurant with Sally Smith and son Michael in the kitchen while daughter Beth waits tables and father Kevin handles the business aspect. It is open at 5:00 P.M., daily except Wednesday. Reservations are appreciated. (828) 645-4700.

Peanut Butter Pie

8 oz. cream cheese
3/4 cup confectioners' sugar
8 oz. peanut butter
1/2 oz. unflavored gelatin
1/4 cup boiling water

3/4 cup milk
1 large container whipped topping
2 graham-cracker crusts
Chopped peanuts for garnish

Beat together cream cheese, sugar, and peanut butter. Dissolve gelatin in water and combine with blended ingredients. Add milk and stir until smooth. Gently stir in topping. Divide ingredients between both crusts. Sprinkle with peanuts and freeze. Each pie serves 6-8.

—Sally Smith, chef, Weaverville Milling Company

The Secret Garden Bed & Breakfast at 56 North Main Street in downtown Weaverville is truly a secret to share. A giant hemlock hedge surrounds the 1904 low country Charleston-style home, which conjures up thoughts of the good old days. Two suites and one room with a king-sized bed have been decorated in a simple, yet elegant style (be sure to see the Mayor's suite). A good library and interesting English chess sets provide quiet entertainment. The 60-foot-long veranda offers an opportunity to relax and enjoy the lovely grounds. Evening turn-down service and gourmet breakfast are included in the reasonable lodging rates. Children 10 years and over are welcome—no pets. (828) 658-9317 or (800) 797-8211. www.secretgardennc.com.

While you are in Weaverville, plan on taking the time to see the beautiful stained-glass windows at the **Weaverville United Methodist Church.** One if them has a very interesting story.

A memorial window called "The Good Shepherd Window" was given to the church by Louise Moore at the death of her husband in 1920. For nearly 60 years the congregation admired the window and enjoyed its beauty. In 1976, seeing the need to repair the church windows, members of the church engaged an expert to estimate the cost. Arriving in the sanctuary, the expert announced, "This window is a Tiffany window!" He pointed to the red robe on the figure of Christ and said, "Only one person in the world could make red glass like this—and that is Tiffany!" The window is indeed a beautiful sight so try to see it. The church is on Main Street.

Golf Courses

This golf course information is courtesy of Journal Communications, Inc.:

Mount Mitchell Golf Course. Located 16 miles east of Burnsville. This course, at an elevation of 3,000 feet, below the peak of Mount Mitchell, is mostly flat with bent grass from tee to green. It is open from April through November. www.burnsville.com.mmgc.

CHAPTER 7

Waynesville

Just west of Asheville and east of Waynesville on U.S. Highway 276 is **Springdale Country Club,** a public country club and resort near Canton. The club has been welcoming guests since 1975—offering golf, relaxation, dining, and Southern hospitality in the Great Smoky Mountains. Sitting up high, the rooms, dining room, and golf course have incredible views. Accommodations are quite varied: cottages, homes, townhouses, and villas, most with fireplaces, decks, and golf cart garages for the cart that Springdale issues you for your stay.

The retreat packages include unlimited golf, a hot breakfast buffet each morning, and authentic Southern dining each evening. The **Sourwood Grill and Patio** offers light grilled Southern specialties for lunch. Springdale provides relaxation and serenity that you can only find at a family-run retreat. You'd best be on your toes when you reach the sixth green. That view of Cold Mountain is distractingly beautiful! (800) 553-3027. www.springdalegolf.com.

Nestled into the serenity of the Smoky Mountains is the **Lake Junaluska Conference and Retreat Center.** Although it is the headquarters for the United Methodist Church in the Southeast and is used mainly for church-related programs, Lake Junaluska is open to the public. Lodging, meals, and recreational amenities are available for individuals and families.

The Terrace Hotel, overlooking the lake, has 100 rooms with private baths. Lambuth Inn, a historic site, has 130 rooms with private baths. Dining rooms in both accommodations serve three meals a day, buffet style. In addition there are lodges and cottages that are open seasonally for groups.

The beautiful 200-acre lake is surrounded by rolling hills and valleys. Recreation includes golf, tennis, a pool, and walking trails. This peaceful place is ideal for a family reunion or a simple getaway. It is located 10 minutes from Interstate 40. It is open all year but is closed to the public during the first two weeks in June. Lake Junaluska is alcohol free. (800) 222-4930. www.lakejunaluska.com.

Few traces remain of the Cherokees who lived in Haywood County. In 1775, the first Anglo-American person settled west of the Blue Ridge Mountains. His name was William Moore and he was a captain in the American militia. In 1811, Waynesville became a township. It was named for "Mad Anthony" Wayne, a soldier known for his bravery during the American Revolution.

Adeline Patrick, owner of the **Open Air Curb Market** on Main Street, is open from 6:00 A.M. until 12:00 midnight, daily. Pots of blooming bedding plants greet you at the front of the store along with boxes of tomatoes, sweet potatoes, apples, bananas, and oranges and racks of vegetable and flower seeds. What a relief from the modern-day minimart! Local and national newspapers are stacked inside among the largest selection of magazines and paperbacks in town. A sign over the magazines reads, *Buy it first—no free reading!* An interesting collection of antique tools decorates the walls and the shelves are filled with staples and snacks. This market is a great place to browse.

At 63 Main Street is **Mast General Store.** These downtown emporiums have become familiar to the locals as well as visitors to Western North Carolina. Their traditional yet unique way of doing business is preserved in historical buildings on many of the main streets across the region. This store features antique display cabinets and has a mezzanine packed with provisions for the entire family. Up front are slat and cane rocking chairs made in North Carolina, as well as the popular Amish handmade rockers and gliders, all at good prices. When asked about the success of these stores, one sales clerk replied, "Variety . . . we strive for customer service and go the distance for what they want." Hours are from 10:00 A.M. to 6:00 P.M., Monday through Saturday, and until 6:00 P.M., Sunday. Winter hours vary. (828) 452-2101.

Next door and under the same roof is the **Candy Barrel,** which features an old-fashioned soda fountain and, as you might expect, barrels and barrels of candy such as maple nut chews and root beer and sassafras drops.

Just around the corner at 171 Montgomery Street is a local favorite, **Lomo's Bakery and Café.** Whether you come in for freshly baked bread or pastries or stop in for lunch, you are sure to be pleased. While you're deciding what to order for lunch, you'll no doubt want to choose something to take home from a variety of croissants, muffins, cookies, and rolls displayed in a glass case. Homemade soups, salads, and sandwiches are the mainstays on the menu along with Lomo's specials, which include a quiche of the day, rotisserie chicken, subs, and focaccias. There is also a nice selection of coffees and teas. It is open from 11:00 A.M. to 3:00 P.M., six days a week. Call (828) 452-1515 or fax your order, (828) 452-1746. No credit cards accepted.

Dick and Elaine Shulman must be doing something right as they have been in business since 1960. **Dick Shulman Company,** at 153 North Main Street, has been in Waynesville since 1988 with great ladies' sportswear at good prices. In addition, Shulman's has monogrammed and engraved gifts and an excellent selection of presents for babies. It is open six days a week. (828) 456-4226.

Around the corner again at 44 Church Street is **Lomo Grill.** The

Argentine chef specializes in Italian and Mediterranean cuisine. Homemade mozzarella cheese and freshly made tomato sauce are used throughout the menu. The Argentine-style wood-burning grill features all natural Angus beef and is served with grilled tomatoes and potatoes. An extensive wine list complements the food. Reservations are recommended and hours are seasonal. (828) 425-5222.

Whitman's Bakery opens at 6:00 A.M. and it might be worth it to be there when the door opens. The bakery makes over a hundred different kinds of breads and piles them high on the countertops until they spill over to the tables. Many of the breads are whole grain, high in fiber, and low in fat (the pumpernickel is a *must* as well as the fresh hoagies). No preservatives are used and everything is made from scratch. If you can make it past the breads, you will see glass cases full of traditional cookies, fried pies, pastries, and doughnuts, with custom-made birthday cakes being the bakery's forte. Next door is the sandwich shop, carrying the same excellent quality as the bakery. It opens at 11:30 A.M.

So few places can boast of over 50 years and three generations in the business that you feel as if you are visiting family here. Whitman's Bakery is located at 18 North Main Street and is open until 5:30 P.M.; lunch is served from 11:00 A.M. to 3:00 P.M. It is closed on Sunday. (828) 456-8354.

The **Old Stone Inn,** Waynesville's historic mountain inn, is a peaceful retreat with gourmet food. Although you'll feel far from civilization in the wooded 3,200-foot-high location, you are actually just a short, brisk walk from downtown. Hundred-year-old oaks, mountain laurel, and rhododendron surround the stone inn and cottages, and chipmunks and rabbits roam freely. Nearby activities include day trips to the Biltmore Estate, Club Car excursions to the Nantahala Gorge, trail riding, and rafting trips.

A full breakfast is served each morning and dinner is served from 6:00 to 8:00 P.M., Monday through Saturday, in the cozy dining room with a fireplace. A different touch is the appetizer plate, a variety of appetizers served before a fire in the Main Lodge—it is a delightful, light meal accompanied by a glass of wine. There is a nice moderately priced wine list and beer is served. Children over 12 are welcome. It is located off of U.S. Highway 276 South on Dolan Road and is open from Good Friday until mid-December. Call about packages. (828) 456-3333.

Twenty minutes west of Waynesville, standing high on a ridge above Balsam Gap, the three-story **Balsam Mountain Inn** has been welcoming guests since 1908. For years, visitors arrived by rail at the old

Balsam depot, formerly the highest railroad station east of the Rockies. After disembarking, they would take a carriage ride up to the inn.

In 1990, innkeeper Merrily Teasley began extensive restoration on the neoclassical Victorian structure. Each of the 50 guest rooms has a private bath, many with antique clawfoot tubs—one enormous bathroom even has a hammock!

You will enjoy the spacious lobby with two beautifully tiled fireplaces, as well as a cozy library and, of course, a front porch lined with rocking chairs. A full breakfast is included in the room rate and dinner is served for overnight guests as well as others by reservation. Merrily's daughter, Noelle, is the chef and she provides a superb regional menu.

Trails for skiing, bicycling, or horseback riding as well as golf courses are nearby. The inn will be happy to drop you off at various elevations and you can "hike home."

Balsam Mountain Inn is located off of U.S. Highway 74/23, about a quarter-mile south of the Blue Ridge Parkway. A small green sign marks the village of Balsam. Turn right up a hill, cross the tracks, and continue until you see the inn. Once here, you are going to have a hard time packing up and leaving! For reservations contact the inn at Box 40, Balsam, North Carolina 28707. (800) 224-9498.

Catfish with Roasted Red Pepper Sauce

1 red pepper
1 pt. heavy cream
¼ tsp. Paul Prudhomme's
  blackening seasoning
¼ tsp. curry powder
⅛ tsp. paprika

¼ tsp. salt
Butter and flour roux to thicken
½ cup lemon juice
½ cup melted butter
4 catfish filets

Cut the red pepper in half, de-seed, and roast in 350-degree oven until tender. Pour the cream in a saucepan over medium heat. Add seasonings and roux, stirring until thickened. Mince the red pepper and add to sauce.

Pour lemon juice and butter over the filets and bake uncovered (or wrapped in parchment paper) in a 350-degree oven until done (slightly firm to the touch). Plate and pour sauce over and around the filets. Serves 4.

—Noelle Teasley, chef, Balsam Mountain Inn

Windsong is a mountain inn located in a secluded mountain cove near Waynesville, just six miles south of Interstate 40. This contemporary log lodge is owned and managed by innkeepers Russ and Barbara Mancini. Russ and Barbara lived throughout Europe for many years and have traveled the world extensively. They have used a unique blend of European antiques and Native American and African furnishings to decorate their home. The main inn has five guest rooms, each with a queen-sized bed, private bath, fireplace, and a spectacular view from a private deck or patio. A gourmet breakfast is formally served on fine English china in the dining room. Pond Lodge is located just a short walk up the mountain and is just right for families or those wanting more privacy. There are two suites and an extensive continental breakfast is served.

Specials are offered throughout the year: Honeymoon Special, Mid-week Seniors Special, Last Minute Getaway, or The Whole Windsong (rent the entire inn). Llama luncheons and dinner treks are also available upon 24 hours' advance request. A half-hour walk, leading a llama along a mountain stream, brings you to a unique picnic table built over the stream. A guide prepares a great dinner on the grill while you enjoy a beverage with your feet dangling over the water. Treks are available May through October, with a minimum of four people. Children over 12 are welcome in the main inn and all ages are welcome in the lodge. Rates are moderately expensive and vary with the season. (828) 627-6111. www.windsongbb.com.

The Swag is a secluded country inn, sitting atop a 5,000-foot private mountain, where your front yard is the Great Smoky Mountains National Park. Dan and Deener Matthews purchased the property in 1969 and built a winding road going up to the inn.

Upon arrival, you will probably get as far as the porch before you stop dead in your tracks—seeing the view stretching miles into the Smokies. This first sight sets the stage for all the pleasures in store for you. The Matthewses have created the perfect sanctuary for people who need to "stop the world and get off" for a few days. Everything is geared for peace and tranquility. The Swag has a total of 15 rooms: 7 are in the main lodge and the rest are in three cabins and a smaller lodge outside. All are decorated individually with handmade mountain crafts, good paintings, and sculptures.

A Country Inn in the Smokies

All meals are served in the wood and stone dining room, unless you want a backpack lunch for hiking. The kitchen is run by chef Jack Keeran, who presents splendid regional meals, while pastry chef Zoe Davis puts the finishing touch to his creations. Almost all the vegetables and greens are taken from the garden and the inn has its own freshwater spring, which pumps 10 gallons of pure, natural water per minute. The spring dates back over 2,000 years and was used by the Cherokee.

All the exploring and hiking you want can begin from The Swag— starting with the gentle, two-mile hike to the longer park trails, which take a big part of the day. Speakers and workshops during selected weeks in summer can add special interest for you; inquire about them when making reservations.

The guest season at the inn is May through October and reservations should be made well in advance. The Swag is expensive, but includes three gourmet meals a day.

It can be reached from Interstate 40. Take Exit 20 to N.C. Highway 276; continue on Highway 276 for 2.8 miles to The Swag sign; turn right on Hemphill Road and travel 4 miles up to the gate; turn left and drive 2.5 miles up the private driveway. (828) 926-0430 or (828) 926-3119.

Life is too short for mediocrity.
　　　　　　　　　　　　　　　—a plaque on the wall of the lodge

Maggie Valley

Maggie Mae Setzer never dreamed that a beautiful valley would be named after her, and that name would stick for years to come. She was 14 years old when the United States postmaster general in Washington gave her father permission to operate a post office and name it the Maggie Post Office in 1904.

A busy U.S. Highway 19 takes you through the heart of Maggie Valley, which, unfortunately, is bordered by many shops, restaurants, motels, etc., that obscure an exquisite view. However, just look past them and you will see one of the prettiest valleys in North Carolina. In summer, many families stay in Maggie Valley because of all the children's activities and the nearness to Asheville and Cherokee. In winter the Cataloochee Ski Area has nine ski slopes with certified ski schools and rentals.

Directly on the strip are three restaurants: J. Arthur's, Granny's Chicken Palace, and Arf's. **J. Arthur's** is the most upscale restaurant in the area, stemming from a well-known family of restaurateurs (Mahoneys and Tiernans) who have been in the business for over 50 years in Florida. Vegetarians are tolerated here but the prime rib is notable far and near; also try the delicious Gorgonzola salad. The address is 2843 U.S. Highway 19. J. Arthur's opens at 5:00 P.M., seven days a week, summer, and Wednesday through Saturday, winter. (828) 926-1817.

Granny's Chicken Palace is down-home eating at its best, with fried chicken being the star attraction. Fried trout is also perfectly cooked and served four times a week—it is deboned at your table. Main dishes are all served with a bowl of fresh green beans and corn. The walls of Granny's honor all the military services with plaques, pictures, and other memorabilia (owner Dick McCarthy belonged to the Marines so a little more attention is given to them). The address is 1168 U.S. Highway 19. Granny's is open from 4:00 to 8:30 P.M., six days a week, and from 11:30 A.M. to 3:00 P.M., Sunday. (828) 452-9111.

With a name like **Arf's,** it better be good. This family restaurant has an interesting recipe for honey pecan catfish that keeps everybody comin'. Hours are 4:30 to 9:30 P.M., seven days a week. Reservations are not required but weekends are crowded. (828) 926-1566.

Stompin' Grounds is reported to be the "Clogging Capital of the World." After you see some of the clogging teams do their "stuff" you will agree. Every Friday and Saturday night, from May to October, clogging is accompanied by live country and bluegrass bands. Bring the family and take part in the fun. Everybody can dance and you will be surprised how quickly you will pick up some of the steps. You can't miss the big red barn with the marquee outside at 3116 U.S. Highway 19. A snack bar serves hot dogs and barbecue, but no alcohol is available. Doors open at 7:00 P.M. Admission is $7 for adults and $3 for children. (828) 926-1288.

Cloaked in deep woods and sitting on a mountaintop is **Smokey Shadows Lodge.** You will drive up a narrow road to a clearing that looks like a miniature settlement from long ago. The lodge was made from mountain stone and hand-hewn logs from a grist mill. Two log cabins complete the setting. Family reunions, special groups, or travelers passing through will find the seclusion they need just five minutes away from the bustling town below. Smokey Shadows has 12 rooms with baths. All are furnished with authentic mountain crafts and some have feather beds. Meals are ethnic, with German night being the favorite. Dining is open to the public but lodgers have first call.

Don't leave Maggie Valley without checking on this rare find. Go straight up Fie Top Road, alongside the Ghost Town entrance, and after two and one-half miles look carefully for the sign to Smokey Shadows Lodge. (828) 926-0001.

Tom and Judy Alexander founded **Cataloochee Ranch** in 1934 as one of the first facilities for tourists in the area. In 1948, the present property was purchased and transformed from a rugged sheep and cattle farm to the rustic, yet graceful facility it is today. The family-owned guest ranch offers 11 cottages, a main ranch house, and a lodge. All rooms have private baths and the cabins and suites have fireplaces. The furnishings are comfortable and the views are spectacular.

"Cataloochee" is an Indian word meaning "wave upon wave," which is apparent from vistas of range after range of the Smokies and Blue Ridge Mountains. Activities here range from relaxing in the heated swimming pool to a peaceful hayride to a vigorous horseback adventure with one of the staff wranglers. There are half-day rides or all-day rides with a picnic lunch. Overnight camping is also available upon request. What a great way to spend some time with your family!

Cataloochee Ranch is open all seasons and offers the closest access to the Cataloochee Valley ski area just one mile away. The moderately expensive rates include breakfast and dinner. One-night reservations are not encouraged and minimum stays are required during certain months. Meals are served family style in the ranch dining room or frequently outside at an outdoor barbecue or "steak-out." Picnic lunches are available upon request. (800) 868-1401.

www.cataloochee-ranch.com.

Miss Judy's Puffed Toast

1 loaf white bread	1 egg
2 cups plain flour	1 tsp. vanilla
4 tsp. baking powder	1½ cups milk
½ cup sugar	2 tsp. oil
½ tsp. salt	Oil for cooking
½ tsp. cinnamon	Confectioner's sugar
½ tsp. nutmeg	Hot maple syrup

Cut slices of bread diagonally and spread out to dry overnight. Make a thick batter with the flour, baking powder, sugar, salt, spices, egg, vanilla, milk, and oil. Coat the slices with batter and sauté quickly in 2 inches of hot oil until golden crisp on both sides. Drain on paper towels. Sprinkle with confectioners' sugar and serve immediately with hot maple syrup.

—Cataloochee Ranch

Cherokee Reservation

The **Cherokee Indian Reservation** consists of 56,000 acres in the heart of the Smoky Mountains. Before Hernando de Soto came on the scene in 1540, the Cherokee Nation included 135,000 square miles of territory, which covered parts of what are now eight states.

Visiting the reservation can be taxing if you don't know your way around. The **Cherokee Visitor's Center** is an excellent one and should be a first stop on your tour. Friendly people will tell you about the best campsites, fishing, tubing, historic landmarks, and motel accommodations on the reservation. The address is Cherokee Visitor's Center, Post

Office Box 460, Cherokee, North Carolina 28719. (800) 438-1601. www.cherokee-nc.com.

All of the Great Smoky Mountains were the territory of the Cherokee Nation long before the first recorded history. The Cherokee named them "The Land of the Blue Mist."

The hot spot in Cherokee is the town itself. Don't be put off by the total tourist atmosphere—the main drag looks like a trading post gone awry with Harrah's, the huge casino, lots of souvenir shops, and live storefront Indians in full regalia. There are several points of interest giving the true history of the Cherokee Nation that are fun as well as informative for everyone, especially school-age children.

Qualla Arts and Crafts Mutual, Inc., is located on U.S. Highway 441 at the entrance of the Mountainside Theater. This cooperative is owned and operated by the Cherokee Indian craftsmen of the Qualla Indian Reservation. It was founded in 1946 as an important source of supplemental income for Indian craftsmen and their families and is recognized as the most outstanding Indian-owned and -operated arts and crafts cooperative in the United States. On display, using a variety of materials and techniques, are stone carvings, Cherokee masks, fabric weavings, baskets, pottery, weapons, and woodcarvings. Many items are for sale. This is open daily, but call for seasonal hours. (828) 497-3103.

Just across from Qualla Arts and Crafts is the **Museum of the Cherokee Indian.** Look for the 20-foot, hand-carved statue of the great leader, Sequoyah, in front of the building. Once inside, you can move about freely, absorbing the history of the Indian and how he lived. A brief film on the life of the Cherokee today will get you up to date on the tribe's entrepreneurial designs for the present and the future. Before you leave, be sure and visit the gift shop and gallery, where there is an excellent book section. John Ehle's *Trail of Tears* is touted as the best history of the rise and fall of the Cherokee Nation. After leaving the museum you will probably understand why the statue of Sequoyah has tears in his eyes.

The museum, located on U.S. Highway 441 at Drama Road, is open every day except Thanksgiving, Christmas, and New Year's Day. There is a small admission fee. (828) 497-3481.

> Probably the most famous Indian leader of all is Sequoyah, who
> created the Cherokee alphabet that was accepted by the chiefs
> in 1821. For the first time, the Cherokee language became writ-
> ten word (called "talking leaves") and was assimilated by the
> people very quickly. In 1827, the first printing press with type set
> in Cherokee produced the first five chapters of Genesis. Great
> strides are being made to preserve this language, which will help
> save the history of the Cherokee culture.

Drama Road takes a big loop outside the town and returns to U.S.
Highway 441 North. You should take advantage of two major sights
along this road—Oconaluftee Indian Village and the long-running
drama, *Unto These Hills.*

The **Oconaluftee Indian Village** is located adjacent to the Mountainside Theater. This village is an authentic replica of a Cherokee
Indian town of 1750 with guides to explain the history, culture, and
lifestyle of the Cherokees. You can see Indian artisans, descendants of
the original inhabitants, creating baskets, woodcarvings, pottery,
finger-woven items, and weapons. What an excellent way to make history come alive for children and adults alike. It is open from 9:00
A.M. to 5:30 P.M., daily, May 15 through October 25. There is an admission fee. For information about group rates call (828) 497-2111.

The 50-year-old play, *Unto These Hills,* tells the story of the Cherokee, beginning with the first encounter with the Spanish explorer
Hernando de Soto in 1540 to the abysmal Trail of Tears in the 1830s
(the journey from the Cherokees' native land to the reservations in
Oklahoma). The play is held in the Mountainside Theater, under the
stars with the Smoky Mountains as a backdrop. Here, in this perfect
setting, with a cast of over 130 actors, singers, and dancers, the sad
drama of the Cherokee Nation unfolds.

Someone once said, "To ignore the mistakes of history is to repeat
them." *Unto These Hills* reminds us to remember. Children especially
love the play. Performances run nightly, except for Sunday, for about
10 weeks in the summer. Tickets may be purchased by phone or at the
box office. The address is Post Office Box 398, Cherokee, North Carolina 28719. (800) 497-2111. www.dnet.net/~cheratt.

After seeing all of the historical sights, you may want to walk into
a few of the many shops located on the reservation. There are plenty
of craft shops where you can buy a pair of moccasins or some Indian
jewelry.

In the middle of town is an unexpected oasis—**Oconaluftee Islands Park.** This small island is surrounded by the Oconaluftee River rapids and can be reached by walking over a wooden bridge. Highway traffic and congestion are all around you but this is a quiet, relaxing place to unwind or let children run and play. The park is beautifully kept and has shaded picnic tables and walking paths. It is located between U.S. Highway 441 and Acquoni Road.

The other big attraction to the Cherokee Reservation is fishing. The main fishing areas are Raven Fork, Soco Creek, and Oconaluftee River. The popularity of Cherokee as one of the country's best places for trout fishing may cause some concern about overcrowding. But it is easy to find a quiet place to enjoy the sport, even in the downtown area on the river.

Expert assistance and supplies abound at **One Feather Fly and Tackle,** located downtown on the river. Although no state fishing license is needed, Tribal Permits are required for persons over age 12 and they are available here. Owner Bob Bradley has been in the business for quite a few years and knows his fishing. Trout season opens the last Saturday of March and continues through February 28 of the following year. Fishing is permitted half an hour before sunrise to half an hour after sunset. Be aware of limits before you fish. The streams are stocked regularly by the Cherokee Fish and Game Management with rainbow, brook, and brown trout of various sizes. (828) 497-3113.

The town of Cherokee is not noted for its gourmet restaurants, but there are lots of fast food places and a couple of family restaurants. The Hungry Bear and Granny's Kitchen are two that have family-style buffets. **Hungry Bear** is said to have authentic Indian corncakes. You can also buy the makings for them at the museum.

A good place to make a hungry crowd happy is **Granny's Kitchen,** a home-cookin' buffet. The fried chicken and veggies are sure to please the crowd as well as your pocketbook. If you want something light there is a good fresh salad bar.

It is located on U.S. Highway 19 just west of the reservation on the road to Maggie Valley. It is open from 11:00 A.M. to 8:00 P.M., Tuesday through Friday, from 7:00 A.M. to 8:00 P.M., Saturday, and from 7:00 A.M. to 3:00 P.M., Sunday.

Don't leave the reservation without going to **Mingo Falls.** Heading north on U.S. Highway 441, bear right onto Big Cove Road and continue for 2.3 miles. Turn right onto a bridge over a river; to the front is a parking lot and trail. The trail walk takes about five minutes. It does have a slight incline and is damp, but it is not difficult and with the proper shoes should be accessible for all ages. Be sure and walk across to the far side for the best view of this beautiful 200-foot waterfall.

(Much of the information about the Cherokee Indian Reservation was freely given to the authors by the Cherokee Visitor's Center. We are grateful for their help in compiling the information on this area.)

Great Smoky Mountains National Park

Just north of Cherokee on U.S. Highway 441 in the Great Smoky Mountains National Park is the **Oconaluftee Visitor Center.** This center is open year round and has information about sights, trails, and picnic areas.

Mingus Mill is one of those "on the way to someplace else" places, but if you see the green marker on the highway don't fail to stop or you will miss a true example of Arcadian life from the 1700s through the 1930s. The Mingus family built a grist mill, powered by a waterwheel, which served the community for years. In 1886, John Mingus contracted Sion T. Early to build the present structure (Mr. Early's initials can be seen under the gable in the front of the building).

The mill is powered by a run of fast-flowing water diverted from Mingus Creek. You will enjoy "walking the race" and feeling the icy water running furiously to the mill. Inside the building you can see all the machinery it took to custom mill the grain and corn for the families in the community. The Great Smoky National Park acquired the mill from the family around 1935. Whole wheat and cornmeal are still ground here and you can purchase them by the sack. Hopefully you will find Mr. L. Winston Hardman, miller, who is there to give you any information you want to know about the mill. He will also tell you about a few "secret" trails you will not find in any travel books on this area. When you finish your tour here, you may not remember where you were going in the first place.

Oconaluftee Visitor Center is an entrance to the fabulous **Great Smoky Mountains National Park.** Following is only a brief guide as volumes are available about the mountains and park. You can even get a trip planning guide to the park by writing to 107 Park Headquarters Road, Gatlinburg, Tennessee 37738, or by calling (865) 436-1200. You can also purchase a copy of the park's road guide at the visitor center.

The Great Smoky Mountains are so named

because they are usually covered by a smoky mist. They are among the highest and most rugged mountains in the Appalachian chain and the slopes are covered with hardwood and evergreen forests. The park, set aside by the federal government in 1930, is the largest protected land area east of the Rocky Mountains, encompassing 500,000 acres with over 270 miles of roads. It lies on either side of the boundary between North Carolina and Tennessee, with about half its area in each state. Most of the roads are paved and highlights include many pullovers with mountain views. **Newfound Gap,** at elevation 5,046 feet, features a large parking area, scenic views, restrooms, exhibits, and access to the Appalachian Trail.

The National Park Service maintains campgrounds at 10 locations in the park and, during the summer and fall, you can make reservations at 3 of them by calling (800) 365-2267. These campgrounds have water but no showers or trailer hook-ups. All other campgrounds are first come, first served. **Le Conte Lodge,** on top of Mount Le Conte, is the only lodging in the park and is accessible only by a half-day hike on a trail. Make reservations for it far ahead by calling (865) 429-5704.

There are picnic areas in the park with tables and fire grates. The park rangers offer campfire programs, guided walks and hikes, and slide programs. In addition to nature study adventures for adults and outdoor youth camps, horseback camps, riding, fishing, and bicycling area available. Fishing for brown and rainbow trout is popular but you must have a license. Fishing for brook trout is prohibited.

During the Ice Age, the Smokies were a refuge for hundreds of plant and animal species retreating before the glaciers. Today the park has more tree species than northern Europe and also contains one of the largest blocks of virgin forests in North America. Many forms of wildlife can be found in the park and this is one of the few places in the eastern United States where black bears can live in wild, natural surroundings. Remember, it is illegal to feed the bears or leave food for them. At least 60 native mammals live in the Smokies along with over 200 species of birds and 58 species of fish.

If you would like to go to the "top of old Smoky," you can get to Clingmans Dome from Newfound Gap. Continue on up Newfound Gap Road, which is a scenic drive across the Smokies' crest. You can park at Newfound Gap where the Appalachian Trail crosses the road or you can drive the spur road to the west out to **Clingmans Dome,** the highest point in the park at 6,643 feet elevation. The observation tower can be reached by a fairly strenuous half-mile hike (resting spots along the trail make the trip a little less arduous). Beetles have invaded the forest killing hundreds of trees, which detracts some from the view, but it is still a spectacular sight. www.nps.gov/grsm.

The Appalachian Trail (AT), a public footpath for hikers and campers, stretches 2,155 miles from Maine to Georgia. The trail passes through 14 states, two national parks, and eight national forests. The trail was designed, constructed, and marked in the 1920s and 1930s by volunteer hiking clubs. The goal of these groups was to preserve the Appalachian crests as an accessible, multipurpose wilderness belt. Open to foot travel only, the AT is blazed in white triangles and boasts a chain of shelters spaced from 8 to 12 miles apart. In the Great Smoky Mountains National Park, camping along the trail is free but requires a permit, which you can get at ranger stations and visitor centers. If you want to camp in the shelters along the trail, you will need to call for reservations: Monday through Friday, (423) 436-1231. Detailed guidebooks are available at (800) AT-STORE. Incidentally, the 70-mile crest-line trail in the park is very primitive and the highest of the entire route. www.atconf.com.

Golf Courses

Here are the area municipal and public golf courses; information courtesy of Journal Communications, Inc.:

Iron Tree Golf Club. Located near Lake Junaluska. This course, open year round, is beautiful mountain golfing at affordable prices. (828) 627-1933.

Lake Junaluska Golf Course. Located in Waynesville. This course, open year round, is owned and operated by the United Methodist Church. Opened in 1919, it is alcohol free and friendly. (828) 456-5777.

CHAPTER 8

Sylva

Sylva, Jackson County's seat and largest town (population 5,000), traces its origins to 1880. Approaching from almost any direction, you can see the imposing courthouse perched atop a high hill in the center of the town. This architectural landmark is one of the most photographed sites in Western North Carolina. The town became the county's focal point when the Western North Carolina Railroad first rolled through during the summer of 1884, and the town was incorporated in 1889.

Sylva's picturesque Main Street is framed at one end by the 1913 Jackson County Courthouse and at the other end by the Great Balsam Mountains. Today, Sylva is home to a growing variety of shops and restaurants. Several annual events draw visitors to this busy town: "Greening Up the Mountains," a spring street festival; fireworks and bluegrass on July 4th; and downtown's traditional Christmas parade. For information call (828) 586-1577 or (800) 962-1911.

Most outstanding artists in the mountains of North Carolina are well represented throughout the region by American Craft schools, galleries, museums, gift shops, and minimalls. **Collene Karcher** has "been there, done that" and the only place you can see her recent works is in her own gallery, Karcher Studio. Her medium is stone carving and hauling her work around the country to exhibit and sell was profitable but exhausting. Karcher bit the bullet and now does business in the circa-1900 chestnut barn just outside her home. Here, her beautiful studies in marble and alabaster are shown in a perfect setting with earth and wood as a background.

Karcher's large and powerful figures are made from Alabama marble, Italian alabaster, and local North Carolina blackstone. Sometimes she introduces steel or wood into her works. She is an accomplished artist who brings an impressive background to the area, including restoration of the state capitol buildings in Michigan, Texas, and Ohio.

Although Karcher is available for commissioned pieces, she always has small works for sale at her gallery, where you can browse to your heart's content through the barn and gardens of her home. She is located at 260 North Beta Road, off U.S. Highway 74, just north of Sylva. Hours are from 10:00 A.M. to 5:00 P.M., Tuesday through Saturday, April through October, or by appointment year round. (828) 586-4813.

The **Coffee Shop** in Sylva has been a coffee shop since before anyone can remember. Gary and Phyllis Gibson have owned it for many years. A photograph hanging on the wall dates back to 1955. Over the years, families have come for breakfast, lunch, and dinner and even a loose curb service is available—drive up, honk your horn, and someone will come out and take your order. A good breakfast is served as well as tasty country dinners, and the friendly service makes you feel right at home. It is open from 6:00 A.M. to 8:00 P.M., daily, except Sunday. (828) 586-2013.

Driving straight through Sylva, you will run into **Cope's Newsstand and Suprette.** A sign boasts the largest selection of magazines in Western North Carolina and you will believe it when you see it. The assortment is most impressive, especially the hunting and sports choices. Ann Cope has owned this store since 1970 and she has newspapers and a good selection of books. This is also a convenience store with the usual staples, including videos! This is a great stop-and-go place.

Set in among the businesses and supply stores is a real "gem," **Lulu's Café,** at 612 Main Street. The outside of the building by no means tells what's inside. Owner Louise Turner has decorated the interior in pink and black with wonderful black and white photographs hanging on the walls.

French chef Didier Crozange and chef Bo Lawsey, a Cherokee Indian, have developed a tantalizing menu. Favorites include Pasta Salad à la Greque (warm pasta with Feta cheese, Greek olives, pepperoncini, tomatoes, red onions, and walnuts served with a lemon-oil dressing) and Catfish Creole (a fresh filet rolled in pecans, baked, and served with Creole sauce). Chef Bo's Carribean Jerk Chicken is a real hit. An excellent wine list and an extensive selection of imported beer complete this exceptional dining place.

The café is closed Thanksgiving and Christmas. Hours are from 11:00 A.M. to 9:00 P.M. during the summer months. Call for other hours. (828) 586-8989.

City Lights Bookstore, upstairs at 3 East Jackson Street and just one block up from Main Street, is an active bookstore with a devoted following. The black and white shop cat, Miss Kitty, a dedicated people-cat, will greet you.

Customers can always find something on the shelves of new books, as well as in the section of used books, which have been turned in for credit. Owner Joyce Moore is devoted to current fiction, but the shop is strong on regional, children's, and travel books. City Lights also carries maps and the shop frequently has readings and book signings. It is open from 9:00 A.M. to 9:00 P.M. (828) 586-9499.

Just below the bookstore is **Spring Street Café.** This café offers healthy, homestyle cooking from around the world. There is also an in-house bakery serving coffee and pastries. It is open from 10:00 A.M. to 10:00 P.M., six days a week, and from 10:00 A.M. to 2:30 P.M., Sunday brunch. (828) 586-1800.

Traveling south out of Sylva on U.S. Highway 107, keep a lookout for **Jack the Dipper** on the west side of the highway at number 944. For a cool treat, this ice cream and coffee shop specializes in exotic sundaes, shakes, coffee, floats, and fruit blasters. Owner Anne Davis says a favorite is the Banana Banshee, made with two dips of vanilla ice cream, one chopped banana, and hot fudge topped with whipped cream and a cherry. After a day of sightseeing, Jack the Dipper can offer a much needed refreshment stop. It is open daily.

Dillsboro

William Dills founded Dillsboro in 1884, just after the coming of the Western North Carolina Railroad. Until the railroad tunnel was completed through Cowee Mountain, the railroad ended at Dillsboro and it became a bustling community in short order. Word spread quickly about the cool summer days and beautiful scenery, and travelers responded.

Whatever the time and whatever the season, the **Dillsboro Smokehouse** will happily satisfy your cravings for hickory-smoked barbecue. The menu offers beef, pork, and chicken with all the trimmings. Other favorites include the pulled chicken sandwich and the baby back ribs. Low-fat items are marked on the menu and everything is available for takeout. The Smokehouse is located on Haywood Street. (828) 586-9556.

Jarrett House, one of the most renowned places in Dillsboro, was designated a National Historic Place in 1984 and is one of the oldest inns in Western North Carolina. It was built in 1884 by William Allen Dills, who founded the town. Just a few years after the Western North Carolina Railroad came to Dillsboro, the first summer visitors arrived to spend several weeks at the inn. This began the ever-growing tourist trade. Although the inn has changed owners over the years, the traditional style has remained the same and the present owners are carrying on with the legendary service.

Early on, Jarrett House became known for its tradition of home-cooked meals served family style. Country ham and red-eye gravy are longtime favorites along with fried chicken, trout, chicken and dumplings, and dishes of seasonal vegetables. Credit cards are not accepted and reservations are not required. Call for hours, as they are seasonal.

After packing in all you can eat, stroll out onto the wide front porch, claim one of the many rocking chairs, and sit a spell. You will probably decide to stay over for a night or two in an antique-furnished room. No children under the age of 12 and no smoking, please. (828) 586-0265 or (800) 972-5623.

Red-Eye Gravy

Red-eye gravy really requires a piece of well-cured country ham with most of the fat left on (but in a pinch, other kinds of ham or bacon could be used). Fry the ham in its own fat in an iron skillet until browned on both sides. Transfer to a plate. Add one-third to one-half cup of strong, black coffee to the skillet, scraping up any ham bits that have stuck to the pan. Stir all this about but do not allow the gravy to boil. Pour over the ham and grits or biscuits.

Dillsboro Chocolate Factory is located at 27 Church Street. Owners Randy and Susan Lyons specialize in homemade fudge, truffles, and fine chocolates. Those lucky enough to visit near Halloween or Thanksgiving will be able to buy pumpkin fudge, a tasty house specialty. (828) 631-0156.

In a 1900 building on the corner of Church and Front streets is

Shirley's of Dillsboro. Shirley Simpson has a fine selection of women's clothes and accessories. If you have forgotten your favorite sweater, you will most assuredly find another one here. Shop hours are seasonal, so in order not to be disappointed, call before you visit. (828) 586-8031.

Those who enjoy needlework know how hard it is to find shops with quality supplies and good choices. **The Yarn Corner,** located at 64 Front Street, will make you happy. Margaret Cogdill has collected a glorious selection of yarns and hand-painted canvases, some locally done. Call for your special needs. (828) 586-3420.

Lots of shops run the length of the depot on Front Street in Dillsboro and one of the best is **Duck Decoys, Ltd.** Nice merchandise for the hunter and fisherman is available, but in the back of the store is an extraordinary selection of handmade furniture that is as beautiful as any in the region. Small dining room tables and occasional tables are handsomely crafted with prices that will surprise you. Of course, given the name of the shop, the decoys are first class as well. Duck Decoys, Ltd. is open all year and has regular store hours.

Who would have more knowledge about good pottery than a fine potter? Rick Uban's shop, **Mountain Pottery,** is exceptional for carrying pieces that are made, not by daubers of clay, but artists with real talent and imagination. Rick has gathered a bunch of creative artisans with a flair and energy you will love. The "fat cats" with real feathers in their mouths are irresistible, miniature crèches are delicate and collector's items, and the vases need stands with spotlights more than flowers. These are true American crafts at their finest. Located at 150 Front Street, it is open from 10:00 A.M. to 6:00 P.M., six days a week, and from 12:00 noon to 3:00 P.M., Sunday. (828) 586-9183.

Gift shops abound in the mountain towns of Western North Carolina. If your time is limited, you can cull through some of these shops by looking in the windows. When you look in **The Golden Carp Gift Shop and Gallery,** it's a cinch you won't pass by.

The Golden Carp

Owners John P. Miele and Bud Smith are dedicated to this business and even have their home upstairs. They have a real knack for knowing what's good, where to get it, and where to put it after you get it. Miele and Smith are way ahead on trends—they have 30 different plate brackets to display your collection of antique pieces or the heavy glass plates so popular now. Their selection of clocks comes in every size from 13 to 31 inches. The shop has vibrant watercolor paintings; some are John Miele's work and some are from Ken Bowser, a well-known regional artist. Prices are surprisingly reasonable.

You can't miss the Golden Carp on Webster Street. It is open from 10:00 A.M. to 5:00 P.M., six days a week, and from 10:00 A.M. to 3:00 P.M., Sunday. (828) 586-5477.

The **Apron Shop** is located in a white house on Webster Street, next to the Golden Carp. It is a snug place packed with handmade aprons in old-fashioned country prints. No, they do not have clever sayings on the front or crazy shapes. If no one is in the shop, just browse; the owner likes to go next door and check on her dog.

When looking for good cottage crafts, you may do well to stick with the co-op shops. These nonprofit stores are usually very well organized. The goods are local mountain crafts made within a 50-mile radius and include quilts, pottery, baskets, wooden toys, jams and jellies, small pieces of furniture, baby clothes, and many more one-of-a-kind items moderately priced. Volunteers usually staff the shops and can put you in direct touch with an artist whose work you particularly like. One of the best co-op craft shops is **Dogwood Crafters**, located on Webster Street, one block south of Main Street. Hours are from 9:30 A.M. to 9:00 P.M. (828) 586-2248.

Riverwood Shops

At the top of the hill in Dillsboro, above the river, is **Riverwood**, where a group of artists have opened shops in front of their studios. This community is very contained and represents many of the mountain crafts in a beautiful and easy atmosphere. After you shop, the **Wellhouse Restaurant** will fortify you with good sandwiches, soups, and all kinds of picnic takeouts. Christmas is a special time in Riverwood. From atop the hill, the whole town of Dillsboro can be seen in all its holiday finery.

Dillsboro is the headquarters for the **Great Smoky Mountains Railroad.** This line has been in existence since 1840. In 1988, it was purchased by a group of investors and shippers for passenger excursions into the mountains during the day. The railroad still hauls freight at night.

Five regular junkets sweep you through the Smokies with panoramic views of rivers, towns, and gaps. The trips can be via steam or diesel engine and you can book open car, coach, crown coach, or club car. Ironically, the least expensive open cars are the most scenic; however, if summer is unseasonably warm, you may want to count on the air-conditioned cars.

The railway trips are seasonal, beginning partially in March and running full steam (pardon the pun) until November with a few Santa Expresses in December. These trips are very popular and you will need to make reservations far in advance by calling (800) 872-4681.

One favorite plan for the energetic family, including grandparents, is the Raft 'n Rail trip to the Nantahala Gorge, which leaves from Bryson City. This seven-and-a-half-hour round trip takes you 22 miles into the gorge, where a guide will then lead you down whitewater rapids to the Nantahala Outdoor Center. After a picnic lunch, you can return to Bryson City by bus. This trip is especially good for the beginning rafter; the Nantahala Power Plant controls the rapids and they are rated a number two (out of five) in difficulty. If you follow the rules, you will have a memorable and safe trip (children must be at least 60 pounds).

There are wonderful picnic grounds along the river. If rafting and/or picnicking are not your thing, there are a couple of good restaurants here and you can return by train, having had an exciting day on the rails. For further information about other trips, call (800) 872-4681.

Five miles south of Dillsboro on U.S. Highway 441 is **The Old School Antique Mall.** The mall rates an A+! This old stone schoolhouse was built in 1939 and closed in 1973. Several years later it became an antique mall with the slogan, "Now you can go to school and love it!" The interior has the ambience of a school with rooms numbered and titled Math, English, and Science. Blackboards remain on some of the walls behind antique-filled counters and there are still lockers in the hall. The large center room, once called the "Gymtorium," now has rows of enticing glass counters filled with collectibles.

The 60 or so dealers range from as far away as Maine, Key West, and Denver. Quality is the first priority of owners Wade and Brenda Ford and the contents measure up from one extreme to the other. Antique sewing items, Shirley Temple dolls, and a Charley McCarthy puppet are next to Dresden figurines, an exquisite 18th-century ivory powder box, and a French inlaid lady's rolltop writing desk. In a room that was probably the library are all manner of books pertaining to antiques. Hours are from 10:00 A.M. to 5:00 P.M., Tuesday through Saturday, and afternoons, Sunday, April through October. (828) 586-8097.

THE OLD SCHOOL
Antique Mall

Bryson City

Just west of Dillsboro in Bryson City are beautiful waterfalls that are not difficult to reach. This particular area is mostly flat and easy to maneuver.

Drive west on U.S. Highway 74 to Exit 67, exit and continue through the first traffic light, and follow the brown signs for **Deep Creek Campground,** which is at one of the entrances of the Great Smoky Mountains National Park. Continue for six-tenths of a mile past the picnic area and enter a gravel parking area. The trail begins at the middle of the parking lot and provides an easy hike to **Tom's Branch Falls** and **Indian Creek Falls.** The trail is parallel to Deep Creek. You can see Tom's Branch Falls across the creek and it is about two-tenths of a mile from the parking lot. Continue half a mile along the creek and, after crossing a bridge and coming up to the next bridge, take the trail to the right. Indian Creek Falls is 200 feet on your left. There is a sign back at the parking lot for a trail leading to **Juneywhank Falls,** which is three-tenths of a mile up the mountain. The park entrance is a great place to picnic, with tables and outdoor grills scattered along the creek bank.

Deep Creek Lodge is located right at the entrance to the national park and provides a perfect place for a family getaway. Owners Bob and Joyce Biggs offer clean, spacious, one- or two-bedroom apartments. Each has a kitchen/dinette/living room with a Laundromat on the premises. The prices are right for the entire family and even some friends. The lodge is open summer months only. (828) 488-2587.

Just outside the lodge is **Creekside Tubing.** You can't miss it—there are stacks and stacks of tubes by the creek. The price for renting a tube depends on comfort level. Some are available with plastic seats (top of the line), others with wood, and some without seats ("bottom" of the line). The most expensive is $5 for the day. If you don't wish to spend the night, this could be a great day trip. Changing rooms are available at no charge and showers are available for $3 per person. The snack bar can take care of your appetite after you have spent the day floating aimlessly down the creek.

Kingfisher's Angling Shop, located at 3 Depot Street in Bryson City, carries a full line of fly-fishing equipment as well as clothing, books, and videos. Owner Edward Chapman grew up fishing the bay and rivers near his home in Point Clear, Alabama, and has extended his love for fishing to the streams and rivers in North Carolina. His shop offers guide services and rentals to North Carolina anglers and has a good selection of decorative accessories with fishing and outdoor motifs. It is open from 9:00 A.M. to 5:30 P.M., Monday through Saturday, and from 12:00 noon to 5:30 P.M., Sunday. (828) 488-4848.

The new kids on the block in Bryson City are Holly Bowick and Julia Hunt, owners of the **Everett Street Diner.** They keep it simple, serving breakfast and lunch favorites with a Southern touch—Holly thinks their grits are superlative. You will be pleased with all of the homemade soups, but the tomato is perfection. For lunch, the catfish sandwich served on a hoagie roll is the café signature. Once a month, the girls show off with a gourmet dinner at night with all the trimmings. The Everett Street Diner, located just down from the courthouse at 52 Everett, is open for breakfast and lunch from 7:00 A.M. to 3:00 P.M.

From Everett Street, cross over U.S. Highway 19 and turn right on Academy Street to the **Randolph House Bed and Breakfast.** This 1895 house has 12 gables overhead and just as many rocking chairs on the front porch. It is listed on the National Register of Historic Places, an honor to the inn's builder, Capt. Amos Frye.

Ruth and Bill Adams began operating Randolph House in 1989. Sitting on a mountain shelf overlooking the town, the inn contains many of the original furnishings dating back to the 1850s. There are six bedrooms, two with private baths. A complete country breakfast is served every morning. Dinner entrees include veal, fish, and prime rib with homemade fruit cobblers among the dessert offerings. It is open from the end of April through October. There are some limitations on children. (828) 488-3472; off-season (770) 938-2268.

Next door is the **Fryemont Inn,** built in 1923 by timber baron Amos Frye. In addition to rooms there are cottage suites with living areas and fireplaces. In the Fryemont's spacious lobby is a huge stone fireplace, large enough to burn eight-foot logs. Help yourself to a cup of coffee and take it out to the rocking chair porch with its breathtaking view of the mountains. If it's after five o'clock, beverages are available in the bar located in the dining area. Call for special rates for families, children, seniors, and stays of one week or longer. The inn is open for Thanksgiving and also for a Halloween party in October.

Notice the unusual exterior of the inn. It is covered with bark from huge poplar trees and the bark is as sturdy today as when the strips were first cut. (828) 488-2159 or (800) 845-4879.

www.fryemontinn.com.

Nantahala Outdoor Center

Nantahala Outdoor Center (NOC) is located at 13077 U.S. Highway 19 West on the Nantahala River. In 1972, NOC was founded by three friends from Atlanta, Horace Holden and Payson and Aurelia Kennedy, with the objective of providing facilities, services, and instruction to help others enjoy the outdoors. They began with an outfitter's store, motel, and small restaurant and offered guided whitewater rafting trips and lessons in canoeing and kayaking on the Nantahala and Chattooga rivers. The number-one goal is still to provide guests with the highest quality and most enjoyable outdoor experience possible.

Today, NOC is one of the world's best-known outfitters, offering rafting trips on the Nantahala, Ocoee, French Broad, Chattooga, Nolichucky, and Pigeon rivers. The Adventure Travel program runs trips all around the world and mountain-biking courses are available, daily and weekends. The Action Learning Department serves the needs of camps, schools, and corporations who come to NOC to work on team-building and leadership skills. On-site are both high- and low-ropes courses and an Alpine Tower.

The center now operates two restaurants and an outdoor café, several motel rooms, group lodging, and private cabin rentals. A 7,000-square-foot outfitter's store has all the gear needed for almost any adventure. The staff members are professionals in their field, enjoy participation in their sports, and love to teach others. For information about rates and courses, call Nantahala Outdoor Center at (888) 662-1662, Extension 600. www.nocweb.com.

Slow Joe's is not slow but a sassy, fast food place that sits just a few feet above the Nantahala River rapids. Place your order for hot dogs, hamburgers, chicken burritos, or anything else that's fast and good, then sit outside until you're called. This is a good place to watch people run the rapids while soaking your tired feet in the cold refreshing water of the Nantahala River. It is open from 11:00 A.M. to 2:00 P.M., Monday through Friday, and from 10:00 A.M. to 6:00 P.M., Saturday and Sunday, spring through October.

High on a hill is **Relia's Garden Restaurant,** a rustic, red-roofed "chalet." It is named for Aurelia Kennedy, creator of the original restaurant. The name also refers to the bountiful organic garden that provides the herbs, flowers, and spices that enhance the restaurant's dishes.

Sitting up high overlooking the garden and the Nantahala, you can enjoy soup, sandwiches, and salads. Catfish, trout, and beef are also available. Relia's can tailor menus for groups or special occasions and has a brown bag license with a minimal corkage fee. It is open from 12:00 noon to 9:00 P.M., daily, June to November. (828) 488-2175.

If you cross the river via the footbridge, you will come to the open, spacious **River's End Restaurant.** Salads, sandwiches, fresh breads, and other hearty and healthy fare for the outdoor appetite are offered. Don't bypass the cheese toast. A bonus is outside seating by the river. If you prefer to come by car rather than rail, take U.S. Highway 19/23 west. The NOC center and restaurants are just over the bridge. River's End is open from 5:00 A.M. to 9:00 P.M.

William Bartram was a Philadelphia botanist who traveled through the Southeast from 1773 to 1777 and published his vivid and mystical descriptions of Indians, plants, and animals in 1791. Today, the nearly 100-mile part of the **Bartram Trail** in Western North Carolina follows his original route. It is maintained by the North Carolina Bartram Society and the U.S. Forest Service.

In several areas, it crosses the Appalachian Trail and, although the Bartram Trail is not as well known, it is becoming more popular as it is less crowded. The Bartram Trail enters Western North Carolina just south of Highlands and ends west of the Nantahala Gorge. For information call (828) 526-4904.

CHAPTER 9

Robbinsville

Robbinsville is a small rural town located on U.S. Highway 129, off of U.S. Highway 19. It serves as a gateway to some of the most glorious country in Western North Carolina. Robbinsville just sits here, being itself, with friendly people to guide you to your destinations. The hangout is **Phillips Restaurant** and you cannot find a more local place—just ask anybody where it is. Country breakfast, lunch, and dinner are served.

Joyce Kilmer Memorial Forest/
Joyce Kilmer-Slickrock Wilderness

One of America's best-loved poems, "Trees," was written by Joyce Kilmer, poet and journalist. He was killed, much too young, while serving as a soldier in World War I, depriving the world of many more beautiful poems of nature.

How fitting that over 17,000 acres in the Nantahala National Forest have been set aside as the Joyce Kilmer Memorial Forest and the Joyce Kilmer-Slickrock Wilderness. Kilmer would be pleased to know that this magnificent virgin forest (where some trees are 100 feet tall and 20 feet in circumference) is dedicated to him and his love of nature.

The only way to see the memorial forest is on foot. The figure-eight **Joyce Kilmer Trail** is a two-mile hike just a short distance from the parking lot. A bridge with rushing water over mossy boulders makes it too inviting to pass up. The forest is an outstanding example of a cove hardwood forest—characterized by thick soil, abundant moisture, and a variety of flora. The trailhead parking area has a flush toilet and picnic tables but camping and overnight parking are not allowed.

Like other wildernesses, Slickrock is managed to protect naturalness and solitude. No motorized or mechanical vehicles are allowed. The miles of trails in the wilderness are maintained to the most primitive standards with few, if any, signs. Wilderness hikers will find no shelters, restrooms, or water faucets and travelers are urged to have a topographic map and a compass. From Robbinsville, take N.C. Highway 1116 off of U.S. Highway 129 North for two miles. At the stop sign turn right onto N.C. Highway 1127 for 10 miles to Joyce Kilmer Road. For more detailed hiking information and a topographic map of the wilderness, stop at the Cheoah District Ranger Office off of U.S. Highway 129 or call the office at (828) 479-6431.

Fontana Dam

Just after Pearl Harbor, construction of the mighty Fontana Dam began in a hurry-up operation to create more power for the war effort. Three years of around-the-clock shifts and 5,000 women and men completed the magnificent structure that you see today; the dam stands 480 feet high and 2,365 feet in length. To see the dam in all its glory, stop at the visitor center's observation towers. The powerhouse, which gives tourists a good knowledge of how it all works, can be reached by a tram.

The Appalachian Trail crosses the top of Fontana Dam. Grateful hikers take full advantage of hot showers, picnic grounds, and camping accommodations available near the visitor center. The Smoky Mountains National Park runs along the border of the dam reservoir with boat launching ramps at various places. The lake has lots of good fishing, with trout, bass, walleye, pike, perch, sunfish, and crappie in abundance; you will need a fishing license.

Fontana is now used for flood control and navigational improvement. Strict environmental laws help in the management of all the natural resources encompassing the dam. It is a perfect example of man's cooperation with nature to create good. An interesting footnote is the unusual sight when the reservoir is being drained, which takes place every five years. When the dam was built an entire town was flooded—it's still down there and is uncovered during this operation. Your timing may be good and you can observe this eerie event.

The Academy Award winning film *Nell*, starring Jodie Foster, was filmed at Fontana Lake.

You may want to spend some time at **Fontana Village.** Located three miles from the dam, this community has been cut out of the deepest forest, placing the Great Smokies at your door. The village is the largest resort property in the mountains, boasting an inn, 200 cottages, a hostel, and campground sites. You can be outfitted for every mountain adventure you choose, with a planned program to go with it.

When you are traveling by car to different spots along the western border, Fontana Village is a perfect place to stay, even for just one night, as it puts you at the entrance to all the sights in the Nantahala Forest. It is open all year. (800) 849-2258. www.fontanavillage.com.

Tail of the Dragon

Heading west on U.S. Highway 129, you will come across the Tail of the Dragon, an 11-mile route that is internationally known, especially to motorcyclists. Someone counted 318 hairpin turns along this road and, although your driver might not find it enjoyable, the views are spectacular. The road is N.C. Highway 28 (Indian Lakes Scenic Byway).

Cherohala Skyway

Take time to drive the **Cherohala Skyway**, a 40-plus-mile trip skipping across the mountains connecting Robbinsville, North Carolina, to Tellico Plains, Tennessee. Definitely pack a lunch and plan to spend at least one to two hours driving the skyway. Allow more time if you want to take advantage of the hikes along the way.

This drive is Western North Carolina at its best—full of planned overlooks that you do not have to leave your car to enjoy. Many of them have picnic tables. Even in the heaviest tourist season, traffic is light and the paved road is heaven to motorcyclists. Stop at the Cheoah District Ranger Office on U.S. Highway 143, pick up a map of the skyway, and choose your own spots to stop. The skyway was named for two forests, "Chero" for Cherokee and "hala" for Nantahala.

Much like a mini-Blue Ridge Parkway, this drive was designed for the tourist to leisurely enjoy nature from the car. The skyway is located on U.S. Highway 143, north of Robbinsville. For more information contact Cheoah Ranger Station, Route 1, Box 16-A, Robbinsville, North Carolina 28771. (828) 479-6431.

Snowbird Mountain Lodge is a state of mind that will haunt you until you come back. If you could describe the perfect inn, Snowbird would be right there at the top of the list. Since the 1930s, guests have come to the lodge for all kinds of occasions—birthdays, anniversaries, honeymoons—but the best reason is rejuvenation.

Innkeepers Karen and Robert Rankin may not be able to take credit for the view of the Snowbird Mountain Range (with a glint of Lake Santeetlah at the bottom), but they can take credit for a beautifully managed inn that leaves no stone unturned to renew you, physically and mentally. The order of the day is peace and tranquillity, but you do not have to be still to enjoy the stillness. From April to November there is a litany of activities—cooking classes, wine dinners, lectures by prominent naturalists, film festivals, kayaking, canoeing, fly-fishing lessons, hiking, and great massage therapy. Schedules change every season so pick the time that offers the most for you.

The lodge itself is a wood and stucco structure with gabled roof. Inside are shiny wooden floors and walls, overstuffed furniture, and oriental rugs. The dining room is simple with snowy white tablecloths and fresh flowers. Three luscious meals are included in daily room rates, which are very reasonable. From Robbinsville, follow U.S. Highway 143 West to Snowbird Mountain Lodge at 275 Santeetlah Road, Robbinsville, North Carolina 28771. (800) 941-9290.

www.snowbirdlodge.com.

Karen and Robert quote Thoreau in one of their schedules: "The woods and fields are a table always spread," as is Snowbird Mountain Lodge.

Driving south from Robbinsville gives you a picture of Western North Carolina different from almost any other region. This route is for people who love to skirt the touristy places and drive aimlessly through wide-open country, hopping from town to town. A picnic lunch is almost compulsory and you will find just the right spot to eat along the way. If Franklin is your final destination along this route, prepare for a long day's drive.

Andrews

Off U.S. Highway 19 is Andrews, which nestles in the foothills of the Snowbird Mountains. One of the excursions of the Great Smoky Mountains Railroad leaves the Andrews Depot and makes the four-and-a-half-hour journey through the Hawksnest Trestle, then climbs the highest railroad grade in Eastern America. Andrews is also a good boat launching area for the serious fisherman. More information can be obtained from the Andrews Chamber of Commerce. (828) 321-3584.

Murphy

From Andrews you will be coming into Murphy on U.S. Highways 19, 129, or 74. Murphy is a hub where you can gas up and chow down, mainly on fast foods. Drive across Lake Hiwassee with pear tree lanes approaching the old downtown area. From your car you can view two interesting buildings: the Cherokee County Courthouse, built in 1927 (this is the only courthouse in the state built of local, regal blue marble), and the United Methodist Church, circa 1922.

Brasstown

Seven miles east of Murphy, off of U.S. Highway 64, is Brasstown. Every lover of mountain crafts must visit this gem. Blink your eyes and you're through it but plan to stop for at least half an hour or more. Before visiting the craft shops in Brasstown, go straight to **John C. Campbell Folk School,** established in 1925. John Campbell and his wife, Olive, came to the mountains in 1908 in a wagon that was their home as well as transportation. They both wanted to do humanitarian work and fashioned their philosophy from the folk schools in rural Denmark. Unfortunately John died in 1919, but Olive and friend Marguerite Butler studied in Europe and returned to Appalachia to finish their work.

From the beginning the school was established not to change the mountain people but to collaborate with them and to this day this tradition has not changed. The catalog states, "Instruction at the Folk School is non-competitive—there are no credits, no grades, no pitting of one individual against another. This method of teaching is what the Danes called, 'The Living Word.' Discussion and conversation, rather than reading and writing, are emphasized and most instruction is hands-on." Courses covered at Campbell are too many to mention, so grab a catalog at Keith House and sign up for a course—it's never too late.

The Craft Shop is in the Olive D. Campbell Building. All of the crafts are made by the instructors at the school and are of excellent quality. Hours at the shop are from 8:00 A.M. to 5:00 P.M., Monday through Friday, and from 1:00 to 5:00 P.M., Sunday. The address is 1 Folk School Road, Brasstown, North Carolina 28902-9603. (828) 837-2775 or (800) 837-8637. www.folkschool.com.

On your way out of town, several craft shops may catch your eye. **Clay's Corner,** the local gas station, is where the artists of the area gather—you may want to drop in.

Hayesville

Back on U.S. Highway 64, continue your jaunt to Hayesville, which has the only stoplight in the county. Swing around the pretty town square and see the courthouse, circa 1889, and the **Old Jail Museum.** Then look for the giant rocking chair in front of **People's Store** and go inside. You will thrill over the wonderful things Mr. Wayne Phillips has collected and you will rub your hands together, thinking you have found the "mother lode" of treasures to buy. Please understand right off that nothing is for sale. He might let you buy a small hornet's nest (not a big one), but anything else he lets you buy will be of no consequence. Mr. Phillips just loves for you to come in and ask about his unique collection. He is a master of trickery so don't touch anything—it might jump out at you.

Golf Courses

This golf course information is courtesy of Journal Communications, Inc.:

Cherokee Hills Golf Club. Located three miles outside of Murphy. This beautiful layout in the foothills of the Smoky Mountains is 18 hole, par 72, and hilly with lots of water. It is open year round. (800) 334-3905.

CHAPTER 10

Franklin

From Hayesville to Franklin is approximately 16 miles and this expanse of road is devoid of any interruptions. You'll enjoy a farmhouse or a convenience store every now and then but mainly you'll just see wide-open spaces.

Franklin is best known for its gem mines. If you are interested in gems, be sure to stop at the **Franklin Gem and Mineral Museum,** located in the old jail at 2 West Main Street. Franklin is host to a large gem and mine show twice a year. The museum is open from 10:00 A.M. to 4:00 P.M., six days a week, and from 1:00 to 4:00 P.M., Sunday, May through October. There is no admission charge. (828) 369-7831.

One of the best restaurants in the area is the **Frog and Owl Kitchen** at 12 East Main Street and it is currently open only for lunch. But, oh, what a lunch you can have here! The menu offers everything from a fabulous pot roast with garlic mashed potatoes to delicious mountain trout cooked to perfection. The gourmet desserts are not to be missed. Try the Gnash (a decadent mint chocolate pie) or the Celeste (a blend of brandy, cream, and sour cream) for a heavenly end to your meal.

Owner Jerri Broyles was a broad jumper in high school, where she acquired the nickname of "Leaping Frog"; she also has a special love for owls—hence the name of the restaurant. Jerri has been cooking good food since the 1970s and has moved her restaurant several times. Her reputation follows her as do her faithful customers. This is open from 11:00 A.M. to 3:00 P.M., Monday through Saturday. (828) 349-4112.

After lunch you can enjoy browsing through the aisles at **Books Unlimited** at 60 East Main Street. New titles, bestsellers, used books, cards, audios, and calendars fill the shelves. It is open from 10:00 A.M. to 6:00 P.M., six days a week.

A fun place to go, even if you are not Scottish, is the **Scottish Tartans Museum and Heritage Center** at 35 Main Street. You enter the gift shop, where large selections of imported Scottish and Celtic items are available—sashes, tams, scarves, dirks (thin daggers), Highland dress items, shawls, kilts—in other words everything Scottish. Downstairs in the gallery you can learn the history of the beautiful tartans woven in plaids to designate a clan. The exhibits are interesting, especially the walls of Scottish names with swatches of the family tartans beside them.

The museum also contains the official registry of all publicly known tartans and is the only extension of the Scottish Tartan Society in Edinburgh, Scotland. It is open from 10:00 A.M. to 5:00 P.M., Monday through Saturday, and from 1:00 to 5:00 P.M., Sunday. (828) 524-7472.

Perry's Water Gardens should be called "Perry's Paradise." This breathtaking, aquatic nursery, the largest in the United States, is the brainchild of renowned gardener Perry Slocum. It began as a hobby for Mr. Slocum in upstate New York. When a highway was scheduled to be built through his gardens, he simply picked up and moved south. The result is 14 acres of sparkling water, filled with tranquil water lilies, glorious irises, and thousands of exotic and rare oriental lotuses. Picnic tables, walking trails, and huge Golden Niobe willow trees surround these spring-fed pools.

In addition to the gardens, there is an aquatic supply store where you may purchase potted water plants, fish ponds, fountains, pumps, etc., for your own garden. Plant sales are held April through September. In the early spring, plant tubers can be shipped anywhere in the world.

The earlier in the day you can visit, the better. In summer it can get quite hot, but more importantly, the lotuses are at their peak in the mornings. The colors tend to lighten as the day lengthens.

Mr. Slocum's son, Ben Gibson, manages the gardens. Organizations are welcome. A consultation service is available and Perry's publishes a color catalog of the plants and equipment to order. There is also an annual Fourth of July Lotus Festival.

From Franklin, drive north on N.C. Highway 28, approximately six miles, to Cowee Baptist Church; just beyond, turn right on Cowee Creek Road; go for two miles, bear left at the fork, and follow the signs to this exotic sunken garden—a true labor of love.

The gardens are open from 9:00 A.M. to 12:00 noon and from 1:00 to 5:00 P.M., Monday through Saturday, and afternoons, Sunday, May through September. Admission is free. (828) 524-3264.

After browsing at Perry's, stop at **Rickman's General Store.** Just watch for wheelbarrows filled with flowers and flags in front of the circa-1895 store. Here are antiques, crafts, sandwiches, and ice cream.

Taking U.S. Highway 64 (N.C. Highway 28) from Franklin to Highlands is the closest thing to hiking by car. This drive is part of the Nantahala National Forest and covers several miles of exquisite natural forests and falls with "catch your breath" vistas. Nothing interferes with this trip except the road, which snakes around hairpin turns—be prepared to go dead slow.

Your first view is Cullasaja Falls, which drops 300 feet to **Lower Cullasaja Falls.** The deep gorge with the majestic waterfall in the background is a sight you will not forget. After a few miles of rapids on one side and tall mountains and forests on the other, you will reach

Dry Falls, which is a big raging waterfall you can walk under; it was used in the film *The Last of the Mohicans.* The last waterfall before Highlands is **Bridal Veil,** a lacy falls you can drive or walk under—in summer, the cold spray feels wonderful.

> "Cullasaja" is a Cherokee word for "honey locust place." The honey locust tree is a religious symbol pertaining to the gods of thunder and lightning.

A diner's dream come true is **On The Verandah,** overlooking tranquil Lake Sequoyah on U.S. Highway 64 (1536 Franklin Road). Deep rose walls welcome you and open timbered ceilings and giant "paper lantern" light fixtures spell sophistication and ease. Slip into the roomy-yet-cozy bar for a glass of wine. On The Verandah has won *Wine Spectator*'s "Award of Excellence" every year since 1987 for their fine wine list. If you prefer, you may brown bag beer or liquor and order set-ups.

Chef Alan Figel opened this rustic, yet contemporary restaurant in 1981. Alan's son, Andrew, is now executive chef while personable daughter Marlene Alvarez is manager. Originally constructed in the 1920s, the building has a colorful history of uses, among them a "speakeasy" in the 1930s. Today comforts abound from good acoustics to live piano music.

On the way to your table on the screened veranda, or the dining room, which is open to the veranda, look over the "hot sauce" collection—shelves of over 1,300 hot sauces from all over the world. Yes, you can sample any of them, including the owner's own Maniac Hot Sauces, which are available for purchase.

Everything on the menu is good, from grilled trout with mango salsa to the seared venison medallions. Don't dare pass up the Thai roasted peanut salad with Romaine and alfalfa sprouts. Fresh seasonal fruit pies melt in your mouth. Year round you can order the Godiva Chocolate Crème Brulee. 'Nuff said! On The Verandah is open for dinner at 6:00 P.M., nightly, and for brunch, Sunday, from March through New Year's Day (the wine bar opens at 5:00 P.M.). Call for reservations and to find out about their special "occasions," including two wine dinners each year. (828) 526-2338. www.ontheverandah.com. Expensive, and worth it.

Highlands

Highlands

The beautiful town of Highlands was founded in 1875 by two friends, Clinton Hutchinson from Kansas and Samuel Kelsey from New York. The adventuresome men drew a line on a map from New Orleans to New York and another from Savannah to Chicago; where the lines intersected, they decided, would be an ideal site for a metropolis. After purchasing 1,400 acres, they laid out the town and built homes for themselves. Hutchinson's home, now a private residence, stands today next to the Hudson Library.

The town's average altitude is 4,118 feet. The pioneers aptly named it Highlands and promoted it as a health resort. Enveloped by the Nantahala National Forest, the Highlands Plateau is botanically and geographically one of the most unique locations in the world.

To serve a super gourmet meal without turning on the stove, try the **Rosewood Market** at 115 Franklin Road. This is a busy takeout and catering shop with a nice selection of wines. Aside from special orders, you'll find delicious ready-to-go soups, bisques, and stews. For hors d'oeuvres you can grab and go with such items as smoked catfish pâté or spinach pesto puff pastries. Wind up dinner with Brie and raspberry phyllo rolls or profiteroles. Chef Holly, from Atlanta, says that everything is made from scratch with the freshest ingredients. Hours are from 11:00 A.M. to 6:00 P.M., Tuesday through Saturday. It is best to call for winter hours. (828) 526-0383.

Should you really want to get into the mountains, rappelling may be the way to go. Rappelling is the art of descending a mountainside by means of a belayed rope. Upper body strength is not necessary and it is said that even the most dedicated couch potato can do it! However, you do need instructions and **Mountain Down Adventures,**

515 Many Road, has certified teachers for this exciting sport; teachers are U.S. Forest Service approved and insured. The first day you begin on the "bunny slope" and as you progress you move on to more difficult terrain. Call (828) 526-3063 for lessons on this very safe and popular sport. www.reiters.net/mountaindown.

The **Mitchell Motel and Cottages,** at N.C. Highway 28 and U.S. Highway 106, has been a well-loved, tried and true lodging location since 1939. This family-owned, stone and log accommodation just outside of the shopping district is in a forest area with a small duck-inhabited lake. In addition to standard rooms and suites, there are four cabins with fireplaces and kitchens. All of the paneled rooms are simply and attractively furnished with quilts, rocking chairs, and nature prints. A whirlpool spa overlooking a mountain stream requires a reservation upon arrival. There is a two-night minimum stay in the cottages. Rates are reasonable and a complimentary continental breakfast is served. No pets, please. Be sure and book early for this popular landmark. (828) 526-2267 or (800) 526-1643.

The **Summer House Gallery** and **Tiger Mountain Woodworks** are at 2089 Dillard Road (U.S. Highway 106). Three white frame buildings contain local art, handcrafted jewelry, and country pine and maple furniture. This place is off the beaten track but worth a trip. It is open six days a week, all year, plus Sunday afternoons during the season. (828) 526-0028.

Dusty Rhodes Suprette, a quiet landmark since 1950, is the type of small store that the local folk like to keep secret. This is because Dusty's carries the most delicious white chocolate chip macadamia nut cookies you have ever tasted! They come frozen, so all you need to do is pop 'em into your oven to bake and no one will ever know that you did not spend at least an hour in preparation.

There is much more . . . Dusty's, a small blue building with cheerful red geraniums out front, also stocks an international gourmet selection of pop-in-the-oven food items. Available are Taco Chalupas, Duckling Leg Confit, Chicken Wellington, Portuguese Bishop Rolls, and French Petit Pan Rolls. In addition, Dusty says he "cuts the best steaks in Western North Carolina." It is located at 493 Dillard Road (U.S. Highway 106) and is open from 8:00 A.M. to 6:00 P.M., six days a week. (828) 526-2762.

A truly picturesque place to stay is the **Old Creek Lodge** on U.S. Highway 106 (Dillard Road). Located half a mile from Highlands' Main Street, it is worth a visit just to see the beautifully landscaped grounds. All 15 cabins, some with two bedrooms, have rocking chairs on the front porches; the rooms are air-conditioned and have Jacuzzis and fireplaces. The lobby has a warm look with wormy chestnut paneling and a plush sofa and chairs. Old Creek Lodge is open all year and children under 12 stay free. Please, no pets. (828) 526-2273 or (800) 895-6343. Rates are strictly seasonal and quite moderate.

It is indeed unusual to find some of the yummiest fudge ever in an Exxon service station, but it's here . . . right at the corner of Main and Dillard! This spot is also known as the **Farmers Market,** as there are often produce and plants sitting outside. Inside on the walls is a colorful collection of bear and deer heads as well as an ancient and grotesque wart hog. Open six days a week, from 7:00 A.M. until 11:00 P.M. (828) 526-4382.

The east end of Main Street is called "Top of the Hill," while the west end is known as the "Gallery End of Town," where you will find Wright Square with captivating galleries and craft shops.

Southern Hands has whimsical, carved wooden bears, in all sizes and shapes, and throws and scarves hand-woven by the renowned Churchill weavers in Kentucky. It is open from 10:00 A.M. to 5:00 P.M., during the season. Winter hours are irregular. (828) 526-4807. **John Collette Fine Arts** features one of the area's finest selections of oils, watercolors, and pastels by regional and national artists. The sculpture and art glass is distinctive. There is something for all tastes. It is open from 10:00 A.M. until 5:00 P.M., daily; open only on weekends in the winter. (828) 526-0339.

Since 1987, **Master Works** of Highlands has represented nearly 300 quality artists and craftsmen from 37 states. Since 1995, the shop has annually been voted one of the top 100 craft galleries in the nation by *Niche* magazine. It is open from 10:00 A.M. to 5:00 P.M., daily; open only on weekends during off-season. Another gallery is **Thomas Kinkade,** a famous painter of luminance, an old style of depicting light. Mr. Kinkade, who lives in California, does not sell his originals. The works here are all lithographs, transferred to canvas, hand highlighted, and signed (his signature is the sign of a fish, a Christian symbol). This is an interesting shop in which to see a masterly portrayal of realism and light in art. Hours are from 10:00 A.M. to 5:00 P.M., six days a week, and from 11:00 A.M. to 5:00 P.M., Sunday. Off-season hours are irregular. (828) 526-9793. **Rarities** is much like a small museum where items are rare and beautiful. The Lucite-encased butterflies from 12 countries are exquisite as is the handcrafted jewelry of gold-colored crystals from Venezuela. Not to be missed are the original works of the famous Western painter, Robert Redbird. This is open seven days a week during the season and on weekends in the winter. (828) 526-8244.

A shop with an international flair is **Narcissus.** Located at 3 Wright Square, this small shop is overflowing with ladies' clothing and accessories. The amber and silver jewelry is eye catching and the Italian scarves are soft and romantic. This is a seasonal store, open from May through October. One of the owners, Giuliana Kaufman, is from Florence, Italy. She spends the winters there after a month of touring the world and searching out distinctive items for her shop. This is open from 10:00 A.M. to 5:00 P.M., Monday through Saturday. (828) 526-9642.

Rosenthals, on Main Street, is a special occasion shop with elegant formal gowns and cocktail suits and pants; however, there are also daytime sportswear lines such as Escada and St. John knits. Some of the costume jewelry are copies of old estate pieces. Other lines are art nouveau styles from Germany and gold filigree from France. It is open from 10:00 A.M. to 5:00 P.M., Monday through Saturday. Call for winter hours. (828) 526-2100.

One of the many landmark shops in Highlands is the **Stone Lantern,** 395 Main Street. It appears tiny, but room after room leads you through a major collection of quality porcelain, bronzes, slate fountains, bonsai containers, and garden statuary. Items range from $10 to $1,000. Owner Ralph DeVille has lived in Japan, Hong Kong, and Thailand and developed a taste and an eye for oriental art. He also has a fine selection of jewelry and pearls.

An added attraction of the Stone Lantern are the Ikebana classes with internationally known instructors. Mr. DeVille opened the Stone Lantern in 1949. Hours are from 10:00 A.M. to 5:00 P.M., Monday through Saturday. (828) 526-2769 or (800) 437-2741.

If you have heard of galax leaves, you know that they are the wonderful rich green leaves that will last for weeks and weeks in water. They are easily found in the local mountain forests.

A favorite local eating spot for a really big, beautiful sandwich is the **Sports Page,** 314 Main Street. Sportsmen can soak up the colorful ambience courtesy of old golf clubs, tennis rackets, and sporting equipment decorating the café walls.

The most popular item on the menu is the Philly steak with grilled onions and peppers. There is also a wide variety of other sandwiches (many are big enough to share), soups, and loaded potatoes. Usually a hungry crowd is waiting, so take a number—the efficient staff will have your order out in good time. It is open for lunch at 11 A.M., six days a week, April through October. For takeouts call (828) 526-3555.

The Village Boutique, 301 Main Street, is a Highlands favorite for casual ladies' clothing and it also has the largest selection of shoes in town, including Donald Pliner and Cole Haan. This shop was born in Cashiers in 1962 and thereafter moved to Highlands. It is open from 10:00 A.M. to 5:00 P.M., daily. Winter hours are from 11:00 A.M. to 4:00 P.M., Thursday through Saturday. (828) 526-8344.

If you have a weakness for soft, luxurious silk, you will want to step into the **House of Wong** at 350 Main Street. Owner Betty Wong has been making Highlands' ladies and visitors happy since 1971 with her colorful silk blouses, pantsuits, and kimonos. In this small boutique you will also find novelty bags and decorative umbrellas. It is open at 10:00 A.M., six days a week. (828) 526-3865.

Scudders Galleries, 352 Main Street, is something of an institution, since it first opened in 1925 in Florida and in 1976 in Highlands. During the summer season, Scudders is a lively antique auction house, open daily for viewing and sales. A nightly auction is held Monday through Saturday at 7:30 P.M. There are always tempting items—oriental rugs, porcelains, bronzes, jewelry, and chandeliers. These are mainly from estates although some are on consignment or from bankruptcy sales. Depending on the "pedigree" of the piece, there are often minimum bids. In the summer, there is an estate-day sale on the second and fourth Saturday of each month. Scudders' winter hours are from 10:00 A.M. to 5:00 P.M., Tuesday through Saturday, but there are no auctions. (828) 526-4111.

Highlands is an "ice cream town" with several serious ice cream shops, and **Kilwins Chocolate and Ice Cream** on Main Street is one of the best. Kilwins make their own cones with waffle-iron steel rollers, then dip a portion of them into chocolate. In addition, the shop creates 11 different fudges, peanut brittle, pecan brittle, pralines, turtles, and chocolate strawberries. A wonderful chocolate fragrance drifts out into the street, so just follow your nose. Kilwins has more than chocolate and ice cream . . . fresh lemonade, limeade, old-fashioned sodas, and malts are also served. They are open from 11:00 A.M. to 5:30 P.M., daily, and to 10:00 P.M., summer weekends. Winter hours are irregular. (828) 526-3788.

The Wit's End Shop has been one of Highlands' tradition since 1940. The shop has a superior collection of sweaters and an extensive array of Vera Bradley's French provincial print handbags. Speculation has it that the name, "Wit's End," is derived from the fact that when you are at your "wit's end" searching for just the right item, you will find it here. The shop is closed from January through March. Summer hours are from 9:30 A.M. to 5:30 P.M., and from 10:00 A.M. to 5:00 P.M., during other months. (828) 526-3160.

One of the best-loved bookstores in the mountains is **Cyrano's,** 390 Main Street. It is said that "good things come in tiny packages" and this is most appropriate for Cyrano's, a small shop that was opened by Randolph Shaffner in 1979. *The Highlander,* a local newspaper, noted that, at Cyrano's "the books are selected by someone with literary taste and not a computer." Book lovers will find this to be true as there is a fine selection of regional, travel, current, and children's books. The staff is always happy to do out-of-print searches for a special volume. It is open from 10:00 A.M. to 5:00 P.M., Monday through Saturday. (828) 526-5488.

Regarding the name of the shop, Mr. Shaffner says, "Cyrano was an unattractive literary character with a heart of gold. Therefore you cannot judge a book by its cover."

An art experience you do not want to miss is the **Ann Jacob Gallery** at the intersection of U.S. Highway 64 and Main Street. The shop has a lively collection of regional, national, and international prints, lithographs, and paintings. There is also serious marble sculpture. Ann began her art career as a collector when she lived in Europe. In 1986 she opened her gallery in Highlands and later another one in Atlanta. This is open from 10:00 A.M. to 5:00 P.M., six days a week, April through December, and weekends only January through March. (828) 526-5550.

A historic landmark is the **Highlands Inn** on the corner of Main and Fourth Avenue. This ideal lodging spot is in the heart of town. The inn was built in 1880, when Highlands was gaining national acclaim as a health resort, and it is listed on the National Register of Historic Places. It was restored in 1989 in the "country manner." All 31 rooms are furnished with antiques.

A continental breakfast is included in the tariff and is actually a full breakfast. The "Highland Nightcap," also included in the price, consists of coffee, tea, or hot chocolate and freshly baked cookies. A nearby golf course is available for guests. Inn rates are quite reasonable and rooms are in demand, so make reservations early. (828) 526-9380. www.highlandsinn-nc.com.

Located in the Highlands Inn, the **Kelsey Place Restaurant,** named after one of Highlands' founders, features a Southern menu with family-style serving. When in season, one of the specialties is a Vidalia onion casserole and the most popular dessert is the spiced apple dish with brown-sugar crust. Meal service is curtailed during the off-season so it is best to check for hours. Prices are moderate. (828) 526-9380.

Dining at **Paoletti's** is a "five star" experience and you will seriously appreciate this fine restaurant at 440 Main Street. The Northern Italian food is excellent and the wine list and cellar inventory have won the *Wine Spectator* award for many years. The Paoletti family knows what they are doing as they have been in the restaurant business since 1955. Everything on the menu is unrivaled. The restaurant is known for the superb ossobuco, and the sea bass is fabulous.

There are quite a few fine restaurants in Highlands, but since 1983 Paoletti's has been the best. Brown bagging is permitted for beer and liquor. The restaurant is open at 5:30 P.M., Monday through Saturday, during the season, and only on weekends during the off-season. Reservations as early as possible are recommended. (828) 526-4906. Expensive, but well worth it.

For another pleasant experience, try **Wolfgang's** at 474 Main Street. This delightful restaurant is located in one of the oldest houses in

Highlands, built in 1880 in a Bavarian style. It is spacious with decks, pavilions, and rooms with fireside seating on cool days. Chef Wolfgang is a former executive chef for the Brennan family of Commander's Palace in New Orleans. He is internationally acclaimed, having won numerous awards, including Chef of the Year in Jamaica and Texas. He·trained in Germany and his background adds freshness and variety to the menu.

Wolfgang's signature soup, a shrimp and lobster bisque, and his crawfish etouffee reflect his New Orleans influence, while the unforgettable Wiener Schnitzel and Rostbraten reflect his German background. To complete your dinner, try the apple strudel, an old family recipe.

Wolfgang's has an extensive wine list (or you may BYOB). There is live music Monday and Thursday nights and a Sunday brunch. It is open at 11:30 A.M., daily, during the season. Reservations are recommended and one check per table is requested. (828) 526-3807. Moderate to expensive.

Birds are lucky critters in the Highlands-Cashiers area, with two **Bird Barns.** Hanging from the ceiling in happy disarray are polished maple bird feeders and squirrel-proof feeders. Birdhouses of all styles, from modern to rustic to Victorian, add to the birder's heaven and a  variety of seed is sure to please any bird's palate. In addition, there is a wide selection of bird-related gift items, including a selection of CDs featuring nature music. Owner Cynthia Strain has been a birder since she received her first pair of binoculars at age nine. She has turned her hobby into a successful business and points out that everything in her shop is made in the U.S.A. Located on Main Street, it is open from 10:00 A.M. to 5:00 P.M., six days a week. (828) 526-3910.

Take time to visit the **Episcopal Church of the Incarnation** on Main Street in downtown Highlands. The church was founded in 1894 and the present church building was completed and dedicated in 1896.

The interior is built of clear chestnut. Before the chestnut tree blight of 1930, these mountains were alive with yellow chestnut tree blossoms in the spring and the brilliant foliage in the fall.

The two brass chandeliers, originally for kerosene, were delivered by ox-cart up the mountain from South Carolina. The beautiful pews are of black walnut and were crafted by Rev. J. T. Kennedy of St. Cyprian's Church in Franklin, North Carolina. The original granite steps are located at the door to the bell tower and the bell is still rung, calling people to worship. Don't miss the Jewell Window in the bell tower—the bottom panel portrays the town of Highlands, including the Church of the Incarnation with its red doors, ministering in the mountains for over a century. Services are held on Sunday and Thursday year round and the church is always open for prayer and meditation. The parish office is open weekdays for you to call about hours for services. (828) 526-2968.

Fond of pearls? Drop into the **House of Lord** at 465 Main Street. Lord's is one of only a few shops in the country to feature rare and magnificent pearls in pale hues of pink, blue, and beige. As you can imagine, these unique jewels are very expensive. Owner Shirley Northrup, a Highlands native, opened Lord's in 1990. She travels the world over several times a year for the beautiful and unusual items in her shop, which is open from 10:00 A.M. to 6:00 P.M., daily, during the season, and from 10:00 A.M. to 5:00 P.M., Monday through Saturday, during winter. (828) 526-9946 or (800) 457-9874.

A spontaneous picnic spread is available at the **Mountain Fresh Market,** 521 Main Street. Since 1986, Mountain Fresh has served locals and visitors with groceries and fresh-baked breads and pies. A deli provides sandwiches, salads, and soups for takeout. There is also a nice selection of wine. It is open from 8:30 A.M. to 7:30 P.M., Monday through Saturday, and from 11:00 A.M. to 5:00 P.M., Sunday. (828) 526-2357. The perfect "picnic-rock spot" is Sunset Rock in Ravenal Park, located only one mile from Highlands.

For outdoor mountain adventures you will need to be outfitted, and in Highlands the place to go is the **Highland Hiker.** There are two stores, one of which is located in a circa-1929 log cabin at 601 East Main Street. Here you will find boating equipment, including canoes. This is also a fly-fishing center with guides, classes, fishing and camping gear, and licenses. (828) 526-0441. The second store is located at 28 Church Street and caters to mountain climbing in a big way. Besides backpacks, footwear, and climbing gear, this store has a $12^1/_2$-foot by 24-foot climbing wall and a belayer who holds the ropes and gives pointers. Both stores are open six days a week and on Sunday afternoon during the season. (828) 526-5298.

Next to golf, fly fishing is the most popular sport in this area. Perhaps more men than women take the fly-fishing courses offered at the Highland Hiker and Brookings Orvis, but according to both shops, women learn faster than men. Instructor Michael Casey of Orvis explained, "It's all timing and finesse and does not require much muscle."

Best place for fly fishing? Chip Sherrill of Highland Hiker believes it is Tuckasegee River because the State Forestry Department regularly stocks two miles of the river; however, he points out that the Chattooga is probably the most scenic.

The most popular fly at Orvis is the "Parachute Adams" and it is guaranteed to catch your limit. A fishing license is required and look carefully for the posted limit of each stream or river. Pleading ignorance of the limit does not impress the local game wardens. Their theory is "If you don't know, don't fish."

The earliest minister at the **First Presbyterian Church** was Rev. A. Melvin Cooper, who arrived in Highlands in 1879. Samuel Kelsey (one of the founders of Highlands) and his wife, Katherine, donated the land for the church. Margaretta Ravenal (the Ravenal family was among the first to have a summer home in Highlands) and her sister Clarissa Burt built the church at their own expense as a memorial to their deceased sister. This building, made of lumber cut from nearby forests, is still used and contains the original pews made of chestnut. The church was dedicated in 1885. This serene place is located on Main Street. You may actually "hear" the church before you see it, for daily the carillon bells ring at 10:00 A.M., 12:00 noon, 3:00 P.M., and 5:00 P.M. Each "miniconcert" lasts for about five minutes (information from Betty Holt's *A History of the First Presbyterian Church*).

Established in 1878, the **Old Edwards Inn** is at Fourth and Main. Over the lobby desk is a sign from the past declaring that there are "19 rooms for ladies and gentlemen." It is listed on the National Register of Historic Places and was thriving when Highlands was still a "frontier" town. There are inviting rocking chairs on the porch and the grounds are a pleasant place for your morning coffee. The **Central House Restaurant** is in the inn and the blue crab soup is memorable. It is open for lunch from 11:00 A.M. to 2:30 P.M. and for dinner from 5:30 to 8:30 P.M., daily The number for both the inn and restaurant is (828) 526-9319.

The **Wild Thyme Gourmet,** 490 Carolina Way, is satisfying in every way. You'll find a tree-shaded courtyard with umbrella tables and a cheerful sun porch where flavorful food is served with efficiency. The luncheon menu may include unusual dishes such as a grilled chicken wrap with artichoke hearts and Kalamata olives or a chèvre cheese sandwich. The soups are heavenly. If it is available, try the cold, light tomato soup topped with crabmeat. Although the service is offered, the Wild Thyme Gourmet is not exactly your average, everyday takeout bistro, but catering is available and it is excellent. Hours are from 11:30 A.M. to 4:00 P.M. for lunch and from 5:30 to 9:30 P.M. for dinner, Wednesday through Saturday, during the season. (828) 526-4035.

Fudge Brownies

4 oz. unsweetened chocolate	¹/₂ cup flour
2 sticks margarine	Dash salt
4 eggs, beaten	1 tsp. vanilla
2 cups sugar	3 tbsp. Kahlua
1¹/₄ cups chopped pecans	

Melt chocolate and margarine together in the microwave, stirring several times. Mix eggs and sugar, then add chocolate mixture, stirring. Add remaining ingredients and pour into a greased 8-inch square pan. Bake at 325 degrees for 30 minutes or until just set. They will be soft in the center. Cool completely before cutting.

—Thanks to the Wild Thyme Gourmet in Highlands

McCulley's, named for one of the owners (a Highlands native), is located at 1 Church Street and is a favorite of locals and tourists. The shop is known for its Scottish cashmere sweaters, as well as its elegant wool, silks, and cottons. This has been a high-end shop for both men and women since 1983. Another specialty is golf wear. It is open from 10:00 A.M. to 5:00 P.M., Monday through Saturday. Winter hours, January through March, are irregular or by appointment. (828) 526-4407 or (800) 526-4407.

Should it be high noon, try the **Highland Hill Deli,** 115 South Fourth Street, which is a quick gourmet sandwich takeout (but there will be a line during high season, as it is a popular spot). The most requested sandwich is the "Highland Hill," with turkey, bacon, avocado, and Havarti cheese. Benches are out front and around the corner on Main Street, so you can rest while you eat. Highland Hill Deli also delivers. It is open from 10:00 A.M. to 10:00 P.M. in summer and from 10:00 A.M. to 5:00 P.M. in winter, daily. (828) 526-9632.

Mirror Lake Antiques, 215 Fourth Street, is an interesting shop for a leisurely browse. Since 1971, it has supplied customers with elusive pieces of sterling silver flatware matching their silver patterns. It is open from 10:00 A.M. to 5:00 P.M., Monday through Saturday, March through December. (828) 526-2080.

Nick's, on Satulah Road, is a good family restaurant where the locals have eaten since 1975. Inside the comfortable, rustic lodge, Nick, the chef, and many of his relatives consistently serve good, fresh food with cheerful efficiency. One of the most popular dishes is the grilled trout with Béarnaise sauce. The trout, raised on a high-protein diet in a mountain-farm lake, are delicious and, incidentally, "good for you." The favorite desserts are an apple-buttermilk pie and Chantilly crepes. Nick's has a good wine list, a children's menu, and a "brown bag" fee for alcohol. It is open for lunch from 11:00 A.M. to 2:30 P.M. and dinner from 5:00 to 9:30 P.M., every day except Wednesday, March to mid-December. (828) 526-2706. Moderate to expensive.

Lakeside Restaurant, on Smallwood Avenue, is a not-to-be-missed place. The fun, whimsical decor will please your eye and the food will please your palate. Aptly named, this small restaurant is situated on the side of pretty Lake Hurris. Owners Marty Rosenfield and Donna Woods opened Lakeside in 1989 after many years of catering in Atlanta. Marty is the major chef and Donna, an artist, decorated the bright, cheerful interior.

The specialty is seafood, so try the local rainbow trout, sauteed in butter, wine, and lemon, or the Maryland crab cakes. If you're a buttermilk pie fan, this is the place for it. There is a brown bag policy for liquor, but wine is available from a quality wine list. You may bring in your own wine, but the corkage fee is substantial. It is open from 11:30 A.M. to 2:00 P.M. for lunch and from 5:30 P.M. until for dinner. No reservations, but there is usually only a short wait. (828) 526-9419.

With picnic basket in hand, head east on Main Street, which becomes Horse Cove Road. On the left is the **Highlands Nature Center and Biological Station,** founded in 1927 and one of the oldest in the country.

At the center, there are programs and lectures for all-age visitors to the Highlands Plateau, renowned for its varied plant and animal life. The center is actually a small nature museum with active bee-hives, bird nests, local plants, animals, and archaeological and geographical exhibits. The friendly, caring staff is frequently nursing injured hummingbirds or orphaned squirrels. The grounds consist of 30 acres of 450 labeled plant and tree specimens planted around Lake Ravenal, where several trails lead visitors through the botanical gardens. The Highlands Nature Center is part of the University of North Carolina and is open from 10:00 A.M. to 5:00 P.M., daily. Winter hours may vary. (828) 526-2623.

Across the street from the center is Ravenal Park and Sunset Rock. The Ravenal family, early Highlands residents from Charleston, South Carolina, donated the land to the city as a recreational park. An extremely bumpy road leads up half a mile, so go slowly whether riding or walking. There is a small parking area and a short path on the right leading to a large outcropping of rock. Here is a magnificent view of Highlands and the southern Blue Ridge Mountains.

About four and a half miles from Highlands is a **giant poplar tree** that you will enjoy seeing. It is located on Rich Mountain Gap, just off Horse Cove Road.

This magnificent poplar is 400 years old and one of the oldest in the country. It is 127 feet high and the girth is 20 feet. The Indians used poplars to make their canoes and what a canoe this tree would have made! At the base is a plaque dedicated to Bob Padgett, a naturalist with the National Park Service, who saved the tree from destruction in 1966.

From the Highlands Nature Center, go 2.1 miles on Horse Cove Road, turn right, and immediately look for the U.S. Forest Service sign on the left. Just across the road are small steps and a short path to the tree.

Deep in the woods, on Horse Cove Road, is the little **Church in the Wildwood,** which holds hymn-sings from 7:00 to 8:00 P.M., Sundays, Memorial Day through Labor Day. The church is located three miles from Highlands. Put your car in low gear when you pass Rich-Gap Road and look on the left for a sign and the church. This small building, built in 1945, served as a community center. In the 1950s, the hymn-sing services began with old-fashioned hymns, a piano, and sometimes a guitar and a banjo. It is nondenominational and, aside from the hymns, there are prayers and a speaker. Singing is always enthusiastic—if sometimes off key—and services are a lovely nostalgic experience.

Richard Guritz Antiques and Interiors, Ltd., 8 Mountain Brook Center, features an eclectic selection of 18th- and 19th-century American and continental antiques. There are also some interesting accessories from the 1920s. Mr. Guritz, a highly regarded decorator with a keen eye for art, represents 80 nationally known portrait artists and carries work of local, regional, and international artists.

Munich, Germany, was home for Richard for 10 years, but he has now put down roots in Highlands. To stock his attractive shop, he makes frequent buying trips to Europe. In-season hours are from 10:30 A.M. to 5:00 P.M., Monday through Saturday, and from 1:00 to 4:00 P.M., Sunday; winter hours are irregular. (828) 526-9680.

During the summer, every other person in Highlands seems to have an ice cream cone. One of the special sources is **Sweet Treats,** located in the Mountain Brook Center. Sweet Treats has a new twist whereby you can make your own creation from 50 or so ice cream and yogurt flavors and you can make some highly pleasing and curious combinations. How about double chocolate, mocha, and raspberry?

Small tables on an outdoor deck look down into Mill Creek with hungry five-pound rainbow trout circling about for treats. Children as well as adults love to feed them and there are several coin-operated machines with fish food. Summer months find Sweet Treats open from 12:00 noon to 9:00 P.M. on weekends and from 12:00 noon to 6:00 P.M. during the week. They are open mainly on weekends in winter. (828) 526-9822 or (800) 350-1786.

There is much more to Highlands than shops and nature activities and visitors might enjoy exploring the cultural aspects of the town: the Highlands-Cashiers Chamber Music Fest, the Bascom-Louise Art Gallery, and the renowned Highland's Playhouse.

Since 1938, the **Highland's Playhouse** has richly entertained residents and visitors with plays and musicals spread over a 10-week period beginning the first of June. The playhouse, built in 1932, is located on Oak Street near the busy intersection of Fourth Street and Main Street, in the old Highlands School Auditorium. The performances are generally popular classic plays featuring Actor's Equity Association members. The playhouse has a significant national reputation and was voted as one of the top 10 playhouses in the country by a national magazine. It is also the second oldest playhouse in North Carolina. The box office opens the first of June at the theater. Tickets can also be reserved by phone. (828) 526-2695.

You will find many of the local and regional artists' work hanging at the **Bascom-Louise Art Gallery,** 554 Main Street. There are some fine artists in the area and this is a worthwhile stop. The nonprofit art center has an active schedule of exhibits, workshops, lectures, and even a film series. It is funded by the Estate of Watson Barratt, a New York theater designer who spent his summers in Highlands. It is named for his wife, Louise, and her parents, the Bascoms, early settlers in Highlands in the 1800s. The gallery shares space with the Hudson Library in a handsome, rustic building. Hours are from 10:00 A.M. to 4:00 P.M., Tuesday through Saturday, April through December. (828) 526-4949.

For music lovers, the **Highlands-Cashiers Chamber Music Fest** holds performances over a six-week period, July through August. In Cashiers, it is usually held in the Albert Carlton Cashiers Library on Grouse Point Road on Monday and Saturday evenings. In Highlands, the fest is held on Sundays and Tuesdays at the Community Baptist Church on Chestnut Street. If world-class string quartets appeal to you, call (828) 526-9060 for tickets or write to Post Office Box 1702, Highlands, North Carolina 28741.

A fine accommodation is the **Kelsey and Hutchinson Lodge** at 450 Spring Street, just a few blocks from Main Street. Named for Highlands' founding fathers, Sam Kelsey and C. C. Hutchinson, the lodge has historic roots. It was built on the site of Lee's Inn, which opened in 1892 and was destroyed by fire in 1983. Today, the lodge has everything a guest could want—35 attractive pine-paneled rooms, most with fireplaces and some with kitchens. Conference rooms and data ports for computers are available. A VIP service is available for your Very Important Pet, with a special "pet package."

An in-house menu is available whereby room service can be ordered from the Wild Thyme, a popular restaurant in Highlands. A long veranda around the lodge makes a very pleasant spot for breakfast, and evening wine with appetizers is served in the comfortable commons area. The location is a perfect place to watch Fourth of July fireworks and all rooms are air-conditioned. Kelsey and Hutchinson is open year round and rates are moderate to expensive, depending on the season. (828) 526-4746. www.k-hlodge.com.

The Elephant's Foot Antiques, at U.S. Highway 64 and Foreman Road, is a must stop if you are in the throes of decorating. European buying sprees as well as consignments provide this shop with a tasteful selection of country French and English antique furniture and accessories. The Elephant's Foot is open from 10:30 A.M. to 5:00 P.M., Monday through Saturday, May to October. (828) 526-5451.

Hanover House Antiques, 802 Fourth Street (U.S. Highway 64 West), is an admirable white frame house built in 1885. For nearly a century it was a private residence, but today it houses a quality collection of English, French, Italian, and American antiques.

Wandering from room to room is a bit like a treasure hunt! One room holds everything blue and white, while another shows off exceptional Majolica. There is a room of primitives—pine furniture, antler plaques, barrels, and baskets. Yet another holds children's clothing and furniture. It all makes for very interesting browsing and buying. It opens at 11:00 A.M., six days a week, and at 1:00 P.M., Sunday. (828) 526-4425.

Antique connoisseurs will be ecstatic over **Toby West Antiques** on U.S. Highway 64 just east of Highlands. It may be a bit pricey, so consider it a trip to a museum of "mountain elegance" as opposed to "mountain rustic." Among many items, you'll find Staffordshire china, English walnut hat and glove forms, and clever antler armchairs covered with bearskin from England. The shop is located in a stately house built in 1895 for Highlands' first chief of police. Seasonal flowers and a spectacular apple tree enhance the yard. Owner and interior designer Toby West lives in Highlands so the shop is open year round, from 10:00 A.M. to 5:00 P.M., Monday through Saturday, and from 12:30 to 5:00 P.M., Sunday. (828) 526-1958.

Alyxandra's is a pleasant ladies' clothing store in a pretty yellow and white cottage on U.S. Highway 64 across the corner from the Highland Falls Country Club. The selection is mainly elegant casual and there is a tempting collection of suits and blouses along with fabulous hand-loomed sweaters. It is open from 10:00 A.M. to 5:00 P.M., six days a week, mid-March through New Year's. (828) 526-4378.

The **Wee Shop,** on U.S. Highway 64 West, is appropriately named. It is indeed a tiny shop stocked with everything Scottish, a strong mountain heritage. Here are traditional kilts, cashmere sweaters and scarves, golf hats, and tartan ties. The shop was originally located in Bournemouth, England, and in 1975 the entire building was shipped intact to the present location. Hours are from 10:00 A.M. to 5:00 P.M., daily, except Tuesday, and from 12:00 noon to 5:00 P.M., Sunday. (828) 526-5357.

Three attractive shops are called the **Apple Mountain Shops. Harold Grant, Inc.** has beautiful Maggie London silk blouses and Anne Crimmons dresses. This shop is for women who like fine sportswear—no blue jeans, designer or otherwise, here! It is closed November to May. (828) 526-0084. **Well Heeled** is a combination clothing and antique store. Most of the antiques are French and there is a nice selection of shoes, cashmeres, and Nicole Miller dresses. (828) 626-8844. **Harold Grant Men's Store** features handsome sports coats. Harold Grant holds a patent on Miracle Slacks with a wonderful expandable waistband—great for vacations. (828) 526-0729. These shops are open from 10:00 A.M. to 5:00 P.M., Monday through Saturday, and most close in winter.

The **Brier-Patch Gifts & Antiques,** on U.S. Highway 64, is a small, white cottage and is one of the most charming gift shops in the mountains, with quality merchandise and good prices. Hours are from 10:00 A.M. to 5:00 P.M., Monday through Saturday, and from 1:00 to 4:00 P.M., Sunday, May through October. (828) 526-4110.

the Brier-Patch
Gifts & Antiques

At the Jackson County-Macon County line, between Cashiers and Highlands, is **Cowee Gap Overlook,** or "The Big View," which is the most famous overlook of the Cashiers Valley. "Cowee," in Cherokee, means "Place of the Deer Clan." Parking is difficult, particularly coming from Highlands, so take care.

On your right is the venerable **Whiteside Mountain,** considered to be the world's most ancient mountain. On the left, rising amidst a breathtaking array of ridges, forests, and valleys, are Chimney Top, Rock Mountain, and Laurel Knob. If you have a sturdy pair of walking shoes and an inclination for a nature hike culminating in another fabulous view, turn off of U.S. Highway 64 onto Wildcat Ridge Road and drive a little over two miles to the Whiteside Mountain Trail, where you will find parking and restrooms.

There are two one-mile trails. One is wide with a gentle slope and the other is more scenic but narrow and difficult. The trails meet at the top, so you may want to go up on the wider one and return on the steeper path. Both trails take you to "Fool's Rock," a flat, table-top rock with a magnificent view. Although difficult to find, an even more spectacular view from the "Devil's Courthouse" is on a short trail to the northern end of the Whiteside summit. Note: There is another Devil's Courthouse on the Blue Ridge Parkway at Milepost 422.4.

The word "mountain" could be relative. People who live in parts of Texas might call a small hill a mountain, while those living in Wyoming would associate the word with high peaks. Generally, geographers and geologists agree that a mountain area is one that is at least 2,000 feet above its surroundings. This kind of region also includes two or more zones of climate and plant life.

The distance between Highlands and Cashiers is only 10 miles, but the serpentine, mountainous U.S. Highway 64 will take twice as long as a flat 10 miles. However, it will not be boring, as there are many pleasant stops to make en route; this means it could take four times as long . . . or more!

Although the **Valley Gift Shop** is small, the selections are large. The shop carries an extensive selection of Portmerion china, including the hard-to-find pattern "Birds of Brittany." It is open from 10:00 A.M. to 5:00 P.M., Monday through Saturday, for most of the year. (828) 743-2944.

For art lovers, the **Whiteside Art Gallery** is a special spot on U.S. Highway 64. The traditional building with a steeple served as the Cashiers Baptist Church for more than a century. It is named for William Whiteside, an art teacher at North Texas University. In addition to works by fine local artists, many of the realistic paintings in this church gallery are William's.

Some interesting commissions have come Whiteside's way from the five paintings he did for Burt Reynolds. One of them is of the Chattooga River, the setting for Burt's well-known movie, *Deliverance*. Whiteside paints in acrylics and egg tempera and teaches classes from May to November. The gallery is open these same months, from 10:00 A.M. to 5:30 P.M., Monday through Saturday, and from 1:00 to 5:30 P.M., Sunday. (828) 743-2269.

To fill out your silver pattern, check out the **Wormy Chestnut** on U.S. Highway 64 West. Owner Charlotte Duval has scads of silver flatware, sterling and plate, but old silver is "her thing." There is a lot more than silver in this quaint building, which served as a country grocery store in the 1930s. Pre-1910 woodworking tools cover half of one wall and there are old prints, furniture, and china. The shop is so named because there was a huge, old wormy chestnut tree on the property when Mrs. Duval opened in 1974. In the 1930s, a blight totally wiped out the big, beautiful chestnut trees so prevalent in the state. She always keeps an eye out for wormy chestnut furniture at auctions and estate sales, mainly around Cocoa Beach, Florida, where she spends the winter. Hours are from 10:00 A.M. to 5:00 P.M., Monday through Saturday, May through October. (828) 743-3014.

In 1819, the early settlers were farmers who tilled crops of cotton and tobacco peacefully with the very first settlers, the Cherokee Indians. Later, local folks had little interest in the Civil War except to avoid the bushwhackers who regularly dragged the men off to battle for either side. Several first-family names you may encounter in the area are the Nortons and the Zacharys, who, in true mountain tradition, shared a lifelong feud. The Zachary house, a handsome Greek Revival frame mansion on U.S. Highway 107, is open for tours.

Cashiers

Cashiers (pronounced CASH-ers) has a population of about 1,500, which blooms to 18,000 in the summer. Much of the annual population explosion are second-home owners attracted to the lush valley of Cashiers with a 3,500-foot elevation, mountain vistas, and a mild, cool climate.

Among the bed and breakfasts in the Cashiers area you'll find two first-rate inns loaded with mountain charm. The **Millstone Inn,** located off of U.S. Highway 64, one mile north of Cashiers, is a "joy forever," with mountain ambience and a friendly, hospitable staff. The inn is situated on a tree-shaded lawn, and Adirondack chairs overlook ancient Whiteside Mountain. Inside are seven rooms and four suites with mountain views and private baths; a few have kitchens. In the warm, inviting living room, a huge millstone, which was found on the property, hangs over the large stone fireplace.

A private residence in the 1930s, the Millstone has been a well-loved inn since 1952. It was voted one of the 12 best inns in the nation by *Country Inn* magazine. A real plus here is the beautiful Silver Slip Falls, only a short hike from the inn. This is an unpublicized waterfall since the only access is through private property. Call well in advance for inn reservations, especially during holiday seasons. Breakfast is included and the inn is not recommended for children. (888) 645-5786. www.Millstoneinn.com.

The Cottage Inn, also built as a family home in 1932, is only half a mile from the Cashiers Crossroads on U.S. Highway 64 East. In addition to four rooms in a main lodge, there are nine rustic small cabins as well as large contemporary A-frames. Almost all of the cottages have fireplaces, decks, kitchens, and cable TV and all are named for the trees surrounding each one. A cozy lobby in the lodge has a stone fireplace, piano, and walls of books. (877) 595-3600. www.cottageinncashiers.com. Rates are moderate depending on the season.

The Crossroads is the one and only intersection of busy U.S. Highways 64 and 107 in Cashiers and it is frequently used as a reference point when giving directions.

The Village Walk is an attractive row of shops behind the Market Basket restaurant on U.S. Highway 107 South. At the southernmost end is the **Bird Barn 'n Garden.** This shop has garden furniture and statuary, as well as everything you need to feed, house, and water your wild birds. Hours are from 10:00 A.M. to 5:00 P.M., Monday through Saturday. (828) 743-3797.

Next door is **The Gem Shop,** with beautiful estate jewelry and a large selection of colored native stones. It has been a fixture in Cashiers since 1952. Hours are from 10:00 A.M. to 5:00 P.M., Tuesday through Saturday, April through December. (828) 743-1074. **Thomas Jacoby Fine Art** is a gallery of handsome works of national as well as local painters and sculptors. It is open from 10:00 A.M. to 5:00 P.M., Monday through Saturday, and afternoons, Sunday, May to November. During the winter, the gallery is open only on weekends. (828) 743-0118. Don't skip the **Bonnie Brae, Ltd.** from Atlanta. This is a pleasant, fragrant shop of aromatherapy, candles, books, linens, and luxurious accessories for the home, open at 10:00 A.M. six days a week. (828) 743-1090.

The **Wild Thyme Gourmet** has fresh-baked breads every morning. An assortment of muffins, scones, bagels, and cinnamon rolls are waiting to be picked up and enjoyed with a steaming cup of coffee.

Lunch brings homemade soups (try the tomato basil) and a variety of sandwiches. Don't forget to take home a few of the decadent dessert pastries to make a perfect ending to your dinner. In fact, if you have come to the mountains to rest and relax, you may want to see more of the Wild Thyme than your kitchen. For special orders and hours, call (828) 743-1065. The original Wild Thyme is located at Fifth Street and Carolina Way in Highlands.

Mountain Slaw

2 pkg. angel-hair slaw	2 tbsp. soy sauce
1 pkg. Ramen noodles, chicken flavor	1 cup sugar
1 pkg. slivered almonds, toasted	$1/2$ cup apple cider
1 cup safflower oil	vinegar

Mix slaw and noodles, breaking up together. Add almonds. Mix oil, soy sauce, sugar, and vinegar. Toss with slaw and refrigerate. Drain before serving. Serves 8-10.

—Mrs. Richard Moore, Sheep Laurel Garden Club, Cashiers

Lyn K. Holloway Antiques, with one of the prettiest gardens in Cashiers, is not to be missed. It is across from the Village Green at the Cashiers Crossroads. The cozy cottage appearance is deceptive as there are 4,500 square feet of space filled with English, French, and American antiques. The charming house was built in 1926 as a private residence. The specialty of the shop is lazy Susan tables, which are becoming increasingly scarce; these are expensive and good quality. It is open from 10:00 A.M. to 5:00 P.M., Monday through Saturday, May to November and Thanksgiving week. (828) 743-2524.

Just across from Lyn K. Holloway Antiques is **Gallery On The Green.** This modest shop was once a small barn with a tiny cottage added. The big surprise inside are the antique prints and engravings—thousands of them—French, English, German, and American. On one wall is an extremely rare, large, copperplate engraving of Karnak's Gate, commissioned by Napoleon after his Egyptian campaign in 1810. There are antique oils and watercolors, many of them by artists listed with auction records. Hours are from 10:00 A.M. to 5:00 P.M., Monday through Saturday, March through November. Call for winter hours. (828) 743-3068.

Captivating is the word to describe **The Not All Country Store.** This antique shop is on U.S. Highway 107 South. Inside this simple tin-roofed house you'll find some elegant pieces of Rose Medallion, Majolica china, and French, English, and American antique furniture. There are also rich decorative accessories to enhance a mountain home as well as a formal townhouse. Owners Runel and Victoria Thompson have called Cashiers home since they opened the shop in the early 1980s. They travel hither and yon to auctions and estate sales to furnish the shop. Hours are from 10:00 A.M. to 5:00 P.M., Monday through Saturday. (828) 743-3612.

Rusticks sits in a snug cul-de-sac with a peaceful lake behind it. Owners Anne and Rody Sherrill have put together groups of tasteful furnishings for mountain homes. Rusticks' main appeal is the beautiful, handmade furniture, in traditional mountain designs, that will stand the test of time. Quality always comes at a price and Rusticks is not cheap; however, for what you get, it's a bargain. It is located just off Highway 107 on Valley Road. Store hours are from 10:00 A.M. to 5:00 P.M., Tuesday through Saturday. (828) 743-3172.

Although you may buy your food in a grocery store, you may never have eaten dinner in one until you try **The Market**

Basket, located on U.S. Highway 107 South, near the Crossroads. In the 1980s, this was a grocery store specializing in gourmet foods and condiments. Later, tables were placed among the shelves and a popular restaurant was born. The shelving, with condiments, sauces, etc., is still there, but now dinner is served nightly, except on Wednesday, and with a different twist—Hot Rocks. Should you choose from the Hot Rock menu, you will be provided with a heated slab of North Carolina granite on which you can cook marinated chicken, shrimp, filet, or a combination; otherwise, there is a regular menu of seafood, steaks, and pasta dishes.

One of the main attractions at The Market Basket is Cy Timmons, who sings and plays his guitar Thursday through Saturday nights. In the past, he has entertained at major restaurants in San Francisco, Los Angeles, and Atlanta and has been the opening act for stars such as Joan Rivers and Peter Nero. Cy is a well-loved entertainment figure in the area. You may BYOB. Dinner is served from 6:00 to 10:00 P.M. Reservations are recommended, especially during the season. (828) 743-2216.

One of the most popular shops in Cashiers is the **Basket Works,** on U.S. Highway 107 South. If it looks like a log cabin, that's because it is. Actually, it is two pre-Civil War cabins that were moved from Tennessee to Cashiers in the late 1980s; they were reconfigured and became the Basket Works. Now, under the ownership of Connie and David Thompson, the log cabins house a fascinating clutter of old stone and marble bowls, Southern antiques, dried flowers, Turkish rugs, and old botanical prints. The Thompsons also make and sell lamps. Every inch of the log and mortar walls is covered with rustic art and whimsical treasures for inside or outside. This is a mountain shop at its best. It is open from 10:00 A.M. to 6:00 P.M., daily, during the season. Call for hours in the winter. (828) 743-5052.

Next door to the Basket Works and down in a small hollow is the **Book & Specialty Shop.** Since 1981 this quaint, blue frame structure has housed rare, used, and new books. The specialty is out-of-print books, but Civil War and World War II buffs will have a field day as there are shelves brimming with books pertaining to these two wars and their military leaders. Owner Else Young has been in the book business since 1940. Her love of books is evident as the shop is neat as a pin, with books dusted and old dust jackets mended. During the winter months, Mrs. Young attends auctions and buys books. She also admires and specializes in Southern authors. Hours are from 10:00 A.M. to 5:00 P.M., Monday through Saturday, May through October. (828) 743-9930.

Book & Specialty Shop

One of the most popular restaurants in Cashiers is **Cornucopia** on U.S. Highway 107 South. It has been pleasing the palates of local folks and tourists since 1979. Owner and chef Scott Peterkin says, "People say they travel a long way just for our crab cakes." They are definitely worth the trip, but so is the Chicken à la Orange. For dessert, try the well-loved Vanilla Buttermilk Pie. This family restaurant is mainly outdoor dining with umbrella tables. A children's menu is available. The service is consistently cheerful and you may bring your own spirits. Lunch is served from 11:00 A.M. to 2:30 P.M. and dinner is served from 6:00 to 9:00 P.M. There are no reservations for lunch and there is usually a short line in the summer. Reservations are recommended for dinner. (828) 743-3750.

People who live in Cashiers say **Tommy's** is strictly a local place where everyone in town goes for breakfast and lunch. In truth, Tommy's is also filled with tourists who know a good thing when they see it. This family-owned restaurant has been in business since 1960, with Irona Madden, now in her eighties, taking care of things as she did when the restaurant first opened.

You cannot find a better country breakfast; every egg is perfect, the ham and bacon are never greasy, the hash browns are good, and the biscuits are lighter than air. The restaurant serves up a good plate lunch with meat, two veggies, and dessert. It is easy to find—being dead center in Cashiers. Hours are from 6:30 to 11:00 A.M. for breakfast and from 11:00 A.M. to 3:00 P.M. for lunch. (828) 743-2010.

While planning to actively enjoy the spectacular great outdoors of the Cashiers-Highlands region, you will want to check in with the **Highland Hiker,** located on the corner of U.S. Highways 64 East and 107 South. This is where you can get all your gear for hiking, biking, backpacking, and mountain climbing. The most popular hiking trails in Cashiers are Horsepasture and Whiteside Mountain, and Highland Hiker carries the tried and true Vasque boot for comfy feet along the paths. Maps are available as well as all kinds of outdoor clothing. Specialties of the shop are bicycles and accessories, in particular Trek and Kona. Hours are from 9:00 A.M. to 5:30 P.M., summer, and from 10:00 A.M. to 5:00 P.M., winter. (828) 743-1731 and (828) 743-1668.

You haven't been to Cashiers if you haven't been to **Cashiers Farmer's Market,** located on U.S. Highway 64 East, right "smack" at the Crossroads. This is a fun stop with all the essence of the mountains. On the side of the walkway to the rustic frame building is a pen that is home to "Biscuit," a miniature pot-bellied pig. She has been a family member of the owners, Tom and Robin Crawford, since 1994.

Inside you'll find fresh fruits and vegetables and, during the summer, freshly frozen shelled peas and beans. On one side are shelves of preserves, jams, jellies, relishes, and sauces (try the blueberry preserves). Don't miss the carrot-pineapple bread or the walnut bread from Annie's Bakery in Franklin, which arrives on Fridays. On Saturday afternoons in the summer, the Farmer's Market occasionally serves old-fashioned, homemade, hand-cranked ice cream, usually with fresh peach syrup. Sinfully good! Hours are from 10:00 A.M. to 5:00 P.M., Monday through Saturday, and from 10:00 A.M. to 4:00 P.M., Sunday, April to Thanksgiving. (828) 743-4334.

Peach Preserves

4 cups peeled, diced peaches	1 pkg. Sure-Jell pectin
$1/2$ cup water	5 cups sugar
1 tbsp. lemon juice	1 block paraffin

Combine peaches, water, lemon juice, and Sure-Jell. Stir constantly while heating. Add sugar, bring to a hard boil, and stir for 5 to 7 minutes. Remove from stove and place pot in sink of cold water. Stir till cool. Pour into sterilized jars. Pour melted paraffin on top of cooled preserves. Boil lids, put hot lids on jars, and seal. Makes 6 8-oz. jars and will keep for a year.

—Faye Stewart, Cashiers

For fresh, tasty takeout lunches or dinners, try **The Chopping Block,** located down a bumpy little lane, off of U.S. Highway 107 North just past the Crossroads. It's tricky to find; look for the sign on the highway. Owner Bruce Cain is a former chef from Florida and a "foodie" from way back. He will prepare almost any meal according to your specifications, but the most popular orders are for his lasagna, stuffed chicken breasts, and beef stroganoff. You'll also find excellent meats, fish, beautiful shrimp, and a variety of good cheeses as well as a nice selection of gourmet goodies. Don't overlook the bread, especially the small, well-seasoned Boule breads. Hours are from 10:00 A.M. to 6:00 P.M., Monday through Saturday, during the season. Bruce plans to stay open most of the year but call ahead. (828) 743-5355.

For a novel dining experience, try **Ezekiel's Barn** on U.S. Highway 107, just north of the Crossroads. It is very much like eating in a friend's house and you'll feel as though you know the owners/chef team, Doug and Debbie Wilgus.

There is only one sitting, with set prices, at 7:00 P.M., Thursday, Friday, and Saturday. Reservations are required and dress is casual, although the waiters are in black tie and the tables are on the formal side. Dinner music is from an old-fashioned player piano, while between courses several waiters sing, including Doug. There is even a game played during the meal and the two-hour dining time flies. Attractive chef Debbie competently masterminds the five-course meal (when you call for reservations they will tell you what's for dinner). You may "bring your own" and set-ups are available. (828) 743-0185. Expensive, but well worth it.

Cashiers Commons on U.S. Highway 107 North, just past the Crossroads, includes several appealing shops. **Zoeller's Hardware** is a large, enticing store where, on entering, the men peel off to the left for nuts, bolts, tools, or paint, while the women gravitate to the right, where there is china, glassware, and kitchenware. This store has something for everyone, including bird feeders, handmade rockers, and duck decoys. Hours are from 8:00 A.M. to 6:00 P.M., Monday through Friday, and to 5:00 P.M., Saturday. (828) 743-5001.

Next door in this shopping compound is the **Cottage Walk,** a sophisticated store with English antiques as well as reproductions. You'll also find great-looking Italian ceramic bowls, ceramic fruit, antler candlesticks, and lamps. Hours are from 9:00 A.M. to 5:00 P.M., six days a week. (828) 743-6728.

Directly across the lane is **Southern Hands,** known mainly for the wooden bear figures, which are made in Big Sky, Montana. The shop carries the beautiful, heirloom furniture of D. R. Dimes from New Hampshire, colorful Gail Pittman china from Mississippi, handsome chimes made from scuba-diving tanks, and much, much more. Hours are from 10:00 A.M. to 5:00 P.M., Monday through Saturday. (828) 743-5499.

Just next door, in the same rustic frame building, is the **Enchanted Bear,** where the owner does chainsaw woodcarvings of . . . you guessed it . . . bears. Here also is silver Indian jewelry and salt-glazed pottery. It is open from 9:00 A.M. to 6:00 P.M., Monday through Saturday. (828) 743-2083.

You should be advised that Cashiers, like quite a few of the towns in Western North Carolina, is dry and spirits are not served in restaurants nor can they be purchased in the area. Most of the cafés and restaurants have a "brown bag" license, which means you may BYOB. For a small fee, the establishments will provide you with either appropriate set-ups or corkage. It is best to inquire ahead.

Happ's Place, on U.S. Highway 107 just north of Cashiers, is the place to go if you've got the *hungries*. Owner Darrell Happ opens for dinner daily plus brunch on Sunday. Happ's is known for fresh seafood specials, country fried steak, chicken livers, and frog legs. The vegetable choices are limitless and if you are there when berries are in season, order the homemade cobbler. Remember, no alcohol can be served in Cashiers, so bring your own. The prices are moderate and the food is great. (828) 743-2266.

In the Glenville community, stop at a little shop called **Main Street Shop,** located at 5071 U.S. Highway 107. The bear carvings here are better than average and are artistically carved by Randy Whaley of Tennessee. Also of note are the handsome, handmade lamps of polished tree slabs with copper shades. The prints of intricate paper-cutting art are quite reasonable. Some of the tables and chests look ancient, but they are locally handcrafted and can be ordered to size. This is open from 11:00 A.M. to 5:00 P.M., Monday through Saturday, and afternoons, Sunday. (828) 743-2437.

On U.S. Highway 107, just north of town, is **Lake Glenville**, the largest lake in the high-country area and, at 3,100 feet above sea level, the highest lake in the Eastern United States. This beautiful lake was built by the Nantahala Power Company in 1941. Take the 20-mile drive around the lake for some of the most breathtaking vistas of the southern Blue Ridge Mountains.

You should enjoy exploring Chestnut Square on U.S. Highway 64 East, just past the Crossroads. This is a pleasant, shady area with a pretty pond and attractive shops. You can recognize **Brookings Orvis** by a life-sized bear in the window. Inside you'll find the famous Orvis fly-fishing rods and a multitude of flies to whet the appetite of any fish. There is also shooting equipment: Browning, Filson, and Orvis, and appropriate apparel. Notice the dog beds and custom engraved collars for your pooch. Fly-fishing schools, guide services, and fishing licenses are available. Shop hours are from 10:00 A.M. to 5:00 P.M., Monday through Saturday. Orvis is open year round, but call for hours during January and February. (828) 743-3768.

The Victorian frame house with a garden bench set among the flowers is **Wild Possessions.** Owner Jill Lewis moved here from St. Croix, where she was an interior designer. In one room, a Victorian parlor heater shares space with vintage hats and antler chandeliers. This is an entertaining shopping spot for men as well as women. Frequently, gentlemen, after looking around, will find the rocking chairs on the pleasant front porch. Hours are from 10:00 A.M. to 5:00 P.M., Monday through Saturday, and from 12:00 noon to 5:00 P.M., Sunday. It is closed Sunday during the winter. (828) 743-1111. Other shops in the complex include the Vogue Shop and Burgess.

Cashiers is lucky to have **Horacio's Restaurant** in Chestnut Square on U.S. Highway 64. This pine-paneled intimate restaurant is cozy and comfortable. Chef and owner Horacio, from Genoa, Italy, claims his signature dish is rack of lamb with caramelized fruit, but he usually specializes in seafood and game. Service is prompt, with Mrs. Horacio adding charm to the efficiency. Hours are from 5:30 to 9:00 P.M., six days a week. Call for off-season hours. Reservations are suggested. (828) 743-2792. Expensive, but worthwhile, and remember to BYOB.

For that magic carpet, look into **Bounds Cave,** 307 U.S. Highway 64 East. Here you'll find all types of rugs imported from various countries. Most of them are orientals—antique and new. If your special rug is not there, owner Judy Brown, an interior decorator, and partner Mark Petrancosta will tap their sources to locate it for you. There are also tapestries and accessories. It is open from 10:00 A.M. to 6:00 P.M., six days, and from 1:00 to 4:00 P.M., Sunday. Call for winter hours. (828) 743-5393.

In 1876, Rev. John Archibald Deal arrived in this area as the first missionary of the Episcopal Church in Western North Carolina. Two years later, with the support of Gen. Wade Hampton, he founded a mission church in Cashiers. Sadly, in 1892 the building was destroyed by fire. A new church was finished in 1895 and it is the present **Church of the Good Shepherd,** the

oldest church structure in Cashiers. The church was restored in 1920 and in 1979 winter services began.

When summer attendance strained the capacity of the church, a Sunday service was begun in cooperation with the Church of the Incarnation in Highlands. Services are held at the old (circa-1918) schoolhouse on Whiteside Cove Road. It is called the **Summer Chapel** and offers another venue of worship more in keeping with the mountain tradition. A gospel band plays old-time music and services are casual. What began over a century ago as a mission outpost beside a dusty dirt road has grown and prospered, reflecting the era of pioneers and early summer residents. The Church of the Good Shepherd is located on U.S. Highway 107 across from the High Hampton Inn and Country Club. (828) 743-2359.

Possibly the most notable and historic landmark in the Cashiers Valley is the High Hampton Inn and Country Club. The history of the property is interesting, as the early owners were colorful characters who figured prominently in the development of our country.

The land was originally purchased by Wade Hampton II in 1845 from Cashiers' first settler, Col. John A. Zachary. The Hamptons, a large aristocratic family from Columbia, South Carolina, built a seven-bedroom "cottage" with various outbuildings on the property. The son, Wade Hampton III, a Confederate general-hero, was governor of South Carolina and served in the U.S. Senate. Today he is listed in the *Guinness Book of World Records* for having killed 86 bears using only a hunting knife—a true mountain man! Wade was an ardent fisherman and early conservationist.

Hampton's niece, Caroline, and her husband, Dr. William Halsted, purchased the property in 1890 and named it "High Hampton." Dr. Halsted planted many unusual specimens of shrubs and trees as well as acres of prizewinning dahlias, which remain a tradition at High Hampton today. Many of Dr. Halsted's trees are still spectacular and designated as national champions. Look for the beautiful and famous Fraser fir, considered the world's largest. In 1922, the estate was sold to Mr. E. L. McKee, a North Carolina industrialist. His son, William McKee, is the current owner and the manager is Will McKee, Jr.

The **High Hampton Inn and Country Club** was built in 1933, using the now extinct chestnut bark shingle siding. A long, wraparound porch with rocking chairs adds to the charm of the lodge. Inside, a great double stone fireplace sits in the center of the huge paneled lobby. High Hampton is frank to say that their accommodations are not plush and are not for everyone. There are no phones or televisions in the 117 rooms; however, guests are fond of it simply because nothing changes. Certainly the 1,400 acres are lovely with rolling green lawns dominated by Rock Mountain and Chimney Top. A 35-acre lake reflects the mountains and trees and is surrounded by a moderate to easy one-mile nature trail.

The hilly, scenic golf course is not difficult and is ideal for golfers with average handicaps. High Hampton has a myriad of activities during the season such as a literary conference, artists' workshops, and bridge tournaments. The rates are reasonable, and High Hampton is child friendly with available babysitters. Coat and tie are required for dinner and there is no tipping. (800) 334-2551. www.highhamptoninn.com.

Granite City is an awesome collection of boulders as large as a small house. This strange outcropping is thought to have been caused by an early earthquake. The climb up to Granite City is about a quarter-mile over rhododendron roots and rocks. The access is moderately strenuous, depending on one's age and agility. Watch out for snakes! From Cashiers, take Whiteside Cove Road, off U.S. Highway 107, for approximately 1.2 miles. Look for a small clearing on the north side of the road. You will see a path, but there is no sign, so look carefully.

Pick a rock spot and open your picnic on the banks under the old **Iron Bridge.** This is a peaceful and interesting landscape with easy paths, rocks, pools, and shimmering currents, which become strong rapids downriver. From Cashiers, take U.S. Highway 107 South; take Whiteside Cove Road and then the primitive Bull Pen Road.

Whitewater Road provides access to wonderful waterfalls. Some are easy to reach; others are more difficult. The entrance to the falls is north of the Horsepasture River Bridge. **Drift Falls** and **Turtleback Falls** are the easiest to reach. Turtleback cascades over a huge flat rock down to a deep pool. **Rainbow Falls** is the most spectacular, with a good railing where you can view or photograph with ease. The trail to **Stairstep Falls**, a series of cascades that resembles steps, is more difficult. Be sue to wear appropriate shoes as the trail is slippery.

Whitewater Falls are the highest falls in eastern North America, boasting a height of 411 feet. These thundering falls are worth a trip and are quite accessible with well-maintained trails and lookout stations. There are many stops, but take them at your own pace and enjoy.

From Cashiers, the falls can be reached from U.S. Highway 107 or by taking U.S. Highway 64 east to Whitewater Road, near the North Carolina-South Carolina state line. Other falls off Whitewater Road are Drift, Horsepasture, and Rainbow.

Some restaurants are established as private clubs or sports clubs and are therefore licensed to serve a full bar. This is the case with **Martines,** located just off of U.S. Highway 107 South, in the middle of Cashiers. With tennis courts on the property, it is considered to be a racquet club. This is an attractive, fairly formal restaurant featuring a varied menu of continental cuisine. It is open from 6:00 to 10:00 P.M. (828) 743-3838.

Micas Restaurant, 4001 U.S. Highway 64 West, just next to the Sapphire Valley Country Club, offers a fully stocked bar. This is the largest restaurant in the area and can seat 300 people inside as well as outside on a deck. Micas is a lively spot with a band on Saturday nights and karaoke on Wednesday and Friday nights. There is also a large room designated as "O'Connell's Pub" with a bar and television. Proprietor Jack O'Connell is a strong military supporter and there is a colorful shelf of hats representing all branches of the armed services.

An added attraction to Micas is a small shop next to the restaurant that sells wine and a large selection of cold beer to go. Simply pay $1 for membership and make your purchases. Micas is open from 11:30 A.M. to 3:00 P.M. for lunch and at 5:00 P.M. for dinner. (828) 743-5740.

Sapphire

If you live or visit in Sapphire, the **Mountain Lilly Restaurant** should be one of your stops for just plain good, fresh, flavorful food. The menu is not large but is tastefully varied—perfect prime rib, moist roasted chicken with a crispy crust, Maryland-style crab cakes, or pan-seared trout with lemon-butter and capers. The Mountain Lilly, named for a 19th-century mountain-river steamboat, also offers a tempting selection of fried seafood. Be aware that there are large, luscious chocolate chip and macadamia cookies lying in wait to tempt you on the way out.

Proprietor Carol Hewitt and her husband, the talented chef, have decades of experience in the restaurant business and the staff is friendly and efficient. There is a full bar and a small wine list but you may bring your own for a corkage or set-up fee. It is open at 5:30 P.M., Thursday through Tuesday, April through October. (828) 883-3546.

Lake Toxaway

During the late 1800s and early 1900s, E. H. Jennings recognized the recreational potential of the area and established the Toxaway Company, which became responsible for the lavish resorts in the area, the most notable of which was the Toxaway Inn. The company was also responsible for the construction of the earthen dam that created Lake Toxaway.

This lavish, six-story inn opened in 1903 but in 1916 a devastating flood cracked the dam and badly damaged the inn. In 1960, Reg Heintish, Sr., decided to restore the area and formed the Lake Toxaway Company. The dam was rebuilt, the lake was restored, and in 1963 the Lake Toxaway Country Club and golf course were built.

The need for a superb, small inn became apparent and, in 1984, Reg and friend Tim Lovelace spotted the stately old Moltz home. Lovelace acquired the property and began extensive renovations. The result was the **Greystone Inn,** which opened in July of 1985 and was listed on the National Register of Historic Places the same year.

The mansion, with its beautiful flagstone veranda overlooking the lake, has small, standard, and luxury bedrooms decorated with antiques and period reproductions. The Hillmont, a separate structure, contains 12 spacious and luxurious rooms. Each room has a view of the lake and a balcony, fireplace, and wet bar. The newer Lakeside Suites are two private suites with mountain views.

Greystone Inn is exclusive and expensive. Daily tariffs are based on double occupancy and include fine dining at the Lakeside Dining Room (breakfast and dinner), a champagne cruise, and complimentary golf at selected times. The inn has received the AAA Four Diamond Award every year since 1985. In 1992, it received the nation's Ten Best Inns award. (828) 966-4700 or (800) 824-5766.

www.greystoneinn.com.

October's End Restaurant, located at 115 Highway 64 West, Lake Toxaway, can be a welcome sight—if you don't pass it. It is located on the right, in the bend of a significant curve, heading east on U.S. Highway 64. A screened-in dining area offers a pleasant spot to dine, seven days a week, from April until "October's end."

Owner Alex Forth has been in the restaurant business since the 1970s and knows how to please customers with good food and good service. At lunch, the pizza or an Italian sub is a good choice, unless you're craving a good hamburger with fries. The dinner menu offers a nice variety of entrees, specializing in Italian dishes. It is open for lunch and dinner, with takeout available. (828) 966-9226.

Just next door is **Maxine's Mountain Gifts,** 115 Highway 64 West. The porch and walkways are running over with baskets, birdhouses, and assorted garden art. Inside, the small shop is filled with local crafts such as button dolls, clocks from Brevard, and wooden toys. On the far end of the front porch, Maxine has a cooler with fresh cut flowers. Shop hours are from 10:00 A.M. to 6:00 P.M., seven days a week, April through November. (828) 966-4847.

www.maxinesmountaingifts.com.

Earthshine Mountain Lodge is a great place for "family camp." Settled in the midst of the Blue Ridge Mountains in the Toxaway resort area, this rustic lodge can accommodate small conference groups or large family groups. The one-and-a-half story, hand-built, cedar log lodge sits on a 1900 homestead and is furnished with log beds covered with handmade quilts. Rockers are in front of large stone fireplaces. The lodge has 10 rooms, each with a private bath and some with sleeping lofts, and Sunrise Cottage has three suites with private baths.

Real adventure awaits in the form of trail rides across the ridges, hiking, sliding on Earthshine's own "mini-Sliding Rock," evening campfires, a climbing wall, a high ropes course, and a zip line course. Rates are reasonable and include three meals, plus taxes and gratuities. There is a two-night minimum. (828) 862-4207.

www.earthshinemtnlodge.com.

Salmonid Farms is a 34-acre beauty. Located near Lake Toxaway, these stocked fishing ponds are popular places for family fun. No licenses are required. One pond is stocked with brook trout and another with rainbow trout (you pay by the pound).

There is a large picnic area and two miles of trails. You can also get postcards and some souvenirs. It is open from 12:00 noon to 5:00 P.M., daily. Call for other hours and directions. (828) 966-4604 or (828) 877-4589.

Twin Streams Bed & Breakfast is located two miles from U.S. Highway 64 West on Twin Ponds Lane on 11 wooded acres, dense with rhododendron and mountain laurel, and with hiking trails for you to explore. Each of the three guest rooms is located on a different level and all have a private bath and private covered deck overlooking a cascading mountain stream. The sound of the water flowing over rocks makes for a unique and restful atmosphere.

Aside from the privacy of the rooms, innkeepers Paul and Celeste Thorington have created a casual place where you can read quietly by the fire in the great room or enjoy watching birds and woodland creatures from the main deck, which overlooks the pond. Another big attraction to Twin Streams is the gourmet breakfast prepared each morning by Celeste—Peaches and Cream French Toast or Cheese Grits Souffle along with creative egg dishes, home-baked breads, and seasonal fresh fruits. No pets, or children under 12, and smoking is restricted to outside grounds. (828) 883-3007. www.brevardnc.com/twinstreams.

St. Andrews-by-the-Lake is an open-air chapel, in the midst of beautiful woods, just off U.S. Highway 281 North. When you enter the church through the only standing wall, you face the altar with a large cross standing on a single beam. With the natural surroundings providing a backdrop and the birds providing the music, it is a special place to worship. The church is nondenominational and rotates ministers each Sunday. Services usually begin around June 1. A schedule is posted denoting speakers.

The church is not easy to find, so a recon the day before is advised. Turn north off U.S. Highway 64 at the intersection with U.S. Highway 281 North, drive two miles, and look for the second dirt drive past Lake Toxaway Realty.

In September of 1999, **Gorges State Park** was dedicated; this is North Carolina's newest state park. Located in Transylvania County on the North Carolina-South Carolina state line, the park has 10,000 acres of Jocassee Gorges, a 7,000-acre park, and a 3,000-acre game land to be managed by the Wildlife Resources Commission. Plans for a parking area and public restrooms, along with a few picnic tables, are in place for the near future. Hiking is allowed, although there are no marked trails, just old logging roads. You can hike to Rainbow Falls; for directions, contact the interim park office on U.S. Highway 64 at the intersection with U.S. Highway 281 South. It is open from 8:00 A.M. to 5:00 P.M., Monday through Saturday. (828) 966-9099.

Yearning for a personally caught, fresh trout dinner? Stop off at the **Morgan Mill Trout Fishing Resort,** a few miles west of Brevard on U.S. Highway 64. Look for the sign high up on the highway at the corner of U.S. Highway 64 West and Morgan Mill Road.

Since 1984, the mill has raised trout for local restaurants. Two ponds are restocked daily and are available for public fishing. A small fee is charged for poles and bait, which is corn; however, fresh, wriggling worms are available if you prefer. The average weight of fish caught is about one and one-half pounds, but the more wary fish have been in these ponds for years and some weigh up to eight pounds.

You are almost guaranteed fish; but should you miss one, by all means take home the smoked trout dip, which is scrumptious! This is a pleasant, clean place with willow trees and picnic tables surrounding the ponds. Your catch can be cleaned for a fee. Some say the fish bite better in cool weather and in the early mornings. A fishing license is not required. It is open from 8:00 A.M. to 6:00 P.M., six days a week, and from 1:00 to 6:00 P.M., Sundays. (828) 884-6823.

The **Morgan Mill General Store,** 201 Morgan Mill Road, is behind the trout farm. This is the source for the famous stoneground grits, cornmeal, bread flour, and pancake and biscuit mixes that are served in the restaurants and sold in many of the stores. Hours are irregular. (828) 862-4048.

Golf Courses

This golf course information is courtesy of Journal Communications, Inc.:

Mill Creek Golf Course. Located five miles west of Franklin. Golfers like these challenging elevations and rolling hills. This 18 hole, par 72, is open year round. (828) 524-6458 or (800) 533-3916. www.mcgolfresort.com.

CHAPTER 11

Brevard

"Transylvania" comes from the Latin, meaning "over the trees" or "across the woods." Transylvania County was settled by Scottish-Irish immigrants in the 1800s. Many of the original settlers were farmers and much of what is now forest land used to be farmland. A rail line built near the turn of the 20th century brought wealthy visitors to vacation at Lake Toxaway and carried timber to the area's sawmills (this information from the *Transylvania Times*). The name Brevard was chosen as a tribute to Ephraim Brevard, an officer in the Revolutionary War and a citizen of renown. There were seven brothers in the Brevard family, all heroes of the Revolution. Ephraim was a medical doctor who helped to establish Queens College in Charlotte.

Brevard Little Theater, the official community theater of Transylvania County, is the resident community theater company at Brevard

College. It was founded in 1935 by a local schoolteacher, Beulah May Zachary, who later became producer of the children's television show, "Kukla, Fran and Ollie." Although the theater was disbanded during World War II, it began again in 1949 under the direction of Robroy Farquhar, the founder of the Flat Rock Playhouse.

Performances are usually Tuesday through Saturday evenings and Sunday afternoons. To get on the mailing list, write to Brevard Little Theater, Post Office Box 544, Brevard, North Carolina 28712. For reservations, call (828) 884-2587.

It is a little spooky to spot a white squirrel perched high above you on a limb, but this rare species is frequently seen on the High Hampton golf course in Cashiers as well as in the woods around Brevard. The local residents cherish these beautiful critters and in 1986 the Brevard City Council unanimously passed an ordinance establishing Brevard as a sanctuary for the white squirrel. Apparently the native gray and brown squirrels are immune to the charms of the white ones, as definite hostility between the species has been observed. Therefore, spotted or striped squirrels are not likely!

O. P. Taylor's is every child's dream—even a grown-up kind of child. Don't be in a hurry when you visit, because every inch of this two-story shop is packed with clothing, gifts, and toys, toys, toys. Stuffed animals hang from the ceiling (on nice days they often hang in the trees outside!) and there are special rooms with trains, model cars, and airplanes. Big floor puzzles and games for *all* ages, fabulous costumes, and even clothes for Beanie Babies are tucked around and over the stairs and shelves.

Little sitting and playing nooks with child-sized tables and chairs are tempting. There is a huge selection of yo-yos as well as Russian nesting dolls and matchbox cars, and the puppets are wonderful. In addition, there is a fabulous selection of expensive but authentic pewter toy soldiers, which will appeal to any age collector. If you are looking for a particular item, chances are you'll find it here. O. P. Taylor's, located at 2 South Broad Street, is open at 10:00 A.M., Monday through Saturday, and at 1:00 P.M., Sunday. (828) 883-2309 or (800) 500-TOYS.

Main Street in the "Heart of Brevard" is filled with interesting stores, and antique shops abound. One of particular interest is the **Open Door Antique Mall** at 15 West Main Street. Greg and Sandy Wagner buy and sell antiques and collectibles. The selection of antique fishing tackle, old records, and books is noteworthy, while classic table-top books are in good condition and go for a fair price. The mall is open from 10:00 A.M. to 5:00 P.M., daily, and from 1:00 to 5:00 P.M., Sunday (but closed Sunday, January to May). (828) 883-4323.

The Fine Arts and Crafts Co-Op, at 7 East Main Street, has 20 local artists who are juried and participate in staffing the gallery. Besides painting and photography, there is a little bit of everything—baskets woven with feathers, paper lanterns, and vivid fabric art. Somewhat unusual are the hand-wrought copper and brass light fixtures and cabinet hardware by metal artist Joe Cooper, who went from pipe welding on oil platforms in the Gulf of Mexico to an art studio in Brevard. It is open from 10:00 A.M. to 5:00 P.M., six days a week. (828) 877-4437.

It may be unusual to discover an exceptional seafood restaurant in a small town in the mountains, but **Falls Landing,** 23 East Main Street, is just that. For lunch, the crab cake on an onion roll is excellent, and a fine choice for dinner would be mahi-mahi, blackened or grilled, and served with Myers rum glazed bananas. Now to confuse the issue, just as good is the trio of lamb chops with ancho chili butter or porterhouse pork chops with mango chutney glaze and a baked, spiced apple. Yum yum.

Proprietor Mike Young has owned a restaurant in St. John and chef Luca Bettini is from Italy; together they give an international flavor to this interesting restaurant. Mike says, "Try it, you'll like it!" So true. A full bar is available. Lunch is served from 11:00 A.M. to 3:00 P.M., Monday through Saturday, and dinner is served from 5:30 to 10:00 P.M., Tuesday through Saturday. Reservations are appreciated. (828) 884-2835.

Chef Mike's Fish "Recipes"
Rainbow Trout Filets

Dip filets in lemon-butter sauce. Dredge in flour seasoned with garlic, salt, and pepper. Saute in butter, 5 minutes each side. Heat chopped pecans and walnuts in bourbon. Pour over fish and pop on a plate.

Atlantic Salmon

Pan sear filets in margarine. Top with fresh ground ginger mixed with soy sauce. Serve.

On most days, people are lined up by 9:30 A.M. in front of **Bracken Mountain Bakery,** at 34 South Broad, enjoying the fragrance while waiting for the bread to come out of the oven. At 11:30 A.M. another group collects for the second oven opening. These mouth-watering breads and pastries are made from organically grown, stoneground flour milled in Graham, North Carolina. The bread contains no preservatives and, although the bakery will slice the bread for you, it is recommended that you slice as you eat to retain freshness.

There are a few tables for enjoying the delicious pastries and scones with your coffee. The most "in demand" breads are the Vidalia onion and cheese bread, the Greek olive flat bread, and the Striata made with Provolone cheese, garlic, and oregano. Keep in mind that eager customers call owners Bill and Debbie Tellman to reserve their favorites. It is open from 8:30 A.M. to 5:00 P.M., Monday through Friday, and from 9:00 A.M. to 5:00 P.M., Saturday. It is open only Tuesday through Friday in the winter. (828) 883-4034.

John A. Reynolds Antiques, at 6 Broad Street, specializes in linens, china, silver, and jewelry. For hours call (828) 884-4987 or (800) 432-GEMS.

If you collect cookbooks and kitchen gadgets, stop by the **Proper Pot** at 44 East Main Street. Larry and Beth Canady have both kitchenware and gourmet food items to make up an enviable gift basket, or you may want to add a special piece to your own cookware. The owners claim that food tastes better when you choose the proper pot! Hours are regular. (828) 877-5000.

Take a break from shopping and stop in at the **Corner Bistro,** on the corner of Broad and Main streets, for a quick lunch. Choose from deli-stacked and gourmet sandwiches, fresh salads, tortilla wraps, quesadillas, and soups. The bistro is open for both lunch and dinner and offers a children's menu plus daily specials. Wine and beer are available. Lunch is served from 11:00 A.M. to 4:00 P.M., six days a week, and dinner is served from 5:00 to 9:30 P.M., Tuesday through Saturday. For takeouts call (828) 862-4746.

Another choice for lunch, and a favorite of the college set, is **Essence of Thyme,** located at 37 Main Street. Here you can relax with an espresso, root-beer float, fresh fruit smoothie, or glass of wine. Sandwiches and salads are always fresh and the pastries are hard to resist. It is open seven days and on weekend evenings with local entertainment. Hours are seasonal. (828) 884-7171.

Essence of Thyme

Rocky's Soda Fountain, 38 Broad Street, has been a landmark in Brevard since it was Varner's Drugstore in 1941. If you just want a "bite" of nostalgic food, pop in and get yourself one of Mrs. Varner's pimento cheese sandwiches and a cherry smash. Hard to beat! (828) 877-5375.

The **Womble Inn and Café,** at 301 Main Street, is a sit-down-and-enjoy-the-atmosphere kind of place. The menu changes daily and usually consists of salads, sandwiches, and daily specials. The dining area is located on the first floor of the inn and lunch is served from 11:00 A.M. to 2:00 P.M., Monday through Friday. The inn will also prepare picnic baskets for dinner on the lawn at the Brevard Music Center or for a lunch in the woods. Twenty-four-hour notice is required. Innkeepers Beth and Steve Womble have six guest rooms, all with private baths and air-conditioning. (828) 884-4770.

In an unassuming building just off of Main Street, at 30 West Jordan, is the **Jordan Street Café.** Ten or so tables with crisp white linen cloths are scattered around a small, light-filled room. Aside from some green plants flanking the doorway, the decor is sparse, with nothing to distract you from the delicious food or your dining companion.

The menu changes often but, hopefully, if you're there for lunch, you'll be able to order the grilled portobello mushroom sandwich with melted bleu cheese and red onion marmalade with a side of sweet potato salad. Outdoor patio dining is available. The café is open from 11:00 A.M. to 2:00 P.M. for lunch and from 10:00 A.M. to 2:00 P.M. for Sunday brunch, during the season. Dinner hours begin at 5:00 P.M. and reservations are strongly recommended. It is closed Tuesday night. (828) 883-2558.

Next door to the Jordan Street Café is the **Jim Bob Tinsley Museum.** Jim Bob was born in Brevard in 1921 and his continuing interests have been Western music, photography, and researching the history of local waterfalls. Tinsley has been performing, and collecting and preserving Western and cowboy memorabilia, since the 1930s. He began as a vocalist on the radio in 1935 and one of his many awards is the prestigious Western Heritage Award for music from the National Cowboy Hall of Fame.

The museum provides free public access to an extensive collection of artifacts, paintings, drawings, and sculptures (you'll want to be sure to see the Remington and the Russell). There are also traveling exhibits. Seasonal hours are from 10:00 A.M. to 4:00 P.M. Call (828) 884-2347 for off-season hours or special tours.

The **Inn at Brevard** has quite a history. In 1885, this Southern mansion was built as the private home for a wealthy widow from Virginia. She enjoyed entertaining nobility in her gracious home, one of whom was her personal friend, Lady Astor.

Today, owners Faye and Howard Yager continue the tradition of entertaining their customers in the style of the Victorian era. With 5 nonsmoking rooms in the main house (3 with private baths) and 10 cabin-style rooms with private showers in the adjacent lodge, there is something for everyone. Rates vary with the season and are moderate to expensive.

The dining rooms are open to the public for dinner and Sunday brunch. To the delight of their customers, the Yagers have hired a four-star chef, whose menu is extensive but not overwhelming. Fresh seafood, steaks, poultry, lamb, and veal are prepared with care and served with traditional sauces. One look at the Sunday brunch menu lets you know that an excursion to the inn would be an excellent idea. It is located at 410 East Main Street. Reservations are recommended and rooms for special parties are available. (828) 884-2105.

Highlands Books is located in a small shopping strip across the street from the main gate of Brevard College. This is quite a large store and it has a widespread reputation for an excellent variety of titles. Highlands has been a fixture in Brevard since 1975 and owners Tim and Peggy Hansen maintain a wide selection of regional books, nature guides, and travel books, as well as the current fiction and nonfiction. This is the place too for maps and hiking guides plus videos and puzzles. It is open at 9:00 A.M., six days a week. (828) 884-2424.

Since 1853, students and teachers at **Brevard College** have formed an educational and spiritual community supported by its affiliation with the United Methodist Church. The college's Paul Porter Center for Performing Arts is one of the premier performing arts spaces on the East Coast. Small classes and a commitment to teaching distinguish Brevard College. The school is also known for the educational opportunities afforded by its natural setting. www.brevard.edu.

The **Brevard Music Center** is the South's most prestigious summer music institution. It began in 1936 when James Christian Pfohl opened a summer band camp for boys on the campus of Davidson College. Fifty young men showed up for the first session. The primary objective of the center was to promote quality music education, and as camp enrollments grew steadily, so did Brevard's reputation among serious music educators.

At the beginning of the center's second decade, the Brevard Music Festival began life as a three-week addition and was an instant success. In addition to stage performances, these early guest artists established the tradition of staying on in Brevard for an extra day to conduct master classes for the students. Legendary names such as Jan Peerce, Isaac Stern, and Beverly Sills entertained and enlightened thousands of music lovers.

Music was and is everywhere on the 143-acre music center campus. On summer evenings, the woods are full of the competing "music" of chirping insects and rehearsing musicians. Rustic cabins bear proud names like Mozart, Beethoven, and Brahms, while faculty cottages along one ridge are fittingly named Fa, La, and Ti.

The music center is now ready for the 21st century. David Effron, artistic director, says that the growth plan "will position Brevard among the finest repertory training programs for serious young musicians anywhere in the world." The very popular concert season begins in late June and continues until early August. For further information, contact the center at Post Office Box 312, Brevard, North Carolina 28712. (828) 884-2011. www.brevardmusic.org. (This information is courtesy of Brevard Music Center.)

There was a camaraderie about singing and working at the Brevard Music Center. We may change; it doesn't. And that, in essence, is Brevard . . . a never-ending wonder of music making!
—Beverly Sills, soprano

One of North Carolina's largest orchid farms, **Owens Orchids LLC,** has seven huge greenhouses filled with half a million plants. It is a breathtaking sight. There are many varieties. One novelty hybrid is called the "Spitting Orchid" because of the way it reacts when touched. The green and white or burgundy and white Lady Slipper of Asian ancestry is one of the most popular.

Orchids are not difficult to grow, according to Bill Owens, and they are an enduring houseplant, susceptible only to cold and over-watering. Owens Orchids is a wholesale and retail business, shipping all over the world. The farm is a little difficult to find; it is located on U.S.

Highway 64, 1.7 miles east of the intersection of U.S. Highway 276 and N.C. Highway 280. Watch carefully for a small pink sign on the highway. It is open from 9:00 A.M. to 5:00 P.M., Monday through Saturday. Call about the orchid lease program. (828) 877-3313. www.owensorchidsllc.com.

Located at 4 Pisgah Highway, **Davidson River Outfitters** is almost at the entrance of the Pisgah National Forest, at the intersection of U.S. Highway 276, U.S. Highway 64, and N.C. Highway 280. Owner David Howell, who took over from his father, has a fine shop. He appears to be ready, willing, and pleasantly able to outfit and/or teach the southern end of Western North Carolina about fishing.

Due to this unique geographical location, you can fish successfully here all year. David says, "Along with 550 miles of water in Transylvania County, there are two blue-ribbon streams nearby, both listed on *Trout Unlimited*'s 'Top 100 Trout Streams in the United States.'" Four hundred miles of world-class trout habitat are within 45 minutes of this shop. Just a few yards behind the shop is the Davidson River, a catch and release area. The South Mills River, a terrific wild trout stream, is just 10 minutes away.

Davidson River Outfitters is a full-service fly shop that carries whatever you need to catch 'em! David has technical quick-dry clothing and a small but good selection of fishing books. He also has everything you need to tie your own flies, including classes. Or you can buy from his extensive fly selection, many locally tied Southern Appalachian patterns. In addition, you can purchase custom-built fly rods. Davidson has recently become a Fly Logic rod dealer. The shop also carries Chota wading sandals and Columbia hiking boots. Guide services are available for any level of experience, as well as rod building, casting instruction, and travel planning. Fishing licenses are here, too. It is open at 8:00 A.M., daily. (888) 861-0111.

www.davidsonflyfishing.com.

> "Fishing is a condition of the mind wherein one cannot possibly have a bad time."

Pisgah National Forest

The Pisgah National Forest, covering 157,000 acres, came into being in 1889 when George Vanderbilt purchased 125,000 acres of then abused and overworked forests and farmland. Today the Pisgah National Forest hosts thousands of visitors who come to hike, camp, picnic, and simply enjoy the abundant beauty of the forest.

The name "Pisgah" comes from the third chapter of Deuteronomy. The Lord ordered Moses to the top of Pisgah and told him to look in all directions, thus revealing the "Promised Land" to the tribes of Israel. James Hall, a chaplain and soldier, and George Newton, a Presbyterian minister, are both credited with naming Mount Pisgah in the late 18th century. The first recorded appearance of the name *Mount Pisgah* was in 1808 (this information courtesy of the Pisgah Inn).

The **Pisgah District Ranger Station and Visitor Center** is located one and a half miles west of N.C. Highway 280 on U.S. Highway 276. Greeting you, as you approach the serene buildings, are forest "critters" footprints painted on the porch steps. This visitor center has informational exhibits (including a short video about the forest), a good gift shop, and restrooms.

Just behind the building is a short (10 minutes each way) nature trail that loops up the hill and through the woods, past the English Chapel and back to the ranger station. Station hours are from 8:00 A.M. to 5:00 P.M., Monday through Friday, and from 9:00 A.M. to 5:00 P.M., weekends and holidays. (828) 877-3265.

The **Pisgah Forest Stables** has guided trips of one, two, and three hours. An easy trail, suitable for ages seven and up, goes into beautiful Perry Cove. The two-hour trip goes up Claw Hammer Mountain on an old logging road, while the three-hour trip takes you near Twin Falls. Weekdays in April, May, September, and October, the stables offer camping trips, furnishing horses, guides, tents, and a cook. From the main entrance to the Pisgah Forest (U.S. Highway 64 and U.S. Highway 276), go north one and three-quarter miles; take the first right past the ranger station; go two miles to the stables. There are two-person minimums for the trips and six-person minimums for the camping. Reservations for the camping trips should be made well in advance. (828) 883-8258.

Davidson River Campground is located just beyond the ranger station on U.S. Highway 276. This very pretty, very popular campground has all facilities including over 150 campsites, warm showers, flush toilets, and dump stations. Although you may reserve a site, get there early and be prepared to line up and wait to get in.

In the fragrant woods alongside the Davidson River, the campground includes hiking trails, picnic areas, fishing streams, and evening programs. Nearby is the English Chapel, a humble little Methodist church that was founded in 1860. It is still active, offering Sunday services for visitors as well as locals. For campground reservations and information call toll free (877) 444-6777 or (800) 280-2267.

The Blue Ridge Mountains are the eastern range of the Appalachian Mountain System. They extend from southeastern Pennsylvania across Maryland, Virginia, North and South Carolina, and northern Georgia. The name comes from the blue tone given these peaks by forests on their slopes when seen at a distance. The highest peaks of the Blue Ridge Mountains are in North Carolina. Grandfather Mountain, at 5,964 feet, is the tallest peak.

The **Pisgah Center for Wildlife Education** opened in the fall of 1998. The center and its activities are programs of the North Carolina Wildlife Resources Commission and are supported through fees collected from hunters and anglers. Therefore, there are no admission fees and no charges for workshops and courses, but pre-registration is required. To register for a course, call the center at (828) 877-4423. The center, which is wheelchair accessible, is located just off of U.S. Highway 276, south of the Cradle of Forestry, in the Pisgah National Forest.

Enter the building through the gift shop. As you continue, you will pass three aquariums with examples of fish found in the mountains, in the piedmont, and on the coast. Just outside is a trail to the Outdoor Exhibit. A paved walk takes you to seven stations, which depict aspects of wildlife conservation, and an information board and an audio will tell the story at each station. At the end of the trail there are butterfly gardens and wild food plots.

The **Pisgah Forest Fish Hatchery** is open from 8:00 A.M. to 5:00 P.M., daily. This fish hatchery has been operated by the North Carolina Wildlife Resources Commission since 1983 and is one of three operated by the commission. The hatcheries, funded by the sale of fishing licenses, produce more than 600,000 fish each year to stock public trout waters. The raceway, where the fingerling trout live until they are large enough to be moved to public waters (usually from one to one and one-half years), is a concrete pond with a constant flow of fresh water. Three kinds of trout are raised here: brook, rainbow, and brown. Only the brook trout is native. Fish food is available for a quarter and makes for lots of fun for kids and adults.

Driving north on U.S. Highway 276, pull off on the right to view **Looking Glass Falls** from the roadside. This 50-foot waterfall is one of the most popular in the Pisgah Forest. There is a stone stairway to the bottom for the more adventuresome. It is not advised to climb to the top, as fast currents and slippery rocks make it quite dangerous. Continuing north, watch on the left for the parking lot for **Sliding Rock.** There is a minimal fee per vehicle unless there are more than 12 people; then there is a small per-person charge. The 150-foot natural water slide provides excitement and fun for all ages. If you are not up for the ride, bring a folding chair and walk down the steps to the bottom, where you can relax and watch. Approximately 11,000 gallons of water flow over this rock every minute. Lifeguards are on duty most of the year, but keep a close eye on the younger ones.

Near Looking Glass Falls and the fish hatchery are two nice picnic areas. Both **Pink Beds Picnic Area** and **Coontree Picnic Area** have quite a few tables. Pink Beds was possibly named for the beautiful pink rhododendrons and mountain laurels that bloom in the spring and early summer. Others say the name comes from the pink rock quarried nearby. There is a large field suitable for a friendly game of kickball.

Cradle of Forestry

In 1895, Dr. Carl Schenck, the German forester, began managing George Vanderbilt's Pisgah Forest. In 1898 he founded America's first forestry school in order to satisfy his questioning apprentices. Winter classes were held at the Biltmore Estate and summer sessions in Pisgah Forest. The "campus" consisted of mountaineer cabins and farm homes from the old Pink Beds community. The one-room school and church building became the school's classroom. This forestry school continued here until 1909; by that time 300 students had graduated from Dr. Schenck's school.

Today, at the site of the school, is the Cradle of Forestry and two trails. The center's displays, some including audio accompaniment, are interesting for every age but especially for children. There are hands-on habitat games, question and answer boards, and places to climb under, over, and into. A simulated helicopter ride including a film of a forest fire is exciting for all ages. During the year, there are special events such as Migratory Bird Days and Smokey Bear's Birthday Party.

The Forest Marketplace showcases everyday objects, such as aspirin and toilet seats, that are made from trees. There is a nice gift shop and a good café that sells sandwiches, snacks, drinks, and baby food. The two trails are short and interesting (each is about one mile of paved path). The Forest Festival Trail is a re-creation of a 1908 Biltmore Forest Fair, which demonstrated the accomplishments of practical forestry. You will see a seedling nursery, tree plantations, and a portable sawmill. The Biltmore Campus Trail leads you past the old schoolhouse, Dr. Schenck's tiny office, student quarters, and rangers' lodges. The Cradle of Forestry is open from 9:00 A.M. to 5:00 P.M., daily from April 15 through the first week in November. There is a small admission fee. (828) 877-3130 or (828) 884-5713. www.cradle-offorestry.com.

A cord of wood is a stack four feet by four feet by eight feet long. One cord will yield 7,500,000 toothpicks, 460,000 personal checks, 61,370 letter envelopes, or 30 rocking chairs.

Almost exactly where U.S. Highway 276 joins the Blue Ridge Parkway is the **Wagon Gap Overlook**, at Milepost 412. Be sure to stop here and look at Cold Mountain, which figures so prominently in Charles Frazier's novel of the same name. If you haven't read *Cold Mountain*, you have a treat in store.

The bare rock profile, named **Devil's Courthouse,** is sinister in appearance and legend. Its "devilish" look has contributed to many folktales. Within the mountain is a cave where legend claims the devil holds court. In Cherokee lore, the cave is the private dancing chamber and dwelling place of a slant-eyed giant, Judaculla. There is a half-mile steep route to the summit; on the way you can see rare and delicate high-altitude plants. Elevation is 5,270 feet. It is located at Milepost 422.4. There is another Devil's Courthouse at Cowee Gap on Whiteside Mountain.

The **Graveyard Fields Overlook** is so named because windthrown tree trunks here, covered with moss and spruce needles, looked like gravestones until destroyed by fire in 1922. There are three trails: two-tenths of a mile, three-tenths of a mile, and one and six-tenths miles. Located at Milepost 418.8, the elevation is 5,120 feet.

The **Pisgah Inn**, located at Milepost 408.6, sits at an elevation of 5,000 feet, overlooking the Blue Ridge Mountains—a truly breathtaking sight, especially considering that all rooms have porches or balconies facing the mountains.

Although the Pisgah Inn has pretty grounds and spectacular scenery, it is not a "luxury resort." What you will not have are phones, coffeepots, or mini-bars in the rooms. What you will have are televisions and VCRs, mountains, hiking trails, a gift shop, laundry facilities, a camp store, a gas station, fax service at the front desk, and an ultrapleasant staff. In addition, the **Pisgah Campground** is across the street. You will also have a serene visit, where you can truly enjoy the "purple mountains' majesty." The dining room has floor-to-ceiling windows and every table has a view. The food is simple, good, and dependable (don't dare leave without ordering the whole grilled mountain trout). Wine and beer are served.

The National Park Service puts on programs during the season, which usually take place in the outdoor amphitheater, at the back of Loop B of the campground. During the summer, the "Christian Ministry in the National Parks" provides interdenominational worship services. Incidentally, it is not only tourists who find Mount Pisgah pleasant; you will possibly see deer and rabbits and you will definitely see the resident skunks. Please do not feed them! The inn and campground are open mid-April through October. For information, write Post Office Box 749, Waynesville, North Carolina 28786. (828) 235-8228.

Hendersonville

Hendersonville was a hunting ground for the Cherokee before Revolutionary War soldier William Mills "discovered" the area in the late 1780s. Mills received one of the first land grants west of the Blue Ridge Mountains and it was dated 1787. Henderson County was named for State Supreme Court Chief Justice Leonard Henderson. The county of Henderson is located on a 75-square-mile intermountain plateau and is almost circled by mountains. It has an elevation of 2,200 feet. William Mills planted hundreds of fruit trees each year. His fellow neighbors did the same and Henderson County now leads the state in the production of apples (information courtesy of the Henderson County Travel and Tourism Bureau).

Hendersonville, with its population of 30,000, is a bustling little town. Downtown Hendersonville was entered into the National Register of Historic Places in 1988. The serpentine street features trees, planter boxes brimming with seasonal flowers, and a thriving array of shops, boutiques, cafés, and restaurants. The historic district offers the visitor traditional Southern hometown charm. Downtown hosts many activities, including the North Carolina Apple Festival held during Labor Day weekend, as well as art shows, street dances, and parades throughout the year. Hendersonville retains its small-town flavor in spite of the seasonal influx of tourists and it is a pleasure to stroll up and down the streets.

There are two historic inns in town that are listed on the National Register of Historic Places and the Historic Hendersonville Walking Tour. The **Claddah Inn,** at 755 Main Street, was originally built for Hendersonville's first mayor in 1888 and in 1906 it became the town's first bed and breakfast. "Claddah" is the name for a Gaelic symbol for love and friendship.

There are 16 rooms with all amenities. A full Irish breakfast is served in the dining room and afternoon tea is served in the spacious parlor. The inn has a no smoking policy and no pets are allowed. (800) 225-4700. www.claddahinn.com.

Next door, the **Waverly Inn** was built in 1898 as an inn. Inside this lovely, old tin-roofed building are 14 rooms with all amenities, including data ports. A full breakfast is served and there is an evening social hour with beverages and hors d'oeuvres. It is open all year. (800) 537-8195. www.waverlyinn.com.

If you've never heard a talking tree, by all means visit the **Holmes Educational State Forest,** located nine miles west of Hendersonville on Kanuga and Crab Creek Road. This will appeal to youngsters as well as adults.

A half-mile trail features seven trees that will tell you their life story—just push their buttons. In addition to the "Talking Tree Trail," there is a wildcat rock trail, a soil and water trail, and scenic over-looks. The 235 acres of forest also include the Forestry Center, well-maintained campgrounds, and horseshoe and volleyball courts. Picnic sites with tables and grills are available.

The forest is named for the first North Carolina forest ranger, who served from 1915 to 1945. It is open Tuesday through Sunday, from mid-March to the Friday before Thanksgiving. (828) 692-0100.

> Thomas Wolfe's famous angel is now residing on the Johnson plot, at the Oakdale Riverside Cemetery. The Johnson family purchased the angel from Wolfe's father and she is still "looking homeward."

At **Jane Asker's Fourth and Main Antique Mall,** you will find various booths with antique christening gowns, vintage clothing, linens, and lace. There is a button booth with antique buttons, including a set made from kudzu. It is open from 10:00 A.M. to 5:00 P.M., six days a week. (828) 698-0018.

In the rear of this mall is **A Moment In Time,** where clocks are bought, sold, and repaired. The clocksmith, John Simons, deals mainly in antique clocks. He is open from 10:00 A.M. to 5:00 P.M., Thursday through Saturday. **Scotties Jewelry and Fine Arts,** 225 Main, has been a family-owned business on this street since 1968. This shop offers a sophisticated blend of listed 19th- and 20th-century paintings and sculpture and some eye-catching jewelry. Scotties holds auctions periodically, with a member of the esteemed Sotheby's officiating. It is open to 5:00 P.M., five days a week, and to 3:00 P.M. (800) 452-4715.

Henderson County is brimming with artists and the **Arts Center,** located at 538-A Main Street, provides a great showcase for them, as well as making studios available. In addition, this very active center has presented significant exhibits on artists such as Ansel Adams, Norman Rockwell, and Salvador Dali. Local exhibits change every month or so and many are juried shows.

The Arts Center is an independent, nonprofit organization dedicated to providing a forum for the visual arts as well as offices and meeting rooms for art organizations. The center, located on the second floor of the historic Skyland Hotel, is open at 10:00 A.M., six days a week. (828) 693-8504.

Arts are obviously important in Hendersonville and quilts are a cherished art form. Georgia Bonesteel, a resident of Henderson County, is an internationally known quilt artist and is considered to be one of North Carolina's talented treasures. She has authored six books on this age-old craft and has appeared as host of "Lap Quilting," a series of 10 programs on North Carolina public television.

One of her beautiful quilts hangs in the county courthouse, which serves as a gallery for many local artists. The First Citizen's Bank, across the street from the Arts Center, houses a permanent collection of quilts, including a quilted picture of the bank itself.

Mountain Lore
Your Personal Bookstore

"Dedicated to the Care and Feeding of Bookworms."

Mountain Lore Bookstore follows in the footsteps of history, location-wise, as there has been a bookstore on this corner at 555 Main Street since 1900. Book lovers will delight in this popular, locally owned store with a slogan of "Dedicated to the care and feeding of bookworms." There are books for all ages and interests in this 1,500-square-foot shop. The shelves hold a wide variety of regional books and a great many volumes by Southern authors. You will also find cards, stationery, and magazines. It is open from 10:00 A.M. to 6:00 P.M., daily, most of the year. (828) 693-5096.

Hannah Flanagan's Pub and Eatery, at 300 North Main, has the typical pub atmosphere with friendly Irish servers and a specialty of corned beef and cabbage; however, the café is known for their Guinness Irish Stew, served mainly on St. Patrick's Day. If you're Irish you will surely want to try the bangers and Irish sausage served with fried cabbage, mashed potatoes, and gravy. This local hangout has live music on Thursday through Saturday nights and stays open until 2:00 A.M. on the weekends. You can choose from over 100 world-renowned beers. Sports fans will love the nine televisions! Takeout service is also available. It is open at 11:00 A.M. for lunch; dinner is served nightly. (828) 696-1665.

One of the many vibrant galleries in town is **Touchstone,** located at 318 North Main Street. This gallery was selected as one of the top 100 retailers of American crafts by *Niche,* a national crafts magazine. Touchstone is loaded with paintings, metal sculptures, pottery, jewelry, and exotic windsocks. The interest is on Southeastern arts and crafts but artists from throughout the United States are also represented. Both the serious collector and the whimsical gift giver will be delighted with this gallery. (828) 692-2191.

Should you need a little "pick-up" from the multitude of shops along Main Street, stop at the **Black Bear Coffee Company.** Some think they have the best coffee in the county with an endless variety of flavors and espresso and cappuccino. They are open from 10:00 A.M. to 6:00 P.M., six days, and to 5:00 P.M., Sunday. (828) 692-6333.

McFarlane Bakery lit its ovens for the first time in 1930 and today it is still baking away using the original recipes. According to baker-owner Michael Cole, over 90 percent of their baked goodies are prepared exactly as they were in 1930. This is a full-service bakery offering cakes, cookies, doughnuts, pastries, and bread. One popular item is the salt-rising bread, which takes two days to prepare and makes wonderful toast. The Danish pastries that are much in demand contain 144 layers. This is open from 7:00 A.M. to 5:30 P.M., Tuesday through Saturday. (828) 693-4256.

Drop into the old corner drugstore, **Days Gone By,** for a step back in time. The present structure was built by Dr. William H. Justus in 1896 and remained in the family until 1956. The elaborate tin-molded ceiling, antique apothecary jars, cash register, and soda fountain are all original. Metal ice cream table and chairs and a marble soda-fountain counter add to the century-old charm. At least 30 ice cream flavors from the Biltmore Ice Cream Company make this a refreshing stop on a warm afternoon.

Breakfast is served and you can jumpstart your day with "Bill's Loaded Waffle," which is, indeed, loaded with ice cream, strawberry or pineapple topping, and whipped cream. Lunches feature old favorites, including a peanut butter and jelly sandwich. Located at 310 North Main, it is open from 9:00 A.M. to 5:00 P.M., Monday through Saturday. (828) 693-9056.

A restaurant down the steps at 321-C North Main Street is **Cypress Cellar,** featuring a "taste of South Louisiana." Choose from fried green tomatoes served over jalapeno cheddar grits or po' boys of fried catfish, oysters, or shrimp on French bread from Gambino's Bakery in New Orleans. Carrying on the Louisiana theme are gumbo, frogs legs, jambalaya, and, of course, red beans and rice. Occasionally on the menu will be alligator and spinach salad! The proprietor and chef, Renee Ellender, is from Bayou Terre Bonne in South Louisiana and the paneling and wood trim in the restaurant is cypress from her family's sugarcane farm. This is open from 11:00 A.M. to 9:00 P.M., Monday through Saturday. (828) 698-1005.

For objets d'art with an international flair, stop in at **Nelly's Treasures** at 333 Main Street. Owner Nelly Attia is originally from France, where she served as a diplomat in the French Embassy. Nelly's features exceptional art jewelry by an Israeli designer. It is open six days a week. (828) 696-4300.

The **Mineral and Lapidary Museum** is located at 400 Main Street. This is also headquarters for the Henderson County Genealogical and Historical Society. It is open at 10:00 A.M., six days a week. (828) 693-1531. Upstairs is the Mineral Museum, displaying minerals and geodes of North Carolina along with gems, Indian artifacts, and fossils. One special exhibit is a 260-pound amethyst geode. The museum also provides services such as mineral identification, reference materials, and a gift shop with hobby-related merchandise as well as gem and mineral jewelry created by the museum's members. The museum is open in the afternoons Monday through Friday, and all day, Saturday. (828) 698-1977.

The very essence of North Carolina folk art can be found at **Wickwire,** 423 Main. This gallery focuses on Western North Carolina art in painting, pottery, hand-painted furniture, quilt "paintings," and three-dimensional wood art of mountain landscapes. Wickwire seeks to blend the emerging artist and established artist. Three Smithsonian artisans and two North Carolina "Living Treasures" are represented in this interesting gallery. This is a good stop for a significant souvenir. It is open from 10:00 A.M. to 5:00 P.M., six days a week. (828) 692-6222.

The **Village Green Antique Mall,** 424 Main Street, is one of the largest antique malls in Western North Carolina, covering a 12,000-square-foot area. Needless to say, a little bit of everything is here. It opens at 10:00 A.M., five days a week, and at 1:00 P.M., Sunday. (828) 692-9057. **Shelly's Diamond Gallery,** 429 Main Street, carries a spectacular selection of Vivian Alexander eggs, which are actually tiny purses. Decorated in the Faberge style, the purses are limited editions as well as dream gifts for Christmas. Since the 1970s, Shelly's has furnished customers with estate jewelry. It specializes in large diamonds and is open six days a week. (828) 692-3615.

Reminiscent of its namesake, Portebello Market in London, the **Portebello** here has a little bit of everything imaginable and not imaginable. There is imported French furniture and national and international art. It is located at 511 North Main. The owner knows the famed Portebello in London well as she lived in that city for many years. (828) 698-7290.

Lilly's, located at 542 Main, is a cozy place to go for a tasty, light lunch such as chicken salad with apricots, walnuts, and raisins, or perhaps Lilly's special salad plate, which includes quiche and tea sandwiches. Dessert is usually an assortment of French pastries and there is a delicious line of exotic teas from which to choose. Lilly, born in 1870 in county Cork, Ireland, never knew when she arrived in this country that she would have a popular tearoom named after her. Owner-chef Toni Gilliam named the tearoom after Lilly, her great-grandmother. It is open at 11:45 A.M. for lunch, Tuesday through Saturday, and at 6:00 P.M. for a gourmet dinner, Friday and Saturday. Tea is served from 3:00 to 5:00 P.M., daily, and brunch on Sunday. (828) 698-1922.

Lilly's Salad Dressing

3 eggs
1 green unpeeled apple,
  cored and sliced
$^1/_2$ cucumber
$^1/_4$ medium onion
1 tbsp. tarragon

1 tbsp. dill weed
3 tbsp. sugar
2 cups oil
$^1/_2$ cup cider vinegar
$^1/_2$ tsp. curry powder

Beat eggs in blender on low. Add apple, cucumber, and onion and blend. Add remaining ingredients and blend until smooth. Refrigerate and serve over a salad of lettuce, quartered tomatoes, and fresh mushrooms.

The **Mast General Store** "is a destination," Charles Kuralt once said on the "Sunday Morning" television program, so do not miss the one at 527 Main Street. It is a look at yesteryear, with a molded-tin ceiling, beaded paneling, and the friendliest clerks in town. There are five Mast General stores in Western North Carolina; the first one opened 1883 in Valle Crucis. This one is open seven days a week.

Take a short jog off of Main Street onto Fourth Avenue West; on the corner, at Number 147, is **Antiques, Etc.,** which specializes in sterling and old silverplate. This is the place to fill in your patterns or purchase lovely old silver vases, trays, and tea sets. One of the proprietors, Joe Ewing, is a recognized silver authority and since the 1970s has traveled the country speaking on antique silver. This is open from 10:00 A.M. to 5:00 P.M., six days a week. (828) 696-8255.

On the corner of Fifth and Main is **Mehri & Company,** with a wide selection of home accessories with a more formal style. You'll also find designer jewelry and estate pieces. Proprietor Mehri is a New Yorker but is originally from Iran. This is open six days a week. (828) 693-0887.

Café Calabria, 123 Fifth Avenue (next to City Hall and half a block from Main Street), is like many of the small bistros in Italy, where a meal is a peaceful respite from busy day activities. When you enter and hear the soft Italian opera music and sniff the aroma of freshly baked bread, cannelloni, and eggplant parmigiana, you will think you have been magically transported to Italy. On the menu you will find homemade baked onion zuppa and traditional tiramisu. A full bar is available and seniors receive a discount. This is open for lunch from 11:00 A.M. to 2:30 P.M., Monday through Saturday, and for dinner from 4:30 to 10:00 P.M., Thursday through Saturday. Reservations are suggested, especially for dinner. (828) 693-4440.

Should you find yourself in Hendersonville on a Tuesday, Thursday, or Saturday morning, you'll want to stop by the **Curb Market** at 221 Church Street. Friendly farmers come to town with mountains of crafts, apple pies, jellies, cakes, fresh fruit and vegetables, plants, and flowers.

The Curb Market began in 1924 on Main Street under eight umbrellas. Today it is a nonprofit organization with 137 booths and many of the vendors are third and fourth generation. The only requirements are that the participants must be residents of

Henderson County and they must grow or make their products. Hours are from 8:00 A.M. to 2:00 P.M., May through December, but you'd best be an early bird at this market. For more information call the Travel and Tourism Bureau at (828) 693-9708 or (800) 828-4244.

Kanuga Episcopal Conference Center is located in Hendersonville and offers "Guest Periods" to the public. These periods are when families, couples, and single persons can gather for a shared time of playing, studying, and Christian community. The beautiful 1,400 acres, with Lake Kanuga in the center, have an inn, cottages, and guesthouses. Privacy, inviting accommodations, good food, and well-chosen programs, all offered in a magnificent mountain setting, are Kanuga traditions.

An especially popular time is the See The Leaves Guest Period held yearly in October. In addition to "oohhing" and "aahhing" over the fall foliage, guests can take advantage of tennis and hiking, the "Leave You Behind" road race and fun run, and nearby golf, complemented by Bible study, vespers, porches, and peaceful views.

You can also go on an apple orchard tour and a motorcade along the Blue Ridge Parkway. It is located about four miles south of Hendersonville on Kanuga Road. For information write to Post Office Box 250, Hendersonville, North Carolina 28793. (828) 692-9136. www.kanuga.org.

The **Fresh Market,** located at 213 Greenville Highway, is one of 24 family-owned markets in the Southeast. The Berry family began the idea of these markets in the 1980s. There are two in the Western North Carolina area, one in Hendersonville and another in Asheville.

This market is a shopper's dream. Literally everything you need for a gourmet meal (beginning with fresh flowers in pots or bunches) is under one roof. Produce bins are overflowing with every imaginable fruit and vegetable; aisles are stacked with oils, spices, and mixes; huge tubs are filled with granola, nuts, snack mixes, dried beans, rice, and coffees. The meat market is a vision with all types of beef, pork, veal, lamb, and poultry ready to be custom cut; some are marinating and awaiting your final touch while others are already prepared and ready for your table.

Fresh seafood adds to the overwhelming number of choices. The bakery has fresh breads of many varieties and shapes, cakes, pies, cookies, crackers, and bagels; choosing is difficult so just fill up your cart and make your choices at home! This is open daily. (828) 693-8223.

There are over 300 commercial apple farms, comprised of 10,000 bearing acres of apple orchards, in the state and many of them are in Western North Carolina. Hendersonville is the state's number-one apple producer and, just outside of Hendersonville on U.S. Highway 64, there are over 20 orchards/markets/fruit stands where you can purchase apples, cider, and jellies. Some markets offer tours, pick-your-own orchards, picnic areas, and opportunities to watch cider being made. For information call the Blue Ridge Direct Market Association at (828) 697-2775, Extension 8. www.ncapples.com.

It is worth the trip up to **Echo Mountain Inn,** 2849 Laurel Park Highway, just for the drive. The road winds up the 3,100-foot elevation of Echo Mountain through an attractive residential area with dense trees and lovely vistas. The inn, a stone and frame structure, was built in 1896 and is situated on the pinnacle, giving the dining room and some of the guest rooms fabulous views. It began as a private summer home, then became a tearoom, before being converted into a summer camp. In 1929, it was purchased, remodeled, and became the Echo Inn.

Today, with 31 rooms, it is not only an inn but a popular restaurant. Local folks as well as visitors come to enjoy a special dinner with an incomparable sunset view. The menu may feature pecan-crusted mountain trout with an orange-rosemary butter sauce or herb-crusted rack of lamb—both delicious. A deluxe continental breakfast is included in the tariff and rates are moderate. The restaurant is open for dinner, Tuesday through Saturday, and rates are moderate to expensive. (828) 693-9626. www.echoinn.com.

At the very end of Laurel Park Highway, just five miles from Main Street, is a view "to die for"; this is **Jump Off Rock Park** (don't let the name give you any ideas), a spectacular scenic overlook encompassing the Blue Ridge and Pisgah mountains as well as rolling green pastures. The name "Jump Off Rock" is derived from a legend of an Indian maiden who, after learning her lover had fallen in battle, jumped from this very rock. Tales have been passed down through the years of various sightings of a lone female on the rock. The park is open from dawn to dusk and there is no admission.

If you have flying in your blood or would simply enjoy a nostalgic visit with old airplanes, look up the **Western North Carolina Air Museum** on Gilbert Street at the Hendersonville Airport. From Asheville or Greenville take Interstate 26 to Exit 22. It is billed as the "First Air Museum in the 'First in Flight' State"; this is appropriate since North Carolina native sons, the Wright Brothers, flew the very first aircraft from Kitty Hawk, North Carolina.

There are 12 beautifully restored planes dating from the 1930s and a replica of a 1917 Nieuport 11. Also among these wonderful old planes is a Stearman N2S, known as the "Yellow Peril," which trained young aviators during World War II. You'll also find a classic North American SNJ-5 Texan and some Piper Cubs.

The guides are friendly and many are former pilots who fly these planes for special events. It is open at 10:00 A.M., Wednesday and Saturday, and at 12:00 noon, Sunday. Admission is free. (828) 693-9708.

Highland Lake Inn is ideal for the Western North Carolina traveler. It is a back-to-nature place with a beautiful lake and 180 acres of unspoiled forest to explore. You may stay in the inn, family cottages, or small cabins sprinkled around the grounds. Large groups can stay in a lodge, which has 20 rooms and is ideal for business groups or family reunions.

Highland Lake is set up much like a camp, where all of the buildings are separate and you walk to the dining room for meals. However, don't get the wrong impression: this place is rustic but not rugged. The dining room is all stone, knotty pine, and brass with a wide-open kitchen you can walk through at any time. Huge roaring fires burn in every room when the chill begins. Most of the fresh greens and herbs are from the small working farm at Highland Lake and the chef's culinary creations will make you glad you are walking home. Activities of all kind are available and the 18-hole golf course, laid out in 1910, was the first one in the area. (828) 693-6812 or (800) 762-1376. www.highlandlake.com.

Flat Rock

Flat Rock began with large summer estates being built by affluent Charlestonians, Europeans, and prominent Southern plantation owners. The first great estate was built in 1827 by Charles Baring of London. The second large estate was built by Judge Mitchell King of Charleston. He later donated the land on which Hendersonville was built.

Other coastal families soon followed. The families of South Carolina's low country came to the Flat Rock area to escape the heat, yellow fever, and malaria.

The whole district of Flat Rock is included in the National Register of Historic Places. Flat Rock is built around a tremendous outcrop of granite, which is said to have been the site of Cherokee gatherings. A great deal of rock has been blasted away and used for highway material. The main "rock" can be found on the grounds of the Flat Rock Playhouse (information courtesy of the Henderson County Travel and Tourism Bureau).

The historic church of **St. John in the Wilderness** is most assuredly a quiet spot you will want to see. Listed on the National Register of Historic Places, the church offers the visitor a unique assembly of families prominent in Southern and national history.

In the 1820s, the Baring family left South Carolina seeking respite from the oppressive low-country heat and settled in Flat Rock. After building their home, Charles and Susan Baring built a private chapel on the grounds. With the formation of the Episcopal Diocese of Western North Carolina in 1836, the Baring family donated their beautiful brick chapel to the diocese.

Inside the church you will want to note the unusual stained-glass windows, the original altar and pulpit, and especially the "box pews." The names engraved on the plaques in the pews are of summer residents who came to North Carolina in those early years from South Carolina, Georgia, and New Orleans.

The unusual and beautiful graveyard, bordered by wrought-iron fencing of many different patterns, provides a stellar summary of famous Southern names. The church and graveyard are open from 9:00 A.M. to 4:00 P.M., daily. They are located on the west side of U.S. Highway 25, three-quarters of a mile north of the Carl Sandburg Historic Site. Stop by the church office for a brochure and a self-guided tour map.

When you go to a play at the **Flat Rock Playhouse,** you are taking part in a tradition that has lasted over 50 years. On the roof of the theater you will see a weathervane with a figure carrying a knapsack and the masks of Comedy and Tragedy. The figure is Robroy Farquhar, beloved founder of the Vagabonds, a group of traveling actors who performed on many stages in many different places. The original group included Jennifer Jones, Robert Walker, Gary Moore, and others (if you are over 50, you will recognize these names). When Robroy came to Henderson County, it was love at first sight and he opened the Old Mill Playhouse, fulfilling his dream for a summer stock theater.

In 1952, the Vagabonds found their final home in Flat Rock; a circus tent was raised and the Flat Rock Playhouse was in business. By 1961, a theater had been erected as well as a dormitory, dining hall, rehearsal hall, and children's theater building. The General Assembly of North Carolina designated Flat Rock Playhouse as the State Theater (one of only three state theaters in the nation) and it is also one of the top 10 summer theaters in the country. Many actors have cut their teeth in Flat Rock; the list reads like a who's who in the legitimate theater.

It takes thousands of people and money to make a theater of this kind work and the lifeblood of this enterprise was Robroy Farquhar, Englishman, playwright, actor, director, and fundraiser. After his death in 1983, his son took up the knapsack and with new energy is keeping the faith for his father. The season at Flat Rock Playhouse usually runs from the end of May through the middle of October. For information and schedules write to the Flat Rock Playhouse, Post Office Box 310, 2661 Greenville Highway, Flat Rock, North Carolina 28731. www.flatrockplayhouse.org.

A worthy site is Connemara, the **Carl Sandburg Home.** The main house sits atop a sloping hill with a lake and woods surrounding it. The trail from the parking lot to the main house is three-tenths of a mile. If you are unable to walk the distance you can call for a shuttle. What a wonderful refuge Connemara must have been for this literary giant who, at the age of 67, brought with him a Pulitzer as well as every other literary award. However, his years at Connemara were just as productive as before he came and he tacked on another Pulitzer and many honors for children's literature, poetry, and songs.

Sandburg's wife, Lillian, was famous in her own right, developing champion dairy goats, improving bloodlines and milk production. Today, the descendants of Lillian's herd still roam the property and the spring, when the baby goats are born, is a peak time to visit.

The house is much like Sandburg left it, very unpretentious and warm with books, papers, and personal belongings scattered everywhere. How fitting for the family to donate this treasure to be preserved as the Carl Sandburg Home National Historic Site. Connemara is located off of U.S. Highway 25 and is well marked. It is open every day of the year. (828) 693-4178.

It is necessary now and then for a man to go away by himself and experience loneliness; to sit on a rock in the forest and to ask of himself, Who am I and where have I been and where am I going?

—Carl Sandburg

On U.S. Highway 25, you will notice a small, two-story building on the east side of the road. This lovely old structure was the Flat Rock Post Office and it dates from 1847. It is now home to the Book Exchange, a secondhand bookstore.

The **Wrinkled Egg** is located in historic Flat Rock at 2710 U.S. Highway 25 South. Yes, there really are wrinkled eggs! When owner Virginia Teel purchased the old Peace Grocery (circa 1890), there were some chickens that had been left on the premises. At one time the chickens were well fed and produced healthy eggs sold at the grocery but, due to poor diet and a calcium deficiency, they began to lay "wrinkled" eggs. Some are on display in the store.

North Carolina is known for its many summer camps and the Wrinkled Egg has become equally well known for making fabulous summer camp surprise packages. This extraordinary little shop is packed with children's clothes and gifts such as diaries, camp stationery, picture frames, magic and pocket games, autograph pillowcases and books, along with some funky American art. The store is open from 10:00 A.M. to 6:00 P.M., Monday through Saturday, February through December (from 1:00 to 5:00 P.M., Sunday, in the summer and October). For orders call (828) 736-3998.

The Secret Garden

Next door to the Wrinkled Egg is a charming shop called **The Secret Garden.** Carolyn Wingerd, owner, has gathered a host of unusual garden accessories for inside and outside the home. The smell of fresh flowers greets you when you walk in the door and the unique cutting garden and collection of perennials for sale are an unexpected bonus. Hours are from 9:00 A.M. to 6:00 P.M., summer, and from 10:00 A.M. to 5:00 P.M., fall. The shop is closed from December 31 until March 1. (828) 697-1331.

Potter David Vorhees and his wife, jeweler Molly Sharp, have indeed joined hands in **Hand in Hand Gallery.** His working studio is on one side, hers on the other; connecting them is their light-filled showroom. David taught himself the potter's skills, then added the painter's touch. Painting is his other love and the legacy of his parents, both professional painters.

The introduction of porcelain was key in the development of his current body of work—colorful floral brush pieces that are fired to a luminous finish. These pieces range from lamps to slab vases to tiny single blossom vases. His tile plaques are exquisite.

Molly began metalworking in the 1970s. Her unusual and beautiful jewelry is crafted using sterling silver, 14-karat gold, semi-precious stones, and local river rocks for a variety of textures and pieces.

The gallery also features other local artists. Some of the more diverse offerings are hand-painted scarves, whimsical fabric character pins, kaleidoscopes, and carved wooden wine stoppers. It is located at 2713 Greenville Highway (U.S. Highway 25). Hours are from 9:00 A.M. to 5:00 P.M., Monday through Saturday. (828) 697-7719.

If sudden hunger should strike while you're in Flat Rock, don't panic; just go straight to the Exxon station on U.S. Highway 25. Inside you will find **Dean's Market and Deli.** Freshly made soups, salads, and sandwiches, along with homemade desserts, await to satisfy and comfort you. The blackberry cobbler is so good you may want to call ahead and reserve a serving! You may take out but there are tables for eating in. It is open daily. (828) 692-5770.

The **Woodfield Inn,** named the "Inn of the South" by the National Register of Historic Places, is located on U.S. Highway 25 South. There are 17 rooms with private baths and all are decorated with elegant antiques. If there is not enough to keep you busy in Flat Rock, the inn has tennis courts and 7 acres of walking trails. A full breakfast is included in the moderately expensive rate. Woodfield sits on 28 acres and the grounds surrounding it include formal English gardens. It is truly a step back in time. (828) 693-6016. www.woodfield-inn.com. The **Squire's Restaurant** in the inn offers regional cuisine and is open to the public for dinner from 5:00 to 8:30 P.M., Wednesday through Sunday.

Golf Courses

Here are the area municipal and public golf courses; information courtesy of Journal Communications, Inc.:

Crooked Creek Golf Club. Located on the old Warner Bros. Estate with tall pines and lots of water and character. Located one and a half miles west of Hendersonville, this course is open all year. (828) 692-2011.

Highland Lake Golf Club. Located two miles south of downtown Hendersonville. This 9 hole, par 35, is very walkable and allows you to use a good club selection. (828) 692-0143.

Orchard Trace Golf Club. Located outside of Hendersonville on Sugarloaf Road. This golf course is fully lighted for night play. It is open year round until 1:30 A.M. (828) 685-1006.

Pine Links Golf Club. Located just one mile from Hendersonville. This 9 hole, par 35, is playable for seniors with easy-to-walk, shorter-length holes. Accuracy is challenged on every hole. It is open year round. (828) 693-0907.

CHAPTER 12

Bat Cave

The community of Bat Cave has been "Bat Cave" since long before the Civil War, according to Mr. J. K. ("Budd") Sumner, who is one of the historians of the area. The granite fissure caves are the longest in North America and used to be the habitat of millions of bats. Recently, the caves have been put under the control of the Nature Conservancy with strict stipulations by owner Margaret Flinsch, who is in her nineties, that tourism should not be encouraged. (Margaret's father could have bought Chimney Rock for $4,500 years ago and she states it would never have been developed as the tourist site it is today.) Conducted tours of Bat Cave by students earning college tuition are allowed. For a small fee, you can sign up for a tour at **Bat Cave Apple House,** where Sarah Lawter, owner, is another font of information. The Apple House is located on U.S. Highways 64 and

74A, just across from an Episcopal church built by the Flinsches. Some bats still abide in these black cavernous caves and no tricks of lighting or other additions have interfered with the total natural setting. The trek is strenuous and takes approximately two and a half to three hours to complete. Because granite caves are unstable you can only venture 300 feet inside. Tours are at 10:00 A.M., Wednesday and Saturday. (828) 625-0380.

What was a hideaway for many famous movie stars and writers in the 1900s can be your hideaway today. Having been twice destroyed by fire, **Esmeralda Inn & Restaurant** is back and running thanks to the perseverance of innkeepers Ackie and Jo Anne Okpych, many loyal friends, and the support of Preservation North Carolina.

The inn was first built in 1890, along an old Pony Express and stagecoach route, then rebuilt in 1917 after a fire. Notable silent-screen stars came to the Esmeralda: Mary Pickford, Douglas Fairbanks, Gloria Swanson, and William S. Hart to name a few. Lew Wallace wrote the script for *Ben Hur* in room number nine and Clark Gable was one of the stars who frequented the inn several weeks a year. Old movie buffs will especially enjoy roaming the area where many movie companies came to film big silent movies of the day. Unfortunately, Esmeralda burned again in 1997, but has reopened and the Okpychs work hard to keep the ambience of the past intact with new modern accommodations.

A balm to soothe the soul . . .

—Dr. Harmon D. Smith,
from his poem about the Esmeralda Inn

Esmeralda sits about 60 feet from U.S. Highway 74 in Hickory Nut Gorge, near Chimney Rock, and it is the perfect place for company retreats or seminars. To stay here is just plain good sense—a great location with nearby attractions, good rates in and out of season, and gourmet meals with complimentary continental breakfast for guests. (828) 625-9105 www.esmeraldainn.com.

Chimney Rock

Some people have dreams of owning a desert island and some dream of owning a mountain. Dr. Lucius Morse had that dream and in 1902 bought himself a towering monolith called Chimney Rock. Today the mountain is still owned by the Morse family and has become one of the top tourist attractions in the country.

After you cross the bridge at Rocky Broad River, pay the admission fee and then snake up the mountain for three miles until you reach the parking area. You have several choices at this point—climb the stairway to Chimney Rock or ride the elevator, which is carved out of the center of the mountain. There is also a 30-minute stroll along the side of the mountain, which ends at the bottom of Hickory Nut Falls. Climbing the stairway to Chimney Rock is an adventure, especially for children. The trek is steep and high but safe, with several rest areas along the way. At times you feel you are standing in midair and, to the novice, this can be unsettling; however, with some coaxing even the beginner can make it to the top. Children feel they have scaled the Chimney and usually do a Rocky Balboa victory dance around the flag. After visiting the gift shop and restrooms, you may want to continue your hike even higher to Exclamation Point and follow the Skyline trail to the top of Hickory Nut Falls. This is an uphill climb, moderate to strenuous, and takes about 45 minutes. You should allow two to three hours to explore Chimney Rock.

From this 500-million-year-old rock, you can see the most beautiful vistas in North Carolina and, on a clear day, you can make out Kings Mountain, which is 75 miles away. Lake Lure is at your feet and is touted to be the most beautiful manmade lake in the world. When you are on the top of Chimney Rock you will believe it. The park has recently announced the opening of a new trail. The Four Seasons Trail is six-tenths of a mile long and it will remain open all year to allow visitors the opportunity of hiking during the winter months. Park hours are from 8:30 A.M. to 4:30 P.M. The park remains open one and one-half hours after the ticket plaza closes. For more information write or call Chimney Rock Park, Box 39, Chimney Rock, North Carolina 28720. (828) 625-9611 or (800) 277-9611.

www.chimneyrockpark.com.

A great ending to the exploration of Chimney Rock is sitting on the deck of **Old Rock Café** with a view of the Rocky Broad River running past you and the great Chimney high above. A good, simple menu appeals to everybody, with fried fish sandwiches, fresh salads, hand-pulled barbecue, and roasted veggies stuffed in pita bread.

Children can walk the path by the river in full view of parents while waiting for their food. Old Rock Café is located just north of the exit from the park on U.S. Highways 64 and 74-A and is open from 11:00 A.M. to 8:00 or 9:00 P.M., during the week. Sunday hours are from 8:00 A.M. to 8:00 P.M., for breakfast, lunch, and dinner. Call for hours after October 1. (828) 628-3393.

An important inn in the 1920s that catered to the "movers and the shakers" of the day was **Lake Lure Inn.** Located in the Western North Carolina hinterlands, the inn has the mountains for a background and Lake Lure in the foreground. The structure is white stucco with a red roof (used to be red tile) and arched breezeways that give it a kind of European influence. "Location, location, location" is usually the primary requirement for booking business conferences and Lake Lure Inn has all the right stuff for successful meetings or retreats— 50 rooms and just 25 miles from Asheville Airport. The inn is great as a base for you to spend a night or two taking in the countryside and enjoying beautiful Lake Lure. Lake Lure Inn is located on N.C. Highway 9, off U.S. Highway 26 from the south, or U.S. Highway 64/74 from Asheville. (828)-625-2525. www.lakelureinn.com.

Before you leave Lake Lure, take a side trip to the Bottomless Pools. Turn right just after the arcade building next to the inn and drive an eighth of a mile; cross over the covered bridge and you will reach the information office, where you will pay a small fee. Park and take a short walk to three cascading waterfalls that drop into basins of such depth that they haven't found the bottom yet! You were told earlier in this book to always carry a picnic basket with you—this perfect spot is the reason why.

Driving through North Carolina you will not be able to miss the vast fields of kudzu, "the vine that ate the South." This prolific vine was originally imported from the Orient to prevent soil erosion, but it was soon deemed an unstoppable menace, growing about a foot a day. With its great green leaves and purple blossoms, kudzu is estimated by the United States Forest Service to cover seven million acres of the South.

An innovative lady in Rutherfordton, North Carolina, Edith Edwards, decided that "if you can't beat it, eat it"—or at least make use of it. Mrs. Edwards, known as the Kudzu Queen, turned the nuisance vine into jelly, quiche, tea, syrup, chiplike snacks, paper, medicine, baskets, wreaths, and fodder for their livestock. Then she tried frying the leaves, which she claims are delicious, and discovered that the kudzu root settles an upset stomach.

Nancy Basket, in Walhalla, South Carolina, turned kudzu into insulation for a room addition. She also makes soap, rugs, and hats as well as pink kudzu jelly, which is quite good and sweet. Perhaps this is the answer: if the population can consume it, we can at last control it!

Kudzu Jelly

Cover 1 gallon of kudzu blossoms with boiling water. Steep overnight or at least 8 hours. Strain. To 3 glasses of strained juice, add 4 cups of sugar. Mix with 1 package of Sure-Jell pectin and follow directions.

Saluda

Whether you're coming from Asheville or Hendersonville, the Carolina Foothills make for wonderful day trips. Besides the glorious scenery, several small towns are nestled between the hills and valleys that will take time to explore. This area is a haven for cyclists and drivers, with good roads leading to the towns and surrounding countryside.

Saluda, formerly called Pace's Gap, was a village in the 1800s that served as a crossroad for commerce between Georgia and South Carolina. A family named Pace provided lodging and supplies for people who delivered goods and livestock. After the Civil War, a young engineer, Charles William Pearson, came to the area to build a railroad, which was known as the Saluda Grade and even today is one of the steepest-class mainline grades in the United States. The tracks cover 50 treacherous curves, with grades from 3.70 to 5.59 degrees, rising 885 feet, three miles in distance. Many lives were lost in the building of this railroad, and even after its completion runaway trains would lose control and careen downhill—from 1878 to 1903, 27 men were killed. Pitt Bellow, one of the injured engineers, devised "side tracks" that routed runaways into steep dead-ends, and the engine, called "The Helper," was placed at the rear of the train to assist in the steep climbs.

In 1881, Pace's Gap was chartered Saluda. After the passenger trains halted in 1968 and the interstate was completed, Saluda lost some of its vitality. Today, downtown Saluda is on the National Register of Historic Places thanks to an energetic community determined to reinvent itself while keeping the past intact. Saluda has everything to make it one of your favorite towns in Western North Carolina. Just driving through, you will get a true picture of what life was like almost a century ago.

The best approach to Saluda is on scenic U.S. Highway 176, which takes you through winding roads and rolling foothills all the way. Stop at High Bridge and look over the side. The depth of the gorge will surprise you, especially if you can find Green River, which looks like a crooked line on a map.

One of the mainstays in Saluda is **Green River Bar-B-Cue Restaurant,** serving Carolina-style barbecue since 1984. Besides fixing barbecue pork or beef a million ways, Green River has smoked turkey, ribs, burgers, and hot dogs. The Saluda Stuffer is a hardy sandwich made with homemade Italian bread hollowed out and stuffed with pork and served with slaw on the side. Just follow your nose and you will find the restaurant—the aroma from the open pit is irresistible. Green River, located at 131 U.S. Highway 176, can accommodate groups of 30 to 300 people with either on-site cooking or catering. It is open from 11:00 A.M. to 8:00 P.M., Tuesday through Saturday, and from 12:00 noon to 3:00 P.M., Sunday. (828) 749-9892.

Follow the highway down Main Street, park close to the old depot, and amble the length of the town, where there is a mix of shops, galleries, and restaurants you will want to explore. Although the businesses are fairly new, most are located in buildings dating back to the 1900s. The antique shop, **Summer House,** would be a good place to start and then continue down to the **Purple Onion Café and Coffee House,** an attractive restaurant that serves good food at lunch and dinner. Try the humus combinations on pita wedges for lunch and delicious pizzas at night. Just a couple of doors down is **Ward's Grill,** a landmark serving hamburgers, hot dogs, pork chops, and homemade sausage. You can eat here or take out. Wander around the annex, which carries hardware, groceries, and meat. Just next door is another favorite restaurant, **Saluda Grade Café,** with two capable chefs serving outstanding rainbow trout dishes. Next door to the café is the **Stamp Peddler,** which carries unusual art stamps and beautiful handmade paper from all over the world. Across the alley is the **M. A. Pace General Store,** which was built in 1910 and is still in business. Most of the shops keep regular business hours.

You cannot leave Saluda without visiting the **Wildflower Bakery,** located at the east end of Main Street. Debi Thomas looks like a walking ad for her health food bakery and will love telling you how the freshest natural ingredients are used for her luncheon menu. The bakery stonegrinds its own wheat every morning and breads are baked and put on big wooden shelves to cool. If you are there at 8:30 A.M. when the bakery opens, pick up the famous Sticky Bun or the herb egg muffin made with fresh herbs, veggies, and a low-cal cream cheese and cheddar blend. For lunch there is always a special of the day as well as "pockets" with all kinds of creative fillings. Tazo is a zesty drink made of apple, pear, and lemon juice with herbs and citrus; you can drink it hot or cold—delicious and different.

Nothing is better than the homemade graham crackers just sweet enough for soft brie and fruit. You can sit at one of the small tables inside the bakery or take in "Nostalgia Courtyard" outside, comprised of five little cubbyhole shops. Hours at the Wildflower Bakery are from 8:30 A.M. to 3:00 P.M., Wednesday through Saturday, and from 10:00 A.M. to 2:00 P.M., Sunday, in season. Call (828) 749-9224 for special orders.

In the 1920s, Capt. Charles William Pearson was a young engineer who discovered a natural falls while spearheading a project for the railroad. The falls and the glen around it were so beautiful he decided to buy the property for his family. Over the years many botanists and birdwatchers have come from all over to study the glen and enjoy one of the most beautiful falls in Western North Carolina.

Pearson's Falls is a natural falls, cascading down stairway boulders, which give it a silvery look. The walk up is an easy quarter-mile.

Picnickers have found the huge tabletop rock at the bottom a perfect place to linger for a while. The Garden House has a collection of plants of the area and is part of the University of North Carolina-Asheville. The property is also a wildlife preserve and laboratory for botany departments in surrounding schools.

Twice the glen has been saved from destruction; first when Captain Pearson saved it from the railroad and second when the Tryon Garden Club saved it from a lumber company in 1931. When you leave you will look up to heaven and thank the man who decided the railroad needed to go somewhere else.

Pearson's Falls is just off U.S. Highway 176, four miles north of Tryon, or three miles south of Saluda. Look for signs. There is a small admission fee. Hours are usually from 10:00 A.M. to 6:00 P.M., Wednesday through Sunday, March through October.

To get the most from the Carolina Foothills, a two-night stay will give you enough time to cover them by car or bicycle. One of the best inns in the area is the **Orchard Inn,** located just outside of Saluda. A long, winding road off U.S. Highway 176 will take you to the Orchard Inn, which sits at the top of a hill. You will instantly be taken with the peaceful surroundings of the foothills and the gracious appearance of this comfortable inn. Built in the 1900s as a retreat for the Brotherhood of Railway Clerks, it has now become a retreat for you. Innkeepers Bob and Kathy Thompson maintain this fine old antique in splendid fashion with modern creature comforts. The inn has nine guest rooms; four cottages are equipped with fireplace, whirlpool, and private deck. The whole downstairs of the inn opens to a big living room with stone fireplace and comfy couches and chairs. Off of this room is the library, where books can be borrowed to read during your stay. The sunny dining room runs the length of the inn with big glass windows for the view. Breakfast is included for guests and dinner is fine dining with four courses. Chicken is not served as the chef prefers lamb, quail, filets, and fish dishes. The flan for dessert is famous. There is full bar service. Dinner is served at 7:00 P.M. and jackets for men are suggested.

Backroads magazine has named the Orchard Inn as excellent headquarters for bicycle tours. Children over 12 are welcome and no pets are allowed. (800) 581-3800. www.orchardinn.com.

Tryon

The expression "thermal belt" has been used to describe parts of North Carolina that enjoy more favorable climates than neighboring sections with the same altitude. Temperature inversions of 20 degrees or more have been noted along some mountainsides in these areas. Inversion is when the temperature is much higher on the mountain slope than at the base. The results of thermal layers are usually evident in the successful growing of fruit. Tryon enjoys thermal belt climate and the grapes grown here are a well-known and delicious product. Other thermal belt areas across Western North Carolina are favored locations for apple orchards.

Tryon is a town that can tell of a great history dating back to the 1700s when the first settlers and the Cherokee were peaceful and brought goods to the old Block House trading post, which is still in existence. When the boundaries between whites and Indians started to get sticky, legend has it that colonial governor William Tryon extended the borders into the foothills for the protection of the Indian hunting grounds. Thus, one side of the boundary was named after a Cherokee chief, and the other side was named "Tryon," after Governor Tryon.

During the American Revolution, the Indians sided with the Redcoats, and a tragic story unfolded of terrible slaughter on both sides before peace came again. In the late 1870s, the railroad came to town and, like its sister city Saluda, everything began to change in Tryon, making it a bustling, prosperous Mecca for tourists escaping city life.

The **Frog and Swan, Inc.,** 1119 North Trade Street, is a worthy stop. Besides charm it is loaded with antique glassware, china, furniture, walking canes, old tools, and an antique sampler or two. The stock, covering 4,000 square feet, is in a 1930s brick building and is mainly handpicked consignment and estate sales pieces. Scattered about on the patio are whimsical garden statuary and plaques—some old, some new. The Frog and Swan is affectionately named after one of the owner's favorite pubs in London. The friendly shop dogs are Fredericka and Geoffrey. Hours are from 9:30 A.M. to 4:30 P.M., Tuesday through Saturday, and during the season on Sunday afternoon. (828) 859-6757.

Antiques On Trade has a double meaning: it is a shop to trade antiques as well as being on Trade Street. C. Frank Sexton, Jr., specializes in estate sales and is a good resource for locating a piece you may be seeking. He is also a good source for information on Tryon since he is a native of the area. The shop has nice collections and, if you hit it right, you can find nifty dessert plates, antique guns, and furniture, and Frank always has a fun selection of antique hats of all kinds. Antiques On Trade is located at 1110 North Trade Street, just before you hit the main drag. (828) 859-9833.

Down by the depot, beside the railroad tracks, is a statue of "Morris," the big polka-dot horse that reached international fame in the early 1900s when Charlotte Yale and Eleanor Vance opened the Tryon Toymakers and Woodcarvers Shop. Morris was the signature piece and became the mascot for the company and Tryon as well.

In the middle of the business district is **Tryon House, Inc.,** called "the source of the horse." You can get all kinds of souvenirs of Morris, lots of equestrian gifts, apparel, and jewelry, prints and posters, Tryon Steeplechase tee shirts, designer hats, music boxes, mugs, and so on. Tryon House, Inc., is located at 220 North Trade Street. (704) 859-9962.

History plays a big part in mountain towns of Western North Carolina. One of Tryon's biggest assets is the old **Pine Crest Inn,** established in 1917 by a well-known equestrian, Carter Brown. Purchased in 1990 by Jeremy and Jennifer Wainwright, the inn has been completely restored in an English Country style with soft leather chairs, shiny hardwood floors, and oriental rugs. Prints and paintings of the hunt and steeplechase line the walls and a drink at the Fox and Hounds Bar makes you feel you are truly in horse country. F. Scott Fitzgerald and Ernest Hemingway liked the Pine Crest and visited often. It is listed on the National Register of Historic Places.

There are 35 guests rooms in the main lodge and cottages and most have fireplaces. Two cabins, over 200 years old, are also part of the inn. Dining is a high note at the Pine Crest, offering grilled mountain trout, Maryland crab cakes, roast duck, and rack of lamb as specialties of the house. Breakfast includes Eggs Benedict, omelets of all kinds, and Belgian waffles (rates include continental breakfast).

FENCE (Foothills Equestrian and Nature Center), the famous equestrian center, is just a few minutes away and, traditionally, many horse lovers stay at the inn for many of the events that take place during the year. The Pine Crest's address is 200 Pine Crest Lane in Tryon. (800) 633-3001 or (828) 859-9135. A little pricey, but worth it.

FENCE signs are all over Tryon—either heralding an equestrian event or just pointing the way. FENCE is 300 acres of woods and fields where horse lovers and nature lovers meet. The Mahler family donated 120 acres to the community in 1985. It has since grown three times the size and is run by volunteers and private donations. The nature part of FENCE includes herb, hummingbird, and butterfly gardens, bird watching, a wildlife pond, hiking paths, and an easy boardwalk trail. Nature classes are offered year round.

Equestrian history lies deep in Tryon and FENCE has become headquarters for over 30 events a year. The famous Block House Steeplechase is held every April, as well as dressage, hunter jumper, and cross-country classics—all kinds of horse-show competitions. The U.S. Pony Club has training rallies during the summer and the North Carolina Dressage and Combined Training Association also has classes. Stop at the information center, where you will find exhibits and a gift shop.

The FENCE center is free to the public and is located at 500 Hunting Country Road, just a short drive from the Pine Crest Inn. The offices are open from 9:00 A.M. to 4:00 P.M., Monday through Friday. (828) 859-9021. www.info@fence.org.

Golf Courses

Here are the area municipal and public golf courses; information courtesy of Journal Communications, Inc.:

Apple Valley Course. This 18-hole, par-72 course shares pools, a fitness center, and beach with the Lake Lure Bald Mountain Course. (828) 625-2888 or (800) 260-1040.

Lake Lure Bald Mountain Course. Located 22 miles east of Hendersonville. Magnificent mountain views and full recreational facilities are offered here. (828) 625-3042 or (800) 260-1040.

Lake Lure Municipal Course. This course opened in 1925. It is 9 holes, par 36. Walking unrestricted. (828) 625-4472.

Meadowbrook Golf Course. Located near Rutherfordton. Meadowbrook has soft rolling hills, Bermuda fairways, and bent grass greens. This course, in excellent condition, is open year round. (828) 863-2690.

Rutherfordton Golf Club. This course is very hilly, with elevated greens, uphill and downhill lies, and beautiful treelined fairways. Tee time booking is not required but call ahead on weekends. (828) 287-3406.

Left to right: *Carolyn Lee Goodloe, Jolane Edwards, Laurel Wilson, Judy Barnes*

Index

Ad-Lib, 31
Albemarle Inn, 44
Albert's Inn, 128
Almost Rodeo Drive, 68
Alpine Village, 128
Alyxandra's, 197
American Folk Art and Antiques, 32
Ann Jacob Gallery, 187
Antique Market Gallery, 20
Antiques, Etc., 236
Antiques On Trade, 256
Anvil Arts Studio, Inc., 61
Appalachian Angler, 77
Appalachian Craft Center, 18
Appalachian Cultural Museum, 83

Appalachian Heritage Museum, 93
Appalachian Rustic Furnishings, 98
Appalachian State University, 84
Apple Mountain Shops, 197
Apple Valley Course, 258
Apron Shop, 161
Arbor, The, 78
Archer's Inn, 73
Archives Antiques, 20
Arf's, 144
Arts Center, 231
Ashe County Cheese Factory, 88
Asheville Antiques, 20
Asheville Art Museum, 14
Asheville Urban Trail, 24

B. B. Barns, 50
B. J.'s Resort Wear, 68
Baba Riche, 35
Back Porch Deli, 79
Back Roads Country Antiques, 69
Baggie Goose, 38
Balsam Mountain Inn, 140
Banner Elk Cafe, 69
Barley's Taproom & Pizzeria, 31
Bartram Trail, 167
Bascom-Louise Art Gallery, 195
Basket Works, 203
Bat Cave, 247
Bat Cave Apple House, 247
Bea Hensley, 117
Beanstreets, 21
Beech Alpen Inn, 72
Beech Tree Bar and Grill, 72
Bellagio, 37
Berliner Kindl German Restaurant, 56
Best Cellar, 94
Bicycle Inn, The, 126
Biltmore Depot, 37
Biltmore Estate, 35
Biltmore Gallery Downtown, 32
Biltmore Village, 36
Biltmore Village Historic Museum, 37
Bird Barn 'n Garden, 201
Bird Barns, 188
Bistro 1896, 16
Black Bear Coffee Company, 233
Black Mountain Bakery, 57
Black Mountain Gallery, 55
Black Mountain Iron Works, 55
Black Walnut Bed and Breakfast Inn, The, 43
Blowing Rock Café, 97
Blowing Rock Stage Company, 96
Blue, 38
Blue Moon Bakery, 32

Blue Ridge Parkway, 109
Blue Spiral Gallery, 31
Bonnie Brae, Ltd., 201
Book & Specialty Shop, 203
Books Unlimited, 178
Boone Golf Club, 107
Boston Pizza, 42
Botanical Gardens, 47
Bounds Cave, 208
Bracken Mountain Bakery, 220
Brevard College, 222
Brevard Little Theater, 217
Brevard Music Center, 222
Bridal Veil, 180
Brier-Patch Gifts & Antiques, 197
Broodmoor Golf Links, 52
Brookings Orvis, 207
Broyhill Inn and Conference Center, 85
Buncombe County Municipal Golf Course, 52
Busy B's Collectibles, 114
Buzz Coren, 130

Café Calabria, 236
Café on the Square, 16
Candy Barrel, 79, 139
Cane Creek Pottery, 127
Captain's Bookshelf, 28
Carl Sandburg Home, 242
Carleton Gallery, 76
Carver's Gap, 127
Casa Rustica, 87
Cashiers Commons, 206
Cashiers Farmer's Market, 205
Cataloochee Ranch, 145
Cathedral of All Souls, 39
Cedar Crest Bed and Breakfast, 33
Cedar Crest Restaurant, 119
Celtic Way, The, 27
Centerpiece, 67

Central House Restaurant, 190
Chalet Restaurant, 114
Chapel Of The Prodigal, 58
Chelseas, 38
Cherohala Skyway, 172
Cherokee Hills Golf Club, 175
Cherokee Indian Reservation, 146
Cherokee Visitor's Center, 146
Cherry Street Kids, 56
Chestnut Street Inn, 44
Chetola Resort, 94
Chevron Trading Post & Bead Company, 22
Chimney Rock, 249
Chopping Block, The, 205
Church in the Wildwood, 193
Church of the Good Shepherd, 208
City Lights Bookstore, 157
Claddah Inn, 230
Clay's Corner, 175
Clear Creek Guest Ranch, 129
CliMax, 26
Clingmans Dome, 152
Coffee Shop, 156
Colburn Gem and Mineral Museum, 14
Collene Karcher, 156
Columbine, 81
Common Ground Distributors, 33
Compleat Naturalist, 36
Complements to the Chef, 42
Constance Boutique, 24
Coontree Picnic Area, 227
Cope's Newsstand and Suprette, 157
Corner Bistro, 220
Corner Palate, 68
Cornucopia, 204

Cottage Inn, The, 200
Cottage Walk, 206
Cowee Gap Overlook, 198
Cradle of Forestry, 227
Craft Pride Gallery, 130
Craft Shop, The, 174
Creekside Tubing, 164
Crippens Country Inn and Restaurant, 96
Crooked Creek Golf Club, 245
Cumberland Falls Bed and Breakfast, 43
Curb Market, 236
Cynthia Bringle, 123
Cypress Cellar, 234
Cyrano's, 186

Dancing Bear Toys, Ltd., 50
Daniel Boone Amphitheater, 84
Daniel Boone Inn, 85
Daniel Boone Native Gardens, 84
Davidson River Campground, 225
Davidson River Outfitters, 224
Days Gone By, 233
de Provence et d'ailleurs, 100
Dean's Market and Deli, 244
Deep Creek Campground, 163
Deep Creek Lodge, 164
Devil's Courthouse, 228
DeWoolfson's Fine Linens, 97
Diane Borde-Sutherland, 127
Dick Shulman Company, 139
Dillsboro Chocolate Factory, 159
Dillsboro Smokehouse, 158
Dogwood Crafters, 161
Dreamfields, 76
Drift Falls, 210
Dry Falls, 180
Duck Decoys, Ltd., 160
Dusty Rhodes Suprette, 182

Earthshine Mountain Lodge, 213
Echo Mountain Inn, 238
Edwina Bringle, 123
Elephant's Foot Antiques, 196
Enchanted Bear, 207
Episcopal Church of the Incar-
    nation, 188
Eseeola Lodge, 63
Esmeralda Inn & Restaurant, 248
Essence of Thyme, 220
Everett Street Diner, 164
Eve's Leaves, 68
Expressions, 97
Ezekiel's Barn, 206

Falls Landing, 219
Family Heirlooms, 100
Faraway Place, A, 26
Farmers Market, 183
Feather Your Nest, 101
FENCE, 257
Fig Leaf, 99
Finders Keepers, 76
Fine Arts and Crafts Co-Op, The,
    219
Fine Arts Theater, 31
Fine Friends, 43
Finishing Touch, The, 19
Fireside Antiques and
    Interiors, 39
First Baptist Church, 30
First Presbyterian
    Church, 30, 190
Flat Rock, 240
Flat Rock Playhouse, 241
Flying Frog Café, 24
Folk Art Center, 51
Fontana Dam, 171
Fontana Village, 171
Fork Mountain Pottery, 126
Foscoe Fishing Company and
    Outfitters, 77

Franklin Gem and Mineral
    Museum, 177
Fred's Backside Deli, 72
Fred's General Mercantile, 72
Freedom Escape Lodge and
    Retreat Center, 133
Fresh Market, 42, 237
Frog and Owl Kitchen, 177
Frog and Swan, Inc., 256
Fryemont Inn, 165

G. Whillikers, 100
Gabrielle's, 48
Gallery, 9, 76
Gallery On The Green, 202
Gamekeeper's Restaurant, 106
Garden Deli, 133
Gardener's Cottage, The, 39
Gardens Of The Blue Ridge,
    62
Gattle's, 100
Gay Smith Pottery Studio, 125
Gem Shop, The, 201
Gem Shoppe, 114
Gentleman's Gallery, 24
giant poplar tree, 193
Gideon Ridge Inn, 104
Gilded Age Antique Shop, 76
Glen Burney Falls, 102
Glen Burney Trail, 102
Glen Mary Falls, 102
Glendale Springs Bed
    and Breakfast, 92
Gold Hill Espresso, 24
Golden Carp Gift Shop
    and Gallery, 160
golf courses, 52, 73-74, 107, 136,
    153, 175, 216, 245, 258
Gorges State Park, 215
Gourmet Gardens Herb
    Farm, 134
Grandfather Mountain, 64

Grandfather Mountain Highland Games and Gathering of Scottish Clans, 65
Grandmother Creek, 64
Granite City, 210
Granny's Chicken Palace, 144
Granny's Kitchen, 150
Grapevine Café, 85
Grassy Creek Golf and Country Club, 119
Grassy Mountain Shop, 115
Graveyard Fields Overlook, 229
Great Smoky Mountains National Park, 151
Great Smoky Mountains Railroad, 161
Green Mansion Village, 76
Green Park Inn, 103
Green River Bar-B-Cue Restaurant, 252
Greenery, The, 49
Greenfield Restaurant, 89
Greystone Inn, 212
Grove Park Inn, 45
Grovewood Café, 46
Grovewood Gallery, 46
Guild Crafts, 50

Ham Shoppe, The, 78
Hand in Hand Gallery, 244
Hannah Flanagan's Pub and Eatery, 232
Hanover House Antiques, 196
Happ's Place, 207
Harold Grant Men's Store, 197
Harold Grant, Inc., 197
Harvest Drive In, 60
Hathaway's Village Café and Market, 38
Hawksnest, 73
Hayden Gallery, 132

Haywood Park Hotel, 25
Health Adventure, 14
Hemingway's Book and Gift Shop, 101
Hickory Ridge Homestead, 83
High Hampton Inn and Country Club, 210
Highland Hiker, 189, 204
Highland Hill Deli, 191
Highland Lake Golf Club, 245
Highland Lake Inn, 239
Highlands Books, 222
Highlands-Cashiers Chamber Music Fest, 195
Highlands Inn, 187
Highlands Nature Center and Biological Station, 193
Highland's Playhouse, 195
Hilltop, 133
Holden's Arts and Crafts, 61
Holmes Educational State Forest, 231
Holy Trinity, 89
Horacio's Restaurant, 208
Horizons, 45
Horn In The West Grounds, 83
House of Lord, 189
House of Wong, 185
Howard's Knob, 86
Hungry Bear, 150
Hunter & Coggins Clothing Co., 19

Ian and Jo Lydia Craven, 131
Indian Creek Falls, 163
Inn Around The Corner, 57
Inn at Brevard, 222
Inn at Elk River, 71
Inn at Ragged Gardens, 96
Inn at the Taylor House, 81
Inn on Biltmore Estate, 36
Interiors Marketplace, 34

Iron Bridge, 210
Iron Tree Golf Club, 153

J & S Beaumont Pottery, 80
J. Arthur's, 144
J W Tweeds, 68
Jabobs, 127
Jack the Dipper, 158
Jackalope's View, 73
Jane Asker's Fourth and Main
    Antique Mall, 231
Jane Peiser, 122
Jarrett House, 159
Jewels That Dance, 23
Jim Bob Tinsley Museum, 221
Joe Nielander, 119
John A. Reynolds Antiques, 220
John C. Campbell Folk
    School, 174
John Collette Fine Arts, 183
Jordan Street Café, 221
Jordan's Restaurant, 72
Joyce Kilmer Memorial Forest,
    170
Joyce Kilmer-Slickrock
    Wilderness, 170
Joyce Kilmer Trail, 170
Julie Mar Needlepoint Studio, 26
Jump Off Rock Park, 239
Juneywhank Falls, 164

Kanuga Episcopal Conference
    Center, 237
Katherine and William Bernstein,
    129
Kelsey and Hutchinson Lodge,
    195
Kelsey Place Restaurant, 187
Kilwins Chocolate and Ice
    Cream, 186
Kingfisher's Angling Shop, 164
Knight's On Main, 95

Kojays, 99
Kress Emporium, 29

La Caterina Trattoria, 17
Lake Glenville, 207
Lake Junaluska Conference and
    Retreat Center, 138
Lake Junaluska Golf Course, 153
Lake Lure Bald Mountain
    Course, 258
Lake Lure Inn, 250
Lake Lure Municipal Course,
    258
Lake Tomahawk Park, 54
Lakeside Restaurant, 192
Laughing Seed Café, 27
Le Conte Lodge, 152
Lexington Park Antiques, 20
Lilith Eberle, 119
Lilly's, 235
Linn Cove Viaduct, 110
Linville Caverns, 60
Linville Falls, 60
Linville General Store, 64
Local Color Weaving Studio, 125
Loft, The, 20
Lollipop Shop, 101
Lomo Grill, 139
Lomo's Bakery and Café, 139
Looking Glass Falls, 227
Louisiana Purchase, 69
Lovill House Inn Bed & Break-
    fast, 86
Lower Cullasaja Falls, 179
Lucy Anne, 19
Lulu's Café, 157
Lyn K. Holloway Antiques, 202

M. A. Pace General Store, 253
McCulley's, 191
McFarlane Bakery, 233
Magnolia Beauregard's, 20

Magnolia's Oyster Bar & Grille, 19
Main Street Shop, 207
Malaprop's Bookstore/Café, 23
Man In The Moon, 98
Manor House Restaurant, 95
Marjon's Antiques, 75
Market Basket, The, 202
Market Place, 28
Martin House, 99
Martines, 211
Mast Farm Inn, 80
Mast General Store, 80, 139, 236
Mast General Store Annex, 79
Master Works, 183
Max Woody Chair Shop, 59
Maxine's Mountain Gifts, 213
Meadowbrook Golf Course, 258
Mehri & Company, 236
Mello Mushroom, 20
Methodist Central Church, 30
Micas Restaurant, 211
Mill Creek Golf Course, 216
Millstone Inn, 200
Mineral and Lapidary Museum, 234
Mingo Falls, 150
Mingus Mill, 151
Mirror Lake Antiques, 192
Mitchell Motel and Cottages, 182
Moment In Time, A, 231
Montreat Conference Center, 58
Moose Café, 41
Moose Mountain Trading Company, 85
Morel's, 68
Morgan Mill General Store, 215
Morgan Mill Trout Fishing Resort, 215
Morning Star Gallery, 97
Moses H. Cone Memorial Park, 105

Mount Jefferson State Park, 90
Mount Mitchell, 116
Mount Mitchell Golf Course, 136
Mount Mitchell State Park, 116
Mountain Aire Golf Club, 107
Mountain Down Adventures, 181
Mountain Fresh Market, 189
Mountain Java, 55
Mountain Lilly Restaurant, 211
Mountain Lore Bookstore, 232
Mountain Pottery, 160
Mulberry Cat, 76
Museum of the Cherokee Indian, 147
Mystery Hill Complex, 92
Mystic Eye, 22

Nantahala Outdoor Center, 166
Narcissus, 184
Natural Home, 22
Natural Selections, 85
Nelly's Treasures, 234
New French Bar, 25
New Morning Gallery, 37
New River, 90
New River Outfitters, 91
New River State Park, 90
Newfound Gap, 152
Nick Joerling, 123
Nick's, 192
Norman Shulman, 124
North Carolina Arboretum, 41
Northwoods Golf Club, 52
Not All Country Store, The, 202
NuWray Inn, 131

O. P. Taylor's, 218
Oconaluftee Indian Village, 148
Oconaluftee Islands Park, 149
Oconaluftee Visitor Center, 151
October's End Restaurant, 213
Old Creek Lodge, 182

Old Depot, The, 56
Old Edwards Inn, 190
Old Europe, 26
Old Hampton Store and Grist Mill, 64
Old Jail Museum, 175
Old Rock Café, 249
Old School Antique Mall, 162
Old Stone Inn, 140
On The Verandah, 180
Once Upon a Time, 39
One Feather Fly and Tackle, 150
Open Air Curb Market, 138
Open Door, The, 24
Open Door Antique Mall, 218
Orchard at Altapass, 112
Orchard Inn, 254
Orchard Trace Golf Club, 245
Owens Orchids LLC, 223
Oz, 98

Pack Place, 14
Pack Square, 14
Pandora's Mailbox, 99
Paoletti's, 187
Pearson's Falls, 253
Penland Gallery, 121
Penland School of Crafts, 120
People's Store, 175
Peppers, 55
Perry's Water Gardens, 178
Phillips Restaurant, 169
Pine Crest Inn, 256
Pine Links Golf Club, 245
Pink Beds Picnic Area, 227
Pisgah Campground, 229
Pisgah Center for Wildlife Education, 226
Pisgah District Ranger Station and Visitor Center, 225
Pisgah Forest Fish Hatchery, 226

Pisgah Forest Stables, 225
Pisgah Inn, 229
Pisgah National Forest, 225
Pleasant Papers/Bookmasters, 99
Portebello, 235
Pottery Garden, 115
Proper Pot, 220
Purple Onion Café and Coffee House, 252

Qualla Arts and Crafts Mutual, Inc., 147

Railroad Grade Road, 87
Rainbow Falls, 210
Randolph House Bed and Breakfast, 165
Rarities, 183
Ravenal Park, 193
Red Rocker Inn, 57
Relia's Garden Restaurant, 166
Reunions, 20
Richard Guritz Antiques and Interiors, Ltd., 194
Richmond Hill Inn, 47
Richmond Inn, 120
Rickman's General Store, 179
Ridgecrest Baptist Conference Center, 59
Rio Doce Gem Mine, 118
River's End Restaurant, 167
Riverwood, 161
Roan Mountain, 127
Roan Mountain Gardens, 127
Robert Levin, 130
"Rock, The," 103
Rocky's Soda Fountain, 221
Rogers Trading Post, 93
Rosenthals, 184
Rosewood Market, 181
Rusticks, 202

Rutherfordton Golf Club, 258

St. Andrews-by-the-Lake, 214
St. John in the Wilderness, 241
St. Lawrence Catholic Church, 30
St. Mary of the Hills Episcopal
  Church, 102
Saint Mary's, 89
Salmonid Farms, 214
Salsas, 17
Saluda Grade Café, 253
Sam's Boutique, 67
Scotties Jewelry and Fine
  Arts, 231
Scottish Tartans Museum
  and Heritage Center, 178
Screen Porch, 33
Scudders Galleries, 185
Secret Garden, The, 243
Secret Garden Bed &
  Breakfast, 135
Serves You Right, 101
Shatley Springs Inn, 91
Sheer Bliss Little Bear Rock
  Shop, 69
Shelly's Diamond Gallery, 235
Shirley's of Dillsboro, 160
Shoppes Of Tynecastle, 67
Shoppes On The Parkway, 93
Silver Tree, 81
Sliding Rock, 227
Slow Joe's, 166
Smokey Shadows Lodge, 145
Snowbird Mountain Lodge, 172
Song Of The Wood Shop, 54
Sorrento's, 68
Sourwood Grill and Patio, 137
Southern Hands, 183, 206
SouthMarke, 101
Sports Page, 185
Spring Street Café, 158
Springdale Country Club, 137

Squire's Restaurant, 244
Stairstep Falls, 211
Stamp Peddler, 253
Starwood Gallery, 98
Stompin' Grounds, 144
Stone Lantern, 184
Stuf Gallery, 20
Sugar Mountain Golf Course, 74
Sugar Mountain Resort, 70
Summer Chapel, 209
Summer House, 252
Summer House Gallery, 182
Sunset Rock, 193
Sunset Terrace, 45
Suze Lindsay, 125
Swag, The, 143
Sweet Treats, 194
Switzerland Café, 115
Switzerland Inn, 113

T. S. Morrison, 22
Tatum Galleries, 77
Thomas Jacoby Fine Art, 201
Thomas Kinkade, 183
Thomas Wolfe Home, 15
Thomas Wolfe Memorial Visitor
  Center, 16
Three Oaks Country Store, 61
Tiger Mountain Woodworks, 182
Toby West Antiques, 196
Todd General Store, 87
Tom Spleth, 122
Tom's Branch Falls, 163
Tommy's, 204
Top Of The Beech, 72
Tops For Shoes, 22
Touchstone, 233
Trevi, 34
Trillium Gallery, 114
Trinity Episcopal, 30
Tryon House, Inc., 256
Turtleback Falls, 210

Tweetsie Railroad, 93
23 Page, 25
Twin Streams Bed &
    Breakfast, 214
Twisted Laurel Gallery, 119
2 On Crescent, 38
Tynecastle Galleria, 67

Unto These Hills, 148
Uptown Café, 26

Valle Crucis Rustic Furnishings,
    81
Valle Fashions, 80
Valle Landing, 81
Valley Gift Shop, 198
Vasarely's Restaurant, 72
Vertu, 32
View Haus, 72
Village Antiques, 35
Village Boutique, The, 185
Village Café, 99
Village Green Antique Mall, 235
Village Grocery, 68
Village Heirlooms, Inc., 69
Village Shops, 68
Vintners Restaurant and Wine
    Shoppe, 98

Wagon Gap Overlook, 228
Ward's Grill, 252
Watauga County Farmer's
    Market, 84
Waverly Inn, 230
We're Good Sports, 101
Weaverville Milling
    Company, 134
Weaverville United Methodist
    Church, 136
Weaving Room Gallery, 62
Wee Shop, 197

Weinhaus, 29
Well Heeled, 197
Wellhouse Restaurant, 161
Western North Carolina Air
    Museum, 239
Western North Carolina Farmer's
    Market, 40
Westglow Spa, 105
Westside Coffee Shop, 133
Whiteside Art Gallery, 199
Whiteside Mountain, 198
Whitewater Falls, 211
Whitman's Bakery, 140
Wickwire, 234
Wilcox Emporium, 85
Wild Possessions, 208
Wild Thyme Gourmet, 191, 201
Wildflower Bakery, 253
Willow Creek, 107
Windmill Restaurant, 49
Windsong, 142
Windwood Antique, 100
Wit's End Shop, The, 186
Wolfgang's, 187
Womble Inn and Café, 221
Woodfield Inn, 244
Woody's Chair Shop, 118
Woolly Worm Festival, 69
Wormy Chestnut, 199
Wrinkled Egg, 243

Yarn Corner, The, 160
Yonahlossee Resort
    and Club, 106

Zambra, 18
Zebulon American Crafts
    Gallery, 132
Zebulon Vance Birthplace, 133
Zoeller's Hardware, 206
Zone One, 31